SINGER
The Complete Photo Guide To
SEWING

**Creative Publishing
international**

First published in the United States of America by
Creative Publishing international, Inc., a member of
Quayside Publishing Group
400 First Avenue North
Suite 300
Minneapolis, MN 55401
1-800-328-389
www.creativepub.com

ISBN-13: 978-1-58923-434-5
ISBN-10: 1-58923-434-0

10 9 8 7 6 5 4 3 2 1

Library of Congress Cataloging-in-Publication Data:
The complete photo guide to sewing : 1200 full-color how-to photos / editors
of Creative Publishing international. – Updated and rev. ed.
     p. cm.
  Includes index.
  ISBN-13: 978-1-58923-434-5
  ISBN-10: 1-58923-434-0
  1. Machine sewing. 2. Dressmaking. 3. Tailoring. 4. House furnishings. I.
Creative Publishing International.
  TT713.C63 2009
  646.2'044–dc22

                                                2008031264

Proofreader: Alyssa Cyphers
Book Design/Page Layout: bradhamdesign.com
Cover Design: John Barnett, 4eyesdesign.com

Printed in Singapore

SINGER

The Complete Photo Guide To
SEWING

1200 Full-Color How-to Photos

Creative Publishing
international

CONTENTS

How to Use This Book

Like any other art or craft, sewing begins with basic techniques. *The Complete Photo Guide to Sewing* gives you the essential information you need for sewing garments and items for your home. In addition to basic techniques, specialty sewing topics, such as fitting, sewing activewear, and sewing home décor projects, are also included.

Getting Started

This section gives you information on the sewing machine and the serger. We show you how to get the perfect stitch and tell you about special features and accessories for both machines. We also tell you about the equipment and notions you will need for all of your sewing, plus some timesaving equipment that will make your sewing easier.

Also covered in the first section is the pattern. You will learn how to take your measurements and select the correct size. A comprehensive guide to fabric selection is included as well as cutting and sewing tips. There is also information on how to choose and apply interfacing.

Sewing Techniques

This section features the basic techniques you will use for nearly everything you sew: garments and home decorating projects. The basic sewing techniques include fitting, seams, darts, gathering, sleeves, collars, waistbands, cuffs, and closures. Each is given an overview, followed by a step-by-step description of how to achieve the best results. Often several methods are presented with guidance as to when and where to use each one.

Home Decorating Projects

We start with the basics of fabric selection and other tips on planning a project. Instructions for many of the projects include alternate methods and suggest timesaving techniques.

The Home Decorating section is divided into five project categories: windows, pillows, bed and bath, slipcovers, and tables. For windows, we give instructions for standard favorites, such as pinch-pleated draperies, Roman shades, and many others. Four basic pillow styles are shown plus variations for closures. Using fabrics of your choice, your options for pillows are endless. Make a comforter cover for your bed, and add pillow shams and a dust ruffle to match. Make new cushions, slipcover your dining chairs, or make a cover for a futon. For tables, learn how to make rectangular and round tablecloths, placemats, and many variations of napkins.

Each category includes an overview and how to take measurements for the projects. For easy reference, fabric and notions required to complete a project are included in a box labeled YOU WILL NEED. The step-by-step instructions are complete: you do not have to purchase additional patterns. The photographs show you how each project should look each step of the way.

Step-by-Step Guidance

The photos add depth and dimension to the instructions, giving you a close-up look at each step. In some cases, the stitches are shown in heavier thread or a contrasting color to make them more visible. Some marking lines have also been exaggerated to show a crucial matching point.

If you are learning to sew or getting back to sewing, you may want to practice your skills on an easy project before starting a larger one. Try sewing simple placemats and napkins to practice a new edge finish. When you sew a first garment, choose a simple style that is easy to fit, with few details.

Whether you are a new sewer, an experienced sewer, or a returning sewer, this book is designed to be a help and an inspiration. Use it as your step-by-step guide to the satisfaction and fun of successful sewing.

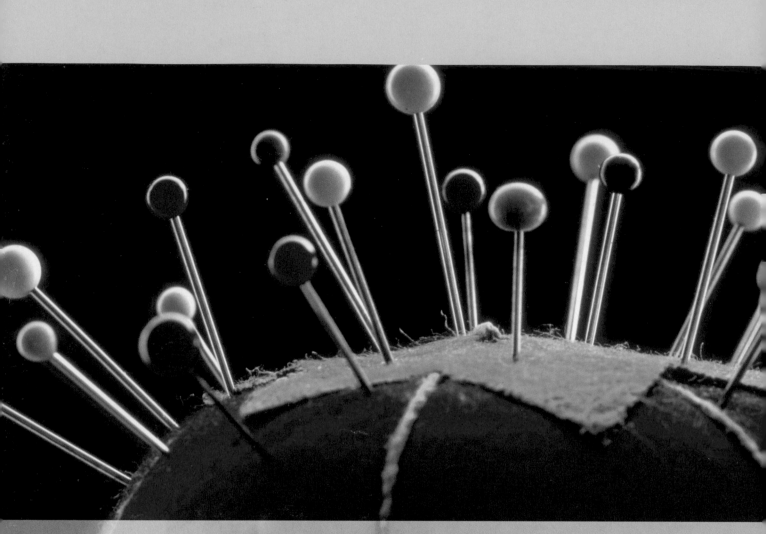

GETTING STARTED

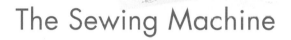

The Sewing Machine

A sewing machine is your most important piece of sewing equipment, so select one with care. A sturdy, well-built machine will give you many years of sewing enjoyment.

If you are buying a new machine, there are a variety of models available to fit any budget or sewing need. Types range from a basic zig-zag with one or two built-in stitches, to the electronic machine that uses advanced computer technology to control and select the stitching.

Available features include built-in buttonholer, color-coded stitch selection, instant reverse, snap-on presser foot, free arm for stitching small round areas (such as pants legs), built-in bobbin winder, automatic tension and pressure adjustment, and automatic stitch length adjustment. Each feature usually adds to the cost of the machine, so look for a machine to match your sewing projects. Buy a machine that satisfies your sewing needs, but don't pay for features you will rarely use. Also consider the amount and difficulty of the sewing you do, and the number of people you sew for. Talk to fabric store personnel and friends who sew. Ask for demonstrations and try out and compare several models. Look for quality workmanship and ease of operation as well as stitching options.

The machine's cabinetry is another factor to consider. Portable machines offer the flexibility of moving to various work surfaces. Machines built into cabinets are designed to be the right height for sewing. They also help you stay organized by providing a convenient place to store sewing equipment and keep it handy.

Although sewing machines vary in capabilities and accessories, each has the same basic parts and controls. Check your manual for specific location of these parts on your machine.

CREATING THE PERFECT STITCH

Perfect stitching is easy to achieve if you thread the machine properly and make the right adjustments in the stitch length, tension, and pressure. These adjustments depend on your fabric and the kind of stitch desired. Consult your machine manual for threading procedures and location of controls.

The stitch length regulator is on either an inch scale from 0 to 20, a metric scale from 0 to 4, or a numerical scale from 0 to 9. For normal stitching, set the regulator at 10 to 12 stitches per inch, or at the number 3 for metric scale machines. On the numerical scale, higher numbers form a larger stitch; if a shorter stitch is desired, dial a lower number. An average stitch length is at number 5.

Bobbins may be built-in or removable for winding. Bobbins with a built-in case are wound in the case. Removable bobbins have a removable bobbin case with a tension adjustment screw. They may be wound on the top or side of the machine. Start with an empty bobbin so the thread will wind evenly. Do not wind it too full or the bobbin thread will break.

In the ideal stitch, both top and bobbin thread are drawn equally into the fabric, and the link is formed midway between fabric layers. The stitch tension control determines the amount of tension on the threads as they pass through the machine. Too much tension results in too little thread fed into the stitch. This causes the fabric to pucker. Too little tension produces too much thread and a weak, loose stitch.

Adjust the pressure regulator for light pressure on heavyweight fabrics, more pressure on light fabrics. Correct pressure ensures even feeding of the fabric layers during stitching. Some machines automatically adjust tension and pressure to the fabric.

Always check tension and pressure on a scrap of fabric before starting to sew. When experimenting with pressure and tension, thread the machine with different colors for top and bobbin thread to make the stitch links easier to see.

Straight Stitch Tension and Pressure

(a) **Correct** tension and pressure makes stitches that are linked midway between the fabric layers. The stitches look even in length and tension on both sides. Fabric layers are fed evenly through the feed and fabric is not marred.

(b) **Too tight** tension results in stitch links that are near the top layer of fabric. Fabric is puckered, and stitches are easily broken. Turn tension dial to a lower number. If pressure is too heavy, the bottom layer may gather up. Fabric may shift or stretch. Stitches may be uneven in length and tension. Dial pressure regulator to a lower number.

(c) **Too loose** tension results in stitch links that are toward the bottom fabric layer. Seam is week. Correct the problem by turning tension dial to a higher number. Too light pressure may cause skipped and uneven stitches, and may pull fabric into the feed. Dial pressure regulator to a higher number.

Zigzag Stitch Tension and Pressure

(d) **Correct** tension and pressure in zigzag stitching produces stitches in which the interlocking link of threads falls at the corner of each stitch, midway between fabric layers. Stitches lie flat and fabric does not pucker.

(e) **Too tight** tension causes fabric to pucker. The thread link falls near the top fabric layer. To correct, decrease the tension. Incorrect pressure is not as apparent in zigzag as in straight stitching. But if the pressure is not accurate, stitches will not be of even length.

(f) **Too loose** tension causes the bottom layer to pucker and the thread link to fall near the bottom fabric layer. Increase tension to balance stitch. The zigzag stitch should be properly balanced in normal sewing. Loosen tension slightly for decorative stitches, and the top stitch pattern will become more rounded.

MACHINE ACCESSORIES FOR SPECIAL TASKS

Every sewing machine has accessories that allow it to perform a variety of special tasks. There are universal accessories that fit any machine, such as the zipper foot, buttonhole attachment and various hemming feet. Other accessories, such as a ruffler attachment, are designed to save time and effort for special types of sewing.

When adding a special accessory or foot to a machine, you must know if your machine has a high shank, low shank, or slanted shank. The shank is the distance from the bottom of the presser foot to the attachment screw. Attachments are specifically designed to fit one of these three styles.

The zigzag plate and the general-purpose foot usually come with the machine. Other accessories often included are the straight-stitch plate and foot, buttonhole foot or attachment, zipper foot, seam guide, various hemming feet, and Even Feed or roller foot. The machine manual explains how to attach the various accessories and achieve the best results with each.

(a) **Buttonhole attachments** allow you to stitch complete buttonholes in a single step. One type stitches and adjusts the buttonhole length to fit the button placed in a carrier behind the foot. Another type of buttonholer for straight-stitch machines makes buttonholes automatically using templates of various sizes. Keyhole buttonholes can be made with this accessory.

(b) **Straight-stitch plate** and foot are used for straight stitching only. The needle hole (arrow) in the plate is small and round. The straight-stitch plate and foot do not allow for any sideways needle movement. Use these features when your fabric or sewing procedure requires close control, such as edgestitching or making collar points. They are also good for sheers and delicate fabrics, because the small needle hole helps keep fragile fabrics from being drawn into the feed.

(c) **Zigzag plate and foot** are the plate and foot on a zigzag machine at time of purchase. They are used for zigzag and multi-needle work as well as plain straight stitching on firm fabrics. The needle hole (arrow) in the plate is wider, and the foot has a wider area for the needle to pass through, allowing for side-to-side needle motion. Use this plate and foot for general-purpose sewing.

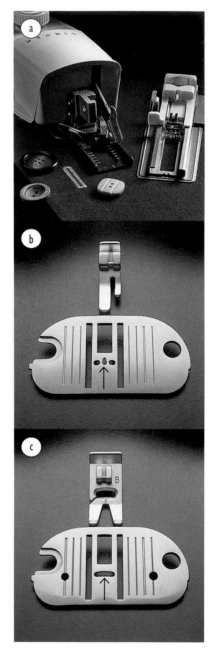

(d) **Zipper foot** is used to stitch cording, insert zippers, or stitch any seam that has more bulk on one side than the other. It adjusts to either side of the needle.

(e) **Special purpose foot** has a grooved bottom that allows for thread build-up in decorative stitches. Seam guide attaches to machine and helps keep seam allowances and hems even.

(f) **Blindstitch hem foot** positions the hem for blindstitch hemming on the machine. This is a fast alternative to hemming by hand.

(g) **Even Feed foot** feeds top and bottom layers together so seams start and end evenly. Use it for vinyl, pile fabrics, bulky knits, or other fabrics that tend to stick, slip, or stretch. This foot is also useful for topstitching and stitching plaids.

(h) **Button foot** holds flat buttons in position for attaching with machine zigzag stitch. This foot saves time when sewing on several buttons.

(i) **Overedge foot** helps keep stitches at full width and prevents curling of flat edges when sewing overedge stitches. Stitches are formed over a hook on the inside edge of the foot.

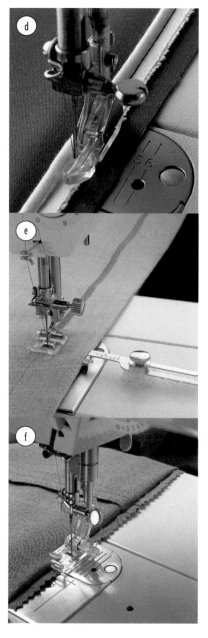

The Serger

A serger is a special-purpose sewing machine that supplements a conventional machine. It is similar to the speed-sewing equipment used by garment manufacturers. A serger cuts sewing time considerably, because it trims and overcasts raw fabric edges as it sews the seam. In addition, it performs this three-in-one operation at high speed. Sergers form 1,500 or more stitches a minute—about twice the rate of conventional sewing machines. As another benefit, all fabrics feed evenly so that even traditionally difficult-to-handle fabrics, such as slippery silks and thin sheers, will not take any extra sewing time.

Because of its unique capabilities, a serger streamlines garment construction. It eliminates time-consuming steps and encourages efficient sewing habits such as flat construction, pinless sewing, and continuous seaming. It also dispenses with routines such as raising and lowering the presser foot, backstitching, and filling bobbins.

Functions and Parts

A serger excels at making self-finished narrow seams, rolled hems, blindstitched hems, and overcast edge finishes. It is also the machine to choose for applying elastic, ribbing, ribbons, and lace. Use a conventional machine whenever straight or zigzag stitching is necessary, such as for topstitching, inserting a zipper, or making buttonholes.

Many different models of sergers are available, each offering different types of stitches. Sergers sew with two, three, four, or five threads. The name of each machine tells which stitches it offers; for example, a 4/3-thread serger can sew either a 4-thread mock safety stitch or a 3-thread overlock stitch. Each stitch type is unique and serves a special purpose.

A serger can be identified by type at a glance. Each type has a certain number of needles and loopers, and the shape of the loopers is easily recognized. For an overview of the sergers available and the stitches they sew, see pages 18 and 19.

Needles may be an industrial type with short or long shaft, or a standard type used on a conventional sewing machine. Use the needle specified for your machine. Industrial needles are stronger and last longer than conventional needles, but they may be more expensive and less widely available. Change conventional needles frequently. Use the finest needle possible to avoid damaging the fabric. Size 11/80 works for most fabric weights.

Knives work like blades of scissors to trim the fabric for the stitch width selected. One knife is high-carbon steel and may last several years. The other knife is less durable and may require replacement three or four times annually. When knives seem dull, first clean them with alcohol; then reposition and tighten the screw. Test by sewing slowly. If a problem remains, replace the less durable knife and test again. As a last resort, replace the other knife.

Principal Parts of the Serger

a. Thread guides
b. Telescoping thread guide holder
c. Spool pins
d. Presser foot lifter
e. Needle, thread tension dials (1 or 2, depending on model)
f. Looper thread tension dials (2 or 3, depending on model)
g. Needle set screws
h. Presser foot
i. Stitch fingers
j. Loopers (2 or 3, depending on model)
k. Needle plate
l. Knives
m. Stitch width regulator
n. Stitch length regulator

o. Handwheel
p. Power and light switch
q. Differential feed control (not on all models)
r. Threading diagrams
s. Looper cover (open)

Location of some machine parts will vary 5-thread serger with cover stitch shown

Serger Thread

A serger uses more thread than a conventional sewing machine, so thread companies offer thread in cones, king tubes, and compact tubes. Tubes and cones have at least 1,000 yd. (920 m) of thread, and cones can have as many as 6,000 yd. (5520 m).

All-purpose thread may also be used on the serger; it is available on parallel-wound or cross-wound spools. Parallel-wound spools require the use of a spool cap for even feeding. There is a wider color selection in all-purpose thread; use it for medium-weight or heavyweight fabrics when color matching is critical.

Serger threads are generally lighter in weight than all-purpose sewing threads. A lightweight thread is recommended for serger use. There is more thread in a serged seam and a lighter-weight thread reduces bulk.

Serger machines sew at a higher rate of speed than conventional sewing machines and create more stress on the threads. Therefore, threads need to be strong and durable. Test thread for strength; poor-quality thread may break easily in some spots. Use the best quality of thread you can; bargain threads sometimes cause more problems than the savings are worth.

Care and Maintenance

Because a serger trims fabric as it sews, it creates more lint than a conventional machine and needs to be cleaned frequently. Use a brush or canned air to remove lint from the looper and throat plate area. Wipe off tension disks, needles, knives, and feed dog with alcohol.

To keep a serger running smoothly and quietly, oil it often. Sergers are lubricated by a wick system and can lose oil by gravity even when they are idle.

THE STITCHES AND THEIR USES

Types of Stitches	2-Thread Overedge Stitch	3-Thread Overlock Stitch	2-Thread Chainstitch	4-Thread Safety Stitch
	• lightweight seam finishes • used for wovens	• stretch seams • durable seams or seam finishes • used for knits and wovens	• stable basting stitch • decorative topstitching • used primarily for wovens	• stable seams with lightweight seam finishes • used primarily for wovens

Types of Sergers

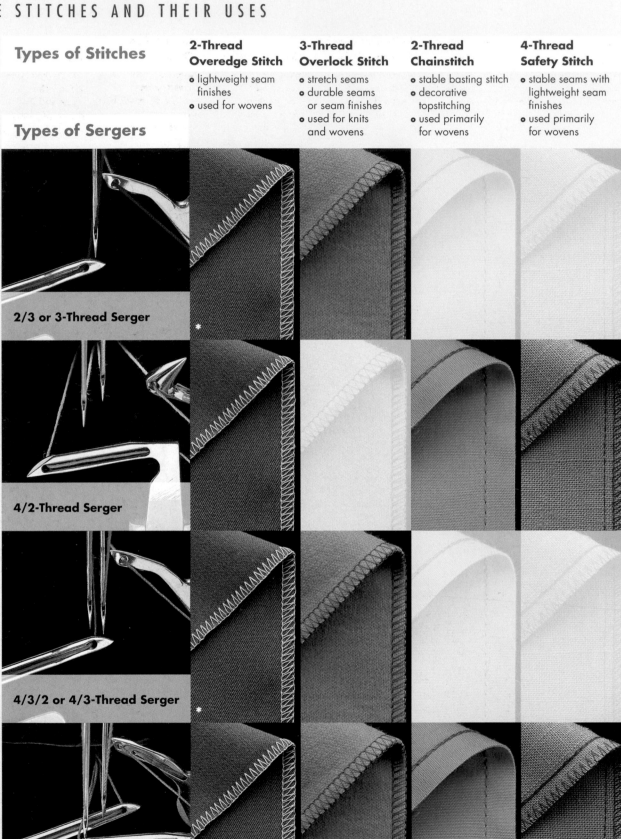

2/3 or 3-Thread Serger

4/2-Thread Serger

4/3/2 or 4/3-Thread Serger

5/4/3/2-Thread Serger

*on some models

5-Thread Safety Stitch

- stable seams with durable finishes
- used primarily for wovens

3-Thread Mock Safety Stitch

- durable ultrastretch seams
- used for super-stretch knits like spandex

4-Thread Mock Safety Stitch

- durable stretch seams
- used for knits and wovens

Flatlock Stitch

- flat, nonbulky stretch seams
- decorative stitching
- used primarily for knits

Rolled Hem Stitch

- narrow hems and seams
- decorative stitching
- used for knits and wovens

Cover Stitch

- stretch hems and seams
- decorative stitching, trims
- used primarily for knits

* on some models

CREATING THE PERFECT STITCH

The tension controls on a serger are actually stitch selectors. Each thread has its own tension control. Changing one or more tension settings affects the character of the stitch, because it changes how the threads loop together. With tension adjustments, the serger can stitch a wide range of threads, fabrics, seams, hems, and decorative treatments.

A good way to become comfortable with serger tension adjustments is to thread each looper and needle with a contrasting thread color. Copy the color code used for the machine's threading diagram. Make several stitch samples, tightening and loosening the tensions in sequence. You will see the effect of each tension adjustment and learn how to use the tension controls to create a balanced stitch. Most of the stitch samples shown below and opposite were made on a 3-thread serger; stitch samples made on other models look similar and are adjusted in the same way.

Correctly Balanced Tensions

(a) 3-thread stitch is formed by two loopers and one needle. Upper (orange) and lower (yellow) looper threads form neat, smooth chain at raw edge. Needle thread (green) forms flat stitches without puckers.

(b) 4/3-thread stitch is formed by two loopers and two needles. Upper (orange) and lower (yellow) looper threads chain neatly at raw edge. Both needle threads (blue, green) form flat stitches that interlock with looper threads.

(c) 4/2-thread stitch makes double row of stitches with two loopers and two needles. Left needle thread (blue) interlocks with lower looper thread (yellow) to make neat, pucker-free chainstitch. Upper looper thread (orange) and right needle thread (green) interlock over raw edge.

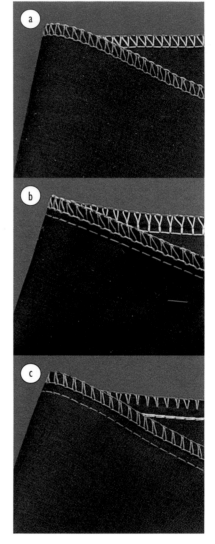

Common Tension Adjustments

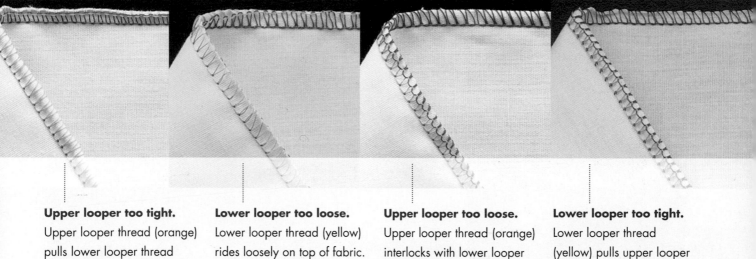

Upper looper too tight.
Upper looper thread (orange) pulls lower looper thread (yellow) to top side of fabric. Loosen upper looper tension so threads interlock at raw edge.

Lower looper too loose.
Lower looper thread (yellow) rides loosely on top of fabric. Tighten lower looper tension until stitches lie flat and smooth on fabric.

Upper looper too loose.
Upper looper thread (orange) interlocks with lower looper thread (yellow) underneath fabric. Tighten upper looper tension so threads interlock at raw edge.

Lower looper too tight.
Lower looper thread (yellow) pulls upper looper thread (orange), causing stitches to interlock under fabric. Loosen lower looper tension so threads interlock at raw edge.

Upper and lower loopers too tight.
Fabric bunches and puckers within stitches. Loosen upper and lower tensions until fabric relaxes.

Upper and lower loopers too loose.
Lower (yellow) and upper (orange) looper threads interlock beyond raw edge and form loose loops. Tighten both looper tensions so stitches hug raw edge.

Needle too tight.
Fabric puckers or draws up lengthwise when needle thread (green) is too tight (a). Loosen needle tension until fabric relaxes. Test knits for thread breakage, loosening needle thread if necessary. On 4/3-thread machine (b), adjust each needle thread (blue, green) individually.

Needle too loose.
Needle thread (green) forms loose loops underneath fabric (a). Tighten needle tension for flat, smooth stitches. On 4/3-thread serger (b), adjust each needle thread (blue, green) individually.

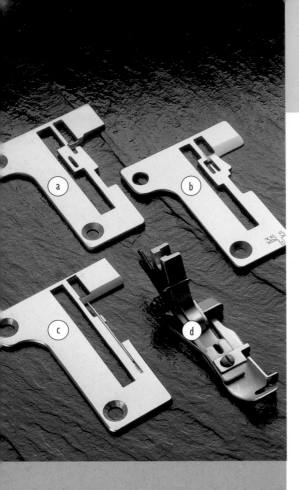

Serger Basics

To begin stitching, run the serger without fabric under the presser foot to create a chain of stitches about 2" (5 cm) long. A thread chain at the start and end of seams prevents stitches from raveling. Operating a serger without fabric does not damage the machine or break threads, because stitches are formed on the stitch fingers (prongs).

The throat plate on most sergers has one (a) or two (b) stitch fingers. Stitches are formed around the stitch finger so that, with the correct tension, the width of the stitch finger determines the width of the stitch. A special throat plate with a narrow stitch finger (c) is used to sew a rolled hem or seam.

The presser foot may also contain a stitch finger (d). Machines with this type of presser foot use a special presser foot for a rolled hem or seam.

How to Change Thread

(1) **Cut** each thread near cone, and remove cone. Tie new thread onto each thread in machine, using small overhand knot. Clip thread ends ½" (1.3 cm) from knot.

(2) **Release** tensions, or set tension controls on 0. Cut needle thread in front of needle. Pull on tail chain to separate threads.

(3) **Pull** threads one at a time through thread guides, upper looper, and lower looper. Pull needle thread until knot reaches needle eye. Cut off knot; thread needle with tweezers.

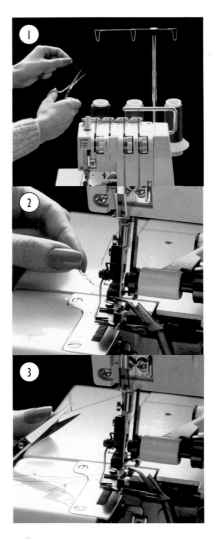

How to Clear the Stitch Fingers

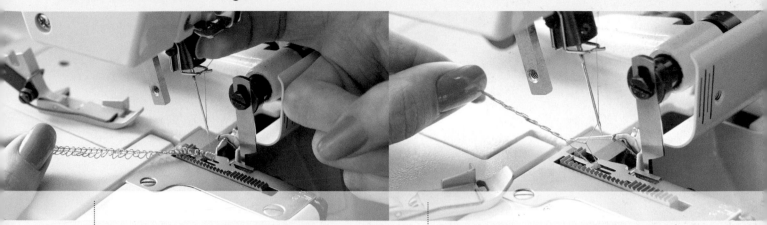

① **Raise** presser foot. Turn flywheel to raise needle. Place left hand on thread chain behind presser foot. To slacken needle thread, pull it gently above last thread guide before needle. (Presser foot has been removed to show detail.)

② **Pull** straight back on thread chain behind presser foot until threads separate and stitch fingers (prongs) of throat plate or presser foot are empty.

How to Start a Seam

① **Make** thread chain. Stitch seam for one or two stitches. Raise presser foot; turn flywheel to lift needle. Clear stitch fingers. Run your fingers along thread chain to make it smooth. (Presser foot has been removed to show detail.)

② **Bring** thread chain to the left, around and under presser foot. Place thread chain between needle and knife. Hold thread chain in position, and lower presser foot.

③ **Stitch** seam over thread chain for about 1" (2.5 cm); then swing thread chain to the right so it is trimmed off as you continue to stitch seam.

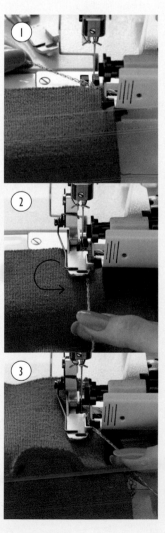

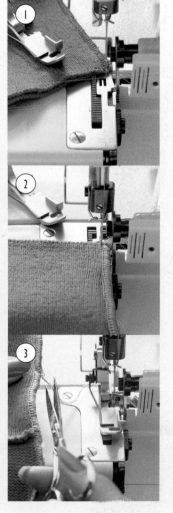

How to End a Seam

① **Stitch** past end of seam by one stitch, and stop. Raise presser foot and needle to clear stitch fingers. (Presser foot has been removed to show detail.)

② **Turn** seam over, and rotate it to align edge of seam with edge of knife. Lower presser foot. Turn flywheel to insert needle at end of seam and at left of edge the width of stitch.

③ **Stitch** over previous stitches for about 1" (2.5 cm). Stitch off edge, leaving thread chain. With scissors or serger knife, trim thread chain close to edge of seam.

How to Stitch Inside Corners and Slits

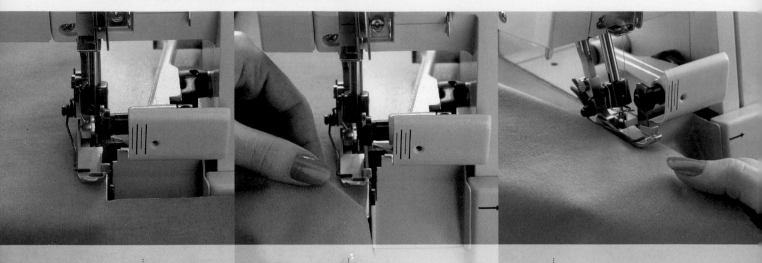

1 **Finish** seams of inside corners by aligning raw edge of fabric with knife of serger. Stitch, stopping before corner.

2 **Fold** the fabric to the left to straighten edge. This may create a tuck, which will not be stitched.

3 **Resume** stitching, holding fabric in straight line. Once past corner, fabric can be relaxed.

How to Stitch Curved Edges

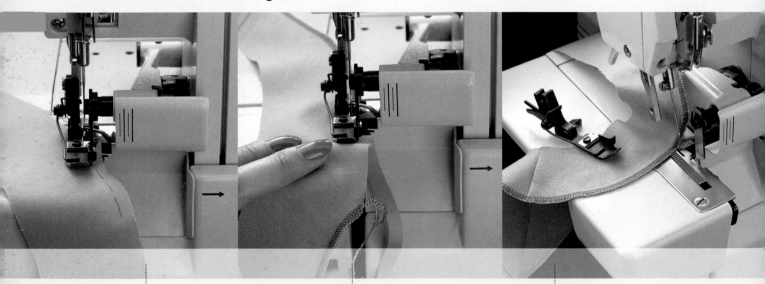

1 **Begin** cutting at an angle, until you reach the desired cutting or stitching line.

2 **Guide** fabric in front of presser foot so knives trim raw edge to curved shape. While stitching, watch knife, not needle.

3 **Stop** when stitches overlap previous stitches. Lift presser foot. Shift fabric so it is behind needle; stitch off edge to prevent gradual looping over edge of fabric. (Presser foot has been removed to show needle position.)

How to Stitch Outside Corners

(1) **Trim off** seam allowance past corner for about 2" (5 cm). If making napkins, placemats, or similar projects, you can cut fabric to finished size and omit this step.

(2) **Sew** one stitch past end of the corner, and stop. Raise presser foot and needle to clear stitch fingers and slacken needle thread slightly. (Presser foot has been removed to show needle position.)

(3) **Pivot** fabric to align raw edge of trimmed seam allowance with knife. Insert needle at serged edge. Lower presser foot, and continue stitching.

How to Remove Stitches

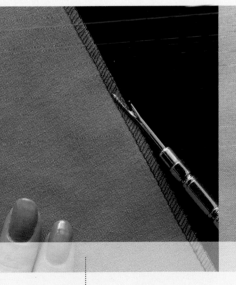
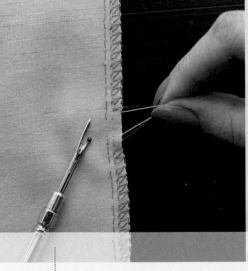
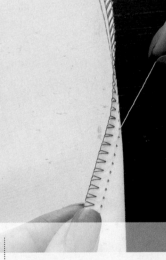

(1) **2-thread stitch.** Cut threads by sliding seam ripper or blade of scissors under the stitches. Remove cut threads.

(2) **3-thread or 4/3-thread stitch.** Clip needle threads every three or four stitches, working from upper side. Pull both looper threads straight out at edge. Remove cut threads.

(3) **4/2-thread stitch.** Working from under side, pull on looper thread to remove chainstitching. Remove overedging as described for 2-thread stitch, left.

Essential Equipment and Supplies

Basic sewing is divided into five processes: measuring, cutting, marking, stitching by hand or machine, and pressing. For each of these tasks, there are essential tools to make the steps easier and the results superior. Build an equipment inventory as you add to your sewing skills.

Sewing-Machine Needles

Select needle size and type according to fabric type and weight and the kind of stitching you will be doing. For general construction, use sharp points (a) for woven and nonwoven fabrics, ballpoints (b) for knits. These are usually distinguished by the color of the shaft. Universal points (c) can be used for many fabric types, knitted and woven, and they are also available with a slip-in thread slot for sewers with poor vision. There are needles designed specifically for sewing leather (d) and denim (e). For decorative sewing, use needles designed for topstitching (f), embroidery (g), metallic threads (h), and quilting (i). Twin and triple needles (j), available in different sizes and widths of separation, are used for stitching two or three parallel rows at a time. Hemstitching, or wing, needles (k) are used for heirloom embroidery. Multiple and hemstitch needles can only be used on zigzag machines that have wide needle holes in the throat plate.

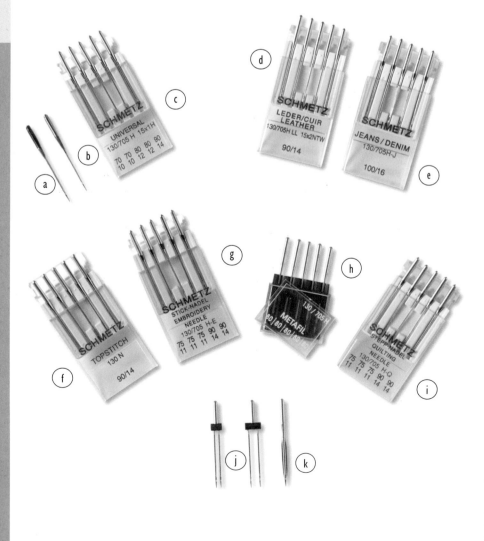

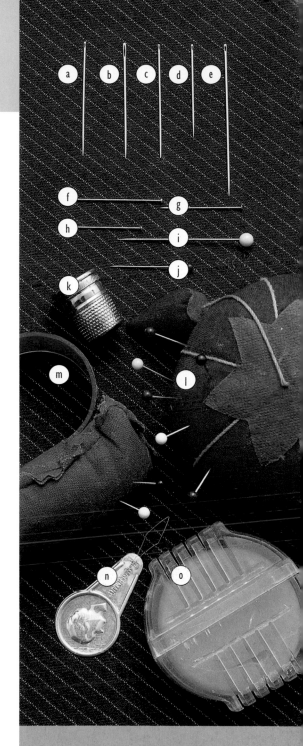

Hand Sewing Equipment

Needles and pins are available in a variety of sizes and styles for different uses. Look for rustproof needles and pins made of brass, nickel-plated steel, or stainless steel. Pins with colored ball heads rather than flat heads are easier to see in fabric and less likely to get lost.

(a) **Sharps** are all-purpose, medium-length needles used for general sewing

(b) **Crewels** are generally used for embroidery. They are sharp and of medium length.

(c) **Ballpoint** needles are used on knits. Instead of a sharp point which may pierce the fabric, the rounded end pushes the knit loops apart.

(d) **Betweens** are very short and round-eyed. They are used to help make fine stitches or for quilting.

(e) **Milliner's** needles are long with round eyes, used for making long basting or gathering stitches.

(f) **Silk** pins are used for light- to medium-weight fabrics. Size 17 is 1 1/16" (2.6 cm) long; size 20 is 1 1/4" (3.2 cm). Both are also available with glass or plastic heads. Extra fine 1 3/4" (4.5 cm) silk pins are easier to see in fabric because of their length.

(g) **Straight** pins in brass, steel, or stainless steel are used for general sewing. They are usually 1 1/16" (2.6 cm) long.

(h) **Pleating** pins are only 1" (2.5 cm) long, for pinning delicate fabrics in the seam allowance.

(i) **Quilting** pins are 1 3/4" (4.5 cm) long, used for heavy materials because of their length.

(j) **Ballpoint** pins are used for knits.

(k) **Thimble** protects your middle finger while hand sewing. It is available in sizes 6 (small) to 12 (large) for individual, snug fit.

(l) **Pin cushion** provides a safe place to store pins. Some pin cushions have an emery pack (an abrasive material) attached for cleaning pins and needles. A wrist pin cushion (m) keeps pins handy.

(n) **Needle threader** eases threading of hand or machine needles.

(o) **Beeswax with holder** strengthens thread and prevents tangling for hand sewing.

Marking Tools

The symbols on a pattern piece are guides for the accurate construction of the garment. Transferring these symbols from pattern to fabric is essential to fitting and sewing. Because you will be working with several types of fabrics, you will need a variety of marking tools.

(a) **Tracing wheels** come in two types: serrated or smooth edge. The serrated edge makes a dotted line marking. It is suitable for most fabrics but may pierce delicate ones.

The smooth-edge tracing wheel protects delicate, smooth fabrics such as silk and chiffon. It makes a solid line marking.

(b) **Dressmaker's tracing paper** transfers the tracing wheel's line to the fabric. Choose a color close to that of the fabric, making sure it can be seen easily.

(c) **Tailor's chalk or marking pencil** marks quickly and easily, directly on the fabric. Chalk rubs off quickly, so use it only when you plan

to sew immediately. A tailor tacker (d) holds two pieces of chalk and marks from both sides.

(e) **Liquid marking pens** make quick work of marking tucks, darts, pleats, and pockets. One type disappears within 48 hours. The other washes off with water but should not be used on fabrics that show water marks. Pressing may set the marks permanently, so remove marking before pressing the area.

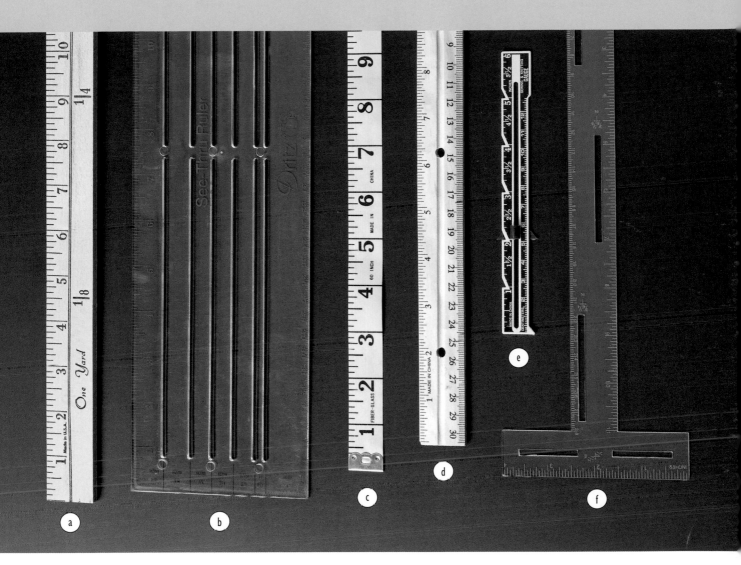

Measuring Tools

Body and pattern measurements both require measuring tools. To ensure a good fit, measure often and accurately with the best tool for the job.

(a) Yardstick is for general marking and for measuring fabric grainline when laying out the pattern. It should be made of smooth hardwood or metal.

(b) See-through ruler lets you see what you measure or mark.

This ruler is used to check fabric grainline and to mark buttonholes, tucks, and pleats.

(c) Tape measure has the flexibility required to take body measurements. Select a 60" (150 cm) long tape with metal tips, made of a material that will not stretch. It should be reversible, with numbers and markings printed on both sides.

(d) Ruler is for general marking. The most useful sizes are 12" or 18" (30.5 or 46 cm) long.

(e) Seam gauge helps make quick, accurate measurements for hems, buttonholes, and pleats. It is a small, 6" (15 cm) metal or plastic ruler with a sliding marker.

(f) See-through T-square is used to locate cross grains, alter patterns, and square off straight edges.

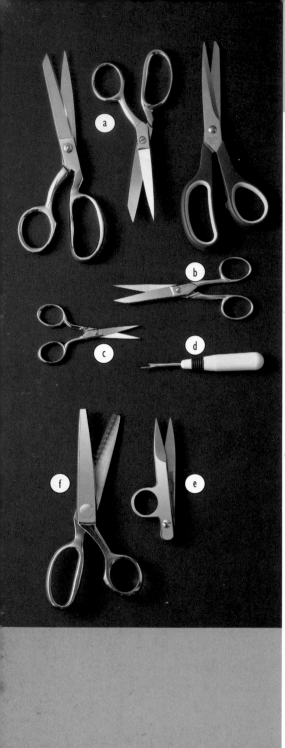

Cutting Tools

Buy quality cutting tools and keep them at their best with periodic sharpening by a qualified professional. Scissors have both handles the same size; shears have one handle larger than the other. Blades should be joined with an adjustable screw (not a rivet) to ensure even pressure along the length of the blade. Sharp shears make clean cuts and well-defined notches. More important, they do not damage fabric. Dull shears slow the cutting process, and make your hand and wrist tire easily. Sewing shears should not be used for other household tasks such as cutting paper or twine. Occasionally put a drop of oil on the screw assembly, wipe them clean with a soft dry cloth after use, and store them in a box or pouch.

(a) **Bent-handled dressmaker's shears** are best for pattern cutting because the angle of the lower blade lets fabric lie flat on the cutting surface. Blade lengths of 7" or 8" (18 or 20.5 cm) are most popular, but lengths up to 12" (30.5 cm) are available. Select a blade length appropriate to the size of your hand. Left-handed models are also available. If you sew a great deal, invest in a pair of all-steel, chrome-plated shears for heavy-duty cutting. The lighter models with stainless steel blades and plastic handles are fine for less-frequent sewing or lightweight fabrics.

Sewing scissors (b) have one pointed and one rounded tip for trimming and clipping seams and facings. The 6" (15 cm) blade is most practical. Embroidery scissors (c) have 4" or 5" (10 or 12.5 cm) finely tapered blades. Both points are sharp for use in hand work and precision cutting.

(d) **Seam ripper** quickly rips seams, opens buttonholes, and removes stitches. Use carefully to avoid piercing the fabric.

(e) **Thread clipper** with spring-action blades is more convenient than shears and safer than a seam ripper.

(f) **Pinking shears or scalloping shears** cut a zigzag or scalloped edge instead of a straight one. Used to finish seams and raw edges on many types of fabric, they cut a ravel-resistant edge.

(g) **Rotary cutter** works like a pizza cutter and can be used by left or right-handed sewers. Use the rotary cutter with a special plastic mat available in different sizes. The mat protects both the cutting surface and the blade. A special locking mechanism retracts the blade for safety.

Pressing Tools

Pressing as you sew is one important procedure that is often neglected. It may seem like a needless interruption, but pressing at each stage of construction is the secret to a perfectly finished garment.

If you need help getting into the pressing habit, locate your pressing equipment near your sewing area. It also helps to press in batches. Do this by stitching as much as possible at the machine. Then press all the stitched areas at one time.

Pressing does not mean ironing. In ironing, you glide the iron over the fabric. In pressing, you move the iron very little while it is in contact with the fabric. Use minimum pressure on the iron, and press in the direction of the fabric grain. Lift the iron to move to another section.

Your pattern directions usually tell when to press, but the general rule is: Press each stitched seam before crossing with another. Press on the wrong side to prevent iron shine, and protect the iron's soleplate by removing pins before pressing.

(a) **Steam/spray iron** should have a wide temperature range to accommodate all fabrics. Buy a dependable, name-brand iron. An iron that steams and sprays at any setting, not just the higher heat settings, is helpful for synthetic fabrics.

Tailor's ham or pressing mitt is used when pressing shaped areas such as curved seams, darts, collars, or sleeve caps. The ham (b) is a firmly packed cushion with rounded curves. One side is cotton; the other side is covered with wool to retain more steam. The mitt (c) is similar to the ham but is especially handy for small, hard-to-reach areas. It fits over your hand or a sleeve board.

(d) **Press cloth** helps prevent iron shine and is always used when applying fusible interfacing. The transparent variety allows you to see if the fabric is smooth and the interfacing properly aligned.

(e) **Sleeve board** looks like two small ironing boards attached one on top of the other. It is used when pressing seams and details of small or narrow areas such as sleeves, pants legs, or necklines.

(f) **Point presser/clapper** is made of hardwood and used for pressing seams open in corners and points. The clapper flattens seams by holding steam and heat in the fabric. This tool is used in tailoring to achieve a flat finish and sharp edges on hard-surfaced fabrics.

(g) **Seam roll** is a firmly packed cylindrical cushion for pressing seams. The bulk of the fabric falls to the sides and never touches the iron, preventing the seam from making an imprint on the right side of the fabric.

SPECIAL EQUIPMENT

Many kinds of special equipment are designed to save time in layout, construction, and pressing. The more you sew, the more these aids will become necessities. Just as you would invest in timesaving devices for cooking and cleaning, invest in sewing equipment to make your wardrobe and home decorating projects go faster.

Before using a new product, read all instructions carefully. Learn what special handling or care is required, and what fabrics or techniques it is suited for. Here is an overview of some of these specialized sewing products.

(a) **Table-top ironing board** is portable and saves space. It is easy to set up near your sewing machine. This ironing board keeps large pieces of fabric on the table so they do not stretch out or drag on the floor. It also helps cultivate the habit of detail pressing while you sew.

(b) **Needle gripper** locks tight to hold the needle, allowing needle to be pulled through heavy fabric.

(c) **Glue** substitutes for pinning or basting by holding fabric, leather, vinyl, felt, trims, patch pockets, and zippers in place for permanent stitching. Use it for craft work as well as general sewing. Glue stick is water soluble, so it provides only a temporary bond. Liquid glue can be dotted in seam allowances to hold layers of fabric together.

(d) **Liquid ravel preventer** is a colorless plastic liquid which prevents fraying by stiffening fabric slightly. It is helpful when you have clipped too far into a seam allowance or want to reinforce a pocket or buttonhole. It darkens light colors slightly, so apply cautiously. The liquid becomes a permanent finish that will withstand laundering and dry cleaning.

(e) **Basting tape** is double-faced adhesive tape that eliminates pinning and thread basting. Use it on leather and vinyl as well as on fabric. The tape is especially helpful for matching stripes and plaids, applying zippers, and positioning pockets and trims. Do not machine-stitch through the tape, because the adhesive may foul your machine needle.

Loop turner is specially designed with a latch hook device at one end to grasp bias tubing or cording and turn it to the right side. It is quicker and easier than attaching a safety pin to one end and working the pin through. Because the wire is so fine, it can be used for very narrow tubing and button loops.

Bodkin threads ribbon, elastic, or cord through a casing without twisting. Some bodkins have an eye through which ribbon or elastic is threaded; others have a tweezer or safety pin closure that grabs the elastic. The bodkin above has a ring that slides to tighten the prongs of the pincers.

Point turner pokes out the tailored points in collars, lapels, and pockets without risking a tear. Made of wood or plastic, its point fits neatly into corners. Use the point to remove basting thread and the rounded end to hold seamlines open for pressing.

Buttonhole cutter makes precision cuts down the center of buttonholes. It comes with a wooden block to place under the fabric, to protect your work surface and accept the sharp thin blade of the cutter. A buttonhole cutter is more accurate than scissors or a seam ripper and less likely to cut the stitches.

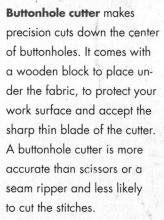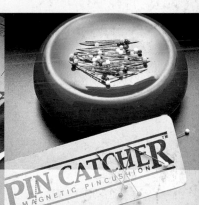

Paper-backed fusible web is sold on rolls, in various narrow widths. It is a timesaving product used for adhering two pieces of fabric together. A protective paper backing is removed from one side after the other side has been heat-fused to the fabric.

Folding cutting board protects a fine table's finish from pin or shears scratches. It also prevents fabric from slipping while cutting, and holds fabric more securely. Stick pins into it for faster pinning, square off fabric against marked lines, and use the 1" (2.5 cm) squares as an instant measure. The folding feature makes storage easy.

Weights hold a pattern in place for cutting. They eliminate time-consuming pinning and unpinning of the pattern and protect fabrics that would be permanently marked by pins. Weights are most easily used on smaller pattern pieces. Some sewers use items like cans of vegetables in place of retail weights.

Magnetic pin catcher and pin cushion keep all-steel pins in their place. The pin catcher attaches to the throat plate of the machine to catch pins as you pull them out while stitching. The magnetic, weighted pin cushion is especially handy for picking pins off the floor. If you have a computerized machine, avoid placing the magnetic pin catcher or cushion on the machine.

are designed for hand and machine sewing on all fabrics: natural fibers and synthetics, wovens, and knits. Heavy thread, designed for machine stitching on denim and canvas, is usually 100% polyester for strength. It can also be used for topstitching to make the stitches more apparent. Button and carpet thread is suitable for hand sewing where extra strength is required. It can also be used for topstitching.

b **Serger thread** is wrapped on large cones and is usually 100% polyester. To use this thread on your conventional machine, place the cone in a jar behind the machine as close as possible to the first thread guide.

c **Polyester thread** is the strongest, longest lasting, given equal weight. It is suitable for most general sewing on medium to heavy fabrics, but avoid using it on lightweight and delicate fabrics. When seams are stressed, polyester thread can tear delicate fibers. Silk thread is slightly elastic and has a high sheen, suitable for machine embroidery. It is a good choice for sewing on fine wool or for hand appliqué and hemming because the stitches sink into the fabric and tend to disappear. Avoid bleach, which weakens silk thread. Mercerized cotton thread is used for natural fiber woven fabrics like cotton, linen, and wool; it does not have enough stretch for knits.

Thread

Thread comes wrapped on short thick spools, long thin spools, or cones. Read the labels carefully to find fiber content and thread weight. Select high-quality thread according to the fiber and weight of the fabric and the purpose of the stitching. As a general guideline, use a natural fiber thread for natural fiber fabrics

and synthetic fiber thread for synthetic fabrics. For perfect tension, use the same size and type thread in the bobbin as you use in the needle.

a **Fine thread** reduces fabric puckering on lightweight fabrics. All-purpose thread may be 100% polyester or have a polyester core wrapped with cotton. Both kinds

Trims and Tapes

Choose trims and tapes that are compatible with your fabric and thread. Most trims and tapes can be machine stitched, but some must be applied by hand. Preshrink trims for washable garments.

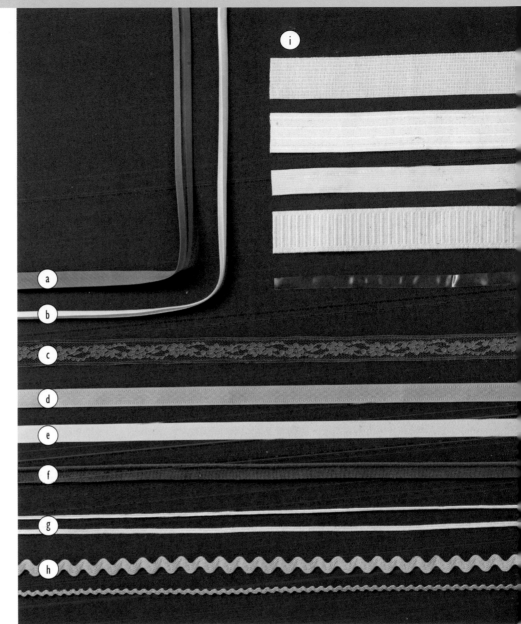

(a) **Single-fold bias tape**, available in ¼", ½", and ⅞" (6 mm, 1.3 cm, and 2.2 cm) widths, comes in a wide range of solid colors. The narrow width is used for "windowpane" quilts. The medium and wide tapes are used for casings, trim, and facings.

(b) **Double-fold bias tape** binds a raw edge. It comes in ¼" (6 mm) and ½" (1.3 cm) folded widths.

(c) **Lace seam binding** is a decorative, flexible lace hem finish.

(d) **Seam tape** is 100% polyester, ½" (1.3 cm) wide, used to stay seams and finish hems.

(e) **Twill tape** is used to stay seams or roll lines. It can also be used for drawstrings or ties. Twill tape is available in various widths from ¼" to 1" (6 mm to 2.5 cm) in black, white, and limited colors.

(f) **Corded piping** is an accent trim inserted in seams to define and decorate edges.

(g) **Braid** is available in soutache and middy styles. Use it for accent, scroll motifs, drawstrings, ties, or button loops.

(h) **Rickrack** comes in ¼", ½", and ⅝" (6 mm, 1.3 cm, and 1.5 cm) widths for accent trim and edging.

(i) **Elastic** is inserted in casings to shape waistbands, wrists, and necklines. Knitted and woven elastics are softer than braided elastics, curl less, and can be stitched directly onto the fabric. Nonroll waistband elastic has lateral ribs to keep it from twisting or rolling. Clear elastic, made of 100% polyurethane, is great for sheer fabrics, lingerie, and swimwear.

c **Self-covered buttons** can be covered with the same fabric as the garment for an exact color match.

d **Toggles** are bar fasteners closed with fabric or cord loops, used on lapped areas.

e **Frogs** are loop-and-ball fasteners that lend a dressy look to special outfits.

f **Snaps** are inside closures for areas that do not receive much stress, such as cuffs.

g **Gripper snaps** are hammered on or applied with a tool on the outside of a garment for a decorative effect.

h **Hooks and eyes** are inside closures available in sizes appropriate to various fabric weights.

i **Heavy-duty hooks and eyes** are used to close waistbands on skirts or pants.

j **Hook and loop fasteners** (Velcro) are available in tapes and small pieces. They are used for closures on lapped areas of garments or home décor items.

k **Snap tape** is often used on leg seams of infant clothes for easy diaper changes. It is also useful for closures on casual clothing and home décor items.

Buttons and Closures

Select these notions either to blend with the garment or stand out and make a fashion statement. Closures can be decorative as well as functional.

a **Sew-through, two-hole or four-hole buttons** are commonly used, all-purpose buttons.

b **Shank buttons** have a "neck" or shank underneath the button.

Zippers

Zippers have metal or plastic teeth, or a synthetic coil attached to a woven tape. Both types come in all-purpose weights. Coil zippers are lightweight, flexible, heat-resistant, and rustproof. Metal zippers come in heavier weights for heavy fabrics and sportswear. Although zippers are usually designed to blend into the garment, some are made to be shown off.

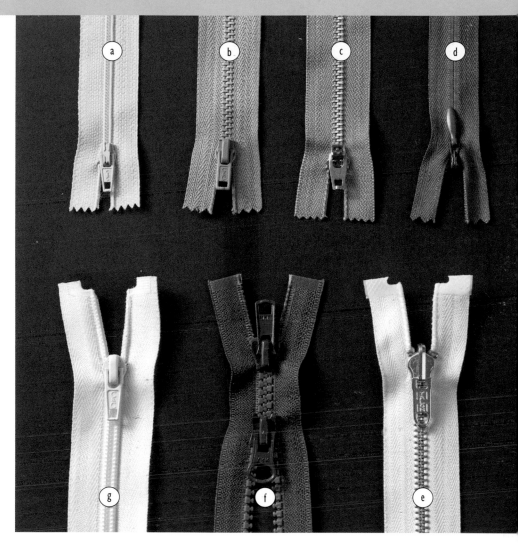

(a) **Polyester all-purpose** zippers are suitable for fabrics of all weights in skirts, pants, dresses, and home decorating items.

(b) **Metal all-purpose** zippers are strong, durable zippers for sportswear as well as pants, skirts, dresses, and home decorating items.

(c) **Brass jean** zippers have brass teeth on blue tapes with a closed bottom, designed for jeans, work, and casual wear in medium to heavyweight fabrics.

(d) **Invisible** zippers are inserted using a special foot designed by the zipper manufacturer. Once installed, the zipper is hidden in the seam and only the slim tab shows.

(e) **Metal** separating zippers, available in medium and heavy weights, are used in jackets, sportswear, and home decorating. Reversible separating zippers have pull tabs that flip to the front and back of the zipper.

(f) **Plastic molded separating** zippers are lightweight yet strong and durable. Their decorative appearance makes them a natural for skiwear and outdoor wear. Two-way zippers have two sliders, so they can be opened from the top and bottom.

(g) **Coil separating** zippers are designed for sweaters and lightweight jackets.

The Pattern

Shopping a pattern catalog is more creative than shopping a ready-to-wear catalog. In a pattern catalog, you aren't limited to the fabric, color, skirt length, or buttons you see on the pages. You are the designer of your own fashion. You can choose the combination that flatters you and expresses your own personal style.

Pattern selection has never been better. Designer styles are available in the same season that they appear in ready-to-wear. There are easy patterns for the sewer with limited time. You will find patterns for accessories, home decoration, evening wear, men's and boys' fashions, and almost every kind of women's or children's garment.

The pattern catalog is divided into categories by size or fashion look. The newest fashions usually appear in the first few pages of each category. Pattern illustrations are accompanied by information on recommended fabrics and yardage requirements. An index at the back of the catalog lists patterns in nu-merical order along with their page numbers. The back of the catalog also includes a complete size chart for every figure type: male, female, children, and infants.

Match the pattern's level of sewing difficulty to your sewing experience. For success, select a pattern appropriate to your sewing skill. If your time or patience is limited, stay with simpler styles.

The number of pattern pieces listed on the back of the pattern is a clue to the complexity of the pattern. The fewer the pieces, the easier the pattern. Details like shirt cuffs, collar bands, pleats, and tucks also make a pattern more difficult to sew. Easy-to-sew patterns feature few of these details.

All pattern companies follow a uniform sizing based on standard body measurements. This is not exactly the same as ready-to-wear sizing. To select the right pattern size, first take your standard body measurements. Wear your usual undergarments and use a tape measure that doesn't stretch. For accuracy, have another person measure you. Record your measurements and compare them with the size chart provided in the pattern catalog.

How to Take Standard Body Measurements

(1) **Waistline.** Tie a string or piece of elastic around your middle and allow it to roll to your natural waistline. Measure at this exact location with tape measure. Leave string in place as a reference for measuring hips and back waist length.

(2) **Hips.** Measure around the fullest part. This is usually 7" to 9" (18 to 23 cm) below the waistline, depending on your height.

(3) **High bust.** Place tape measure under arms, across widest part of back and above full bustline. Pattern size charts do not include a high bust measurement, but this measurement should be compared with the full bust to choose the right size pattern.

(4) **Full bust.** Place tape measure under arms, across widest part of the back and fullest part of bustline. Note: If there is a difference of 2" (5 cm) or more between high and full bust, select pattern size by high bust measurement.

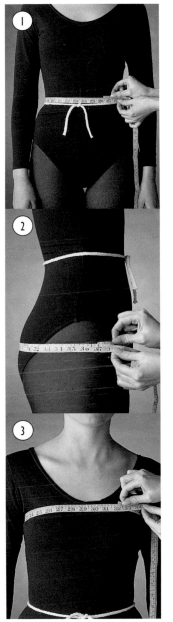

(5) **Back waist length.** Measure from middle of the most prominent bone at the base of the neck down to waistline string.

(6) **Height.** Measure without shoes. Stand with your back against a wall. Place a ruler on top of your head and mark the wall. Measure from the mark to the floor.

THE PATTERN ENVELOPE

The pattern envelope contains a wealth of information, from a description of the garment to the amount of fabric needed. It gives ideas for fabric and color selection. The envelope helps you determine the degree of sewing difficulty with labels that indicate whether the style is a designer original, easy-to-sew or only suitable for certain fabrics. On the pattern envelope, you'll also find all the information needed to select fabric and notions.

The Envelope Front

Views are alternate designs of the pattern. They may show optional trims, lengths, fabric combinations or design details to appeal to a beginner, or challenge an experienced sewer.

Pattern company name and style number are prominently displayed on the pattern envelope.

Fashion photograph or illustration shows the main pattern design. It suggests suitable fabric types such as wool or cotton, and fabric designs such as print or plaid. If you are unsure of your fabric choice, use the pattern illustration as your guide. It is the designer's interpretation of the fashion.

Designer original patterns, indicated by the designer's name, often contain more difficult-to-sew details such as tucks, topstitching, linings, or underlinings. For sewers who have the time and skill, these patterns provide designer fashions that duplicate ready-to-wear.

Labels may identify a pattern that has easy construction methods, is designed for timesaving sewing, has special fitting or size-related information, or shows how to handle fabrics like plaids, knits, or lace. Each pattern company has special categories and names for these designs.

Size and figure type are indicated at the top or side of the pattern. If the pattern is multi-sized, such as 8–10–12, you will find cutting lines for all three sizes on one pattern.

The Envelope Back

(a) **Body measurement and size chart** is a reference to determine if you need to make alterations. For a multi-sized pattern, compare your measurements with those in the chart to decide which cutting line to use.

(b) **Garment descriptions** include information on style, fit, and how the garment is constructed.

(c) **Style number** is repeated on the back of the envelope.

(d) **Yardage block** tells you how much fabric to buy for the size and garment view you have selected. Yardage for lining, interfacing, and trims is also listed. To determine how much fabric you need, match the garment or view and the fabric width at the left with your size at the top of the chart. The number where the two columns meet is the number of yards to buy. The most common fabric widths are given. If the width of your fabric is not given, check the conversion chart at the back of the pattern catalog. Some patterns list the extra yardage required for napped fabrics or uneven plaids.

(e) **Metric equivalents** of body measurements and yardage are included for countries that use the metric system.

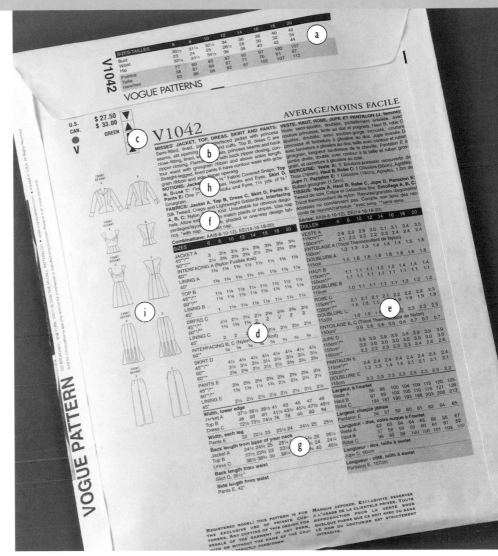

(f) **Fabric types** suitable for the garments are suggested. Use them as a general guide to fabric selection. The special advice, such as "unsuitable for stripes or obvious diagonals," alerts you to fabrics that are not appropriate.

(g) **Finished garment measurements** indicate finished length and width. You may need to make length adjustments. The "width at lower edge" is the measurement at the hemmed edge, indicating the fullness of the garment.

(h) **Notions**, such as thread, zipper, buttons, and seam binding, which are required for garment construction are listed. Purchase them at the same time as the fabric to ensure a good color match.

(i) **Back views** show the details and style of the garments' back.

Number of pattern pieces gives an idea of how easy or complicated the pattern is to sew.

INSIDE THE PATTERN

Open the pattern envelope to find the printed pattern pieces and the direction sheet which guides you, step-by-step, through the construction of the garment. Read through the direction sheet before cutting or sewing. Use it to plan and organize your sewing time, and alert you to the techniques you need to know as you progress.

Views of a single garment are labeled by number or letter. Patterns which include several different garments such as a skirt, jacket, and pants (called wardrobe patterns) usually feature only one version of each. In this case, each garment is identified by name only. All pattern pieces are identified with a number and name, such as skirt front.

Fashion drawings and views are featured prominently on the direction sheet, sketched as they appear on the front of the envelope or as detailed line drawings. Some patterns illustrate each garment separately with the pattern pieces used in its construction. Most patterns illustrate all the pattern pieces together, with a key to identify the pieces used for each garment or view.

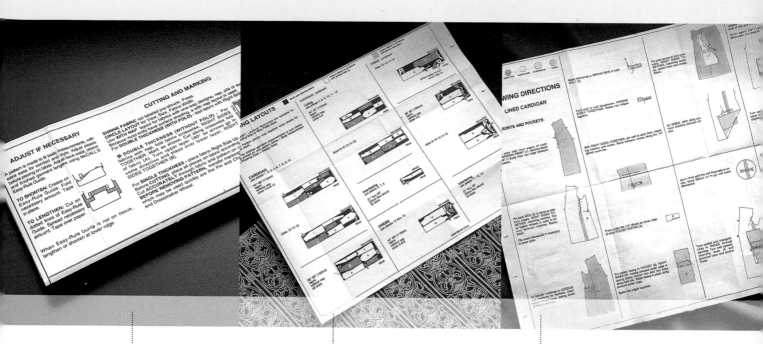

General instructions are given as a short refresher sewing course. These instructions may have a different name on each pattern, but they generally contain tips on how to use the pattern. Included is information on pattern and fabric preparation; explanation of pattern markings; cutting, layout, and marking tips; and a short glossary of sewing terms. The easy-to-sew and beginner patterns often incorporate these tips into the step-by-step instructions.

Cutting layouts are shown for each garment view. They differ according to the width of the fabric, pattern size, and whether the fabric has nap. Layouts for interfacing and lining are also included. When the fabric is to be cut in a single thickness or on the crosswise grain, the pattern layout indicates this with a symbol, explained in the general instructions. A pattern piece, right side up, is illustrated without shading; wrong side up, it is shaded or scored. Circle the layout for the correct pattern size, fabric width, and view.

Sewing directions are a step-by-step guide to constructing the garment, arranged by views. Beside each instruction is a sketch illustrating the sewing technique. The right side of the fabric usually appears shaded; the wrong side, plain. Interfacing is indicated with dots. Together, the sketch and the directions give you a clear picture of exactly what to do. Remember that these are only general directions. An alternative technique may be more effective for the fabric you are using.

The Pattern Pieces

The pattern piece tissue may look like it is printed with secret symbols but, like international road signs, these markings are universal symbols used by all pattern companies. Pattern symbols are used from the time you start to lay out the pattern until you finish the hem or sew the last button in place.

Pattern pieces have instructions as well as symbols printed on them. Follow these instructions just as carefully as you follow those on the direction sheet.

Layout and cutting symbols such as grainlines do not need to be transferred to the fabric. Construction symbols must be transferred to the fabric for accurate garment construction (page 81).

Symbol	Description	How to Use
	**Grainline.** Heavy solid line with arrows at each end.	Place pattern piece on fabric with arrow parallel to selvage.
	Fold bracket. Long bracket with arrows at each end or "place on fold" instruction.	Place pattern piece with arrows or edge exactly on fold of fabric.
	**Cutting line.** Heavy solid line along outer edge of pattern. May also designate a "cut-off line" for a certain view.	Cut on this line. When more than one size is printed on one piece, use the cutting line for size that fits best.
	Adjustment line. Double line indicating where pattern can be lengthened or shortened before cutting.	To shorten, make a tuck in pattern between lines. To lengthen, cut pattern between lines and spread apart.
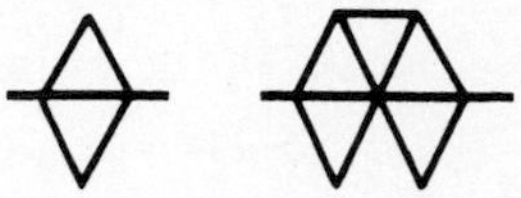	**Notches.** Diamond shapes along cutting line, used for matching seams. Numbered in order in which seams are joined.	Cut out into margin of pattern or make short snips into seam allowance. Match like-numbered notches accurately.
	**Seamline.** Long, broken line, usually ⅝" (1.5 cm) inside cutting line. Multi-sized patterns do not have printed seamlines.	Unless otherwise specified, stitch ⅝" (1.5 cm) from cut edge.
	Foldline. Solid line marking where garment is to be folded during construction.	Fold along this line when sewing facings, hems, tucks, or pleats.
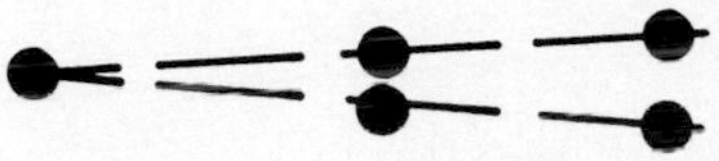	**Dart.** Broken line and dots forming a "V" shape, usually at hipline, bustline, or elbow.	Mark, fold along center line and carefully match lines and dots. Stitch to a point.
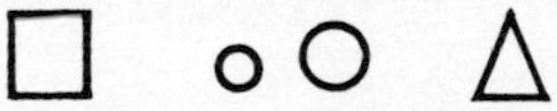	**Dots (large and small), squares, or triangles.** Usually found along seamlines or darts.	Areas of construction where precise matching, clipping, or stitching is essential.
	**Easing line.** Short, broken line with small dot at each end, marking area to be eased.	Easestitch larger piece; pull up stitching to match smaller piece.
	Gathering lines. Two solid or broken lines, or small dots at each end, marking an area to be gathered.	Make two rows of easestitching between dots of larger piece; pull up stitching so dots match with those on smaller piece.
	Hemline. Hem allowance is printed on the cutting line.	Turn hem up the specified amount, adjusting as necessary.
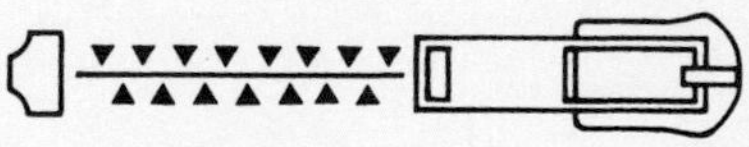	**Zipper placement.** Parallel rows of triangles along seamline where zipper is to be inserted.	Insert zipper so pull tab and bottom stop are positioned where indicated.
	Detail positions. Broken lines indicating placement of pockets, tucks, or other details.	Mark and position detail where indicated.
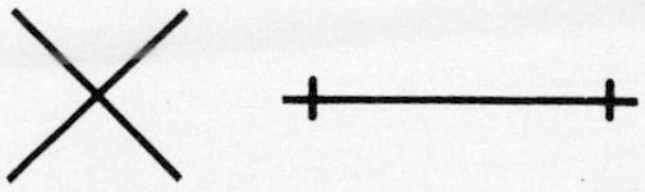	**Button and buttonhole placements.** Solid lines indicate length of buttonhole; "X" or illustration shows button size and placement.	Mark and position where indicated.

Fabric Essentials

All fabrics are based on two kinds of fibers: natural or man-made. Natural fibers are those derived from plants or animals: cotton, wool, silk, and linen. Man-made fibers are produced by chemical processes. They include polyester, nylon, acetate, spandex, and many others.

Combining natural and man-made fibers produces blends which give you the best qualities of several fibers. For example, the strength of nylon may be added to the warmth of wool, the easy care of polyester to the comfort of cotton.

There is an almost endless variety of blends available, and each one behaves differently. Check the fiber content on the bolt end for the kinds and quantities of fibers used. Care instructions are also listed. Examine the hand of the fabric—how it feels, how it drapes, whether it crushes easily or ravels, whether it stretches. Drape the fabric over your hand or arm to determine if it is as soft or crisp, heavy or light, as you need for a particular project.

Fabrics are also classified by fabrication, meaning how they are made. All fabrics are either woven, knit, or nonwoven. The most common woven is the plain weave construction. This is found in fabrics such as muslins, poplin, and taffeta. Denim and gabardine are diagonal weaves. Cotton sateen is a satin weave. Knits also have several classifications. Jersey is an example of a plain knit. Sweater knits can be made by the purl, patterned, or raschel knit processes. Felt is an example of a nonwoven fabric.

Selecting the right fabric for your sewing project takes a little practice. Refer to the back of the pattern envelope for suggestions, and learn to feel the hand of fabric. Quality fabric doesn't have to be expensive. Choose well-made fabric that will wear well and stay looking good.

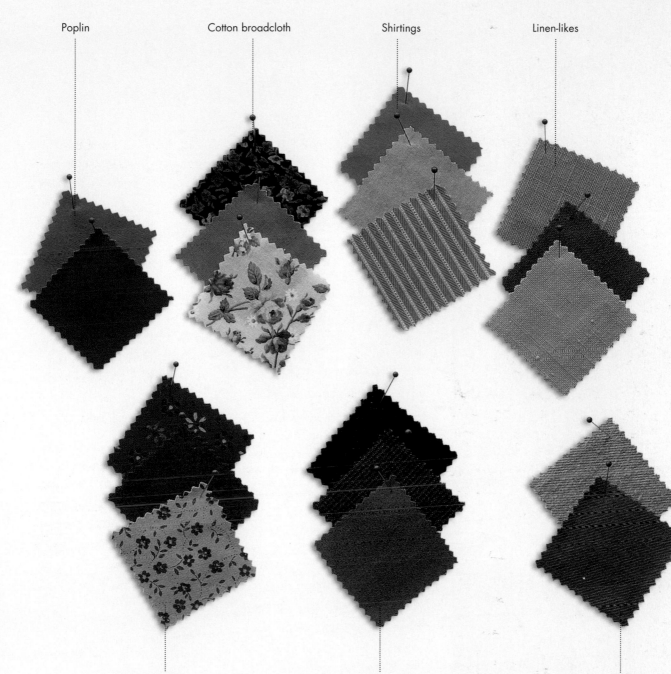

Poplin

Cotton broadcloth

Shirtings

Linen-likes

Firm knits

Firm wool

Denim

Easy-to-Sew Fabrics

There are many fabrics that are easy and quick to sew. These fabrics are generally plain weave or firm knit, of medium weight. Most do not require complicated seam finishes or special handling, since they ravel very little.

Small prints, overall prints, and narrow stripes are easy to sew because they do not require matching at the seams. Prints, especially if they are dark, hide stitching imperfections.

Plain-weave fabrics, such as poplin or cotton broadcloth, are always good choices. Stable or moderate-stretch knits do not need seam finishing, and their stretchability makes fitting easier. Natural-fiber fabrics, such as cottons and lightweight wools, are easy to sew because stitching blends into these fabrics.

For more examples of easy-to-sew fabrics, consult the suggested fabrics that are listed on the backs of easy-to-sew patterns.

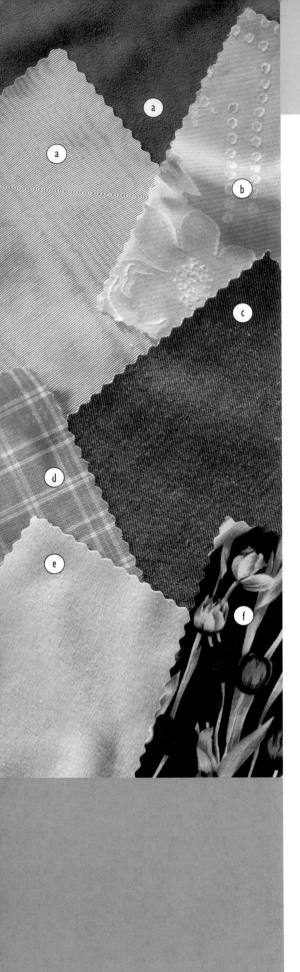

HANDLING SPECIAL FABRICS

Certain fabrics, because of their design or fabrication, need special attention during layout and construction. Some easy-to-sew fabrics fall into this category. The special handling required is usually not difficult. Often you need only add one more step, such as a seam finish, or exercise a little more care.

(a) **Napped and pile** fabrics such as velvet, velveteen, velour, flannel, and corduroy require special care in cutting out. These fabrics appear light and shiny when brushed in one lengthwise direction, and dark when brushed in the other direction. To prevent your garment from having a two-toned look, you must follow the "with nap" layouts on the pattern instruction sheet. Decide which way you want the nap to lie, and cut all pattern pieces with the top edges facing the same direction.

Although satin and moiré taffeta are not napped fabrics, their surfaces reflect light differently in each lengthwise direction. Decide which effect you prefer, and use a one-way layout.

(b) **Sheer** fabrics look best with special seams and seam finishes. Unfinished seam allowances detract from the fragile, see-through look

of voile, batiste, eyelet, or chiffon. French seams are a classic choice, but other seam finishes can also be used.

(c) **Twill weave** fabrics such as denim and gabardine have diagonal ridges. If these ridges are very noticeable, use a "with nap" layout for cutting, and avoid patterns that are not suitable for obvious diagonals. Denim ravels easily and requires enclosed seams.

(d) **Plaids and stripes** require special care in layout and cutting (pages 76 to 80). To match plaids and large stripes at seams, you need to buy extra fabric. Buy ¼ to ½ yd. (0.25 to 0.5 m) more than the pattern calls for, depending on the size of the design.

(e) **Knits** must be handled gently during construction to keep them from stretching out of shape. Special stitches and seam finishes (page 109) are needed to maintain the right amount of stretch.

(f) **One-way design** fabrics, such as some flower and paisley prints, require a "with nap" cutting layout so the design does not go up one side of the garment and down the other. Border prints are cut on the crosswise rather than lengthwise grain of the fabric. They usually require more yardage. Select patterns which show a border print view and specify the correct yardage.

Guide to Fabrics and Sewing Techniques

Type	Fabric	Special Seams	Machine Needle	Thread
Sheers	Crisp: organdy, organza, voile Soft: batiste, lawn, chiffon, China silk, georgette, gauze	French, mock French, self-bound, double-stitched	8 (60), 9 (65), or 11 (75)	Extra-fine: mercerized cotton, cotton-covered polyester, or long-fiber polyester
Lightweight	Silk shirtings, broadcloth, calico, oxford cloth, chambray, lightweight linens, challis, seersucker, eyelet, charmeuse	French, mock French, self-bound, stitched-and-pinked or multi-zigzag, double-stitched	8 (60), 9 (65), or 11 (75)	Extra-fine: mercerized cotton, cotton-covered polyester, or long-fiber polyester
Light to medium-weight knits	Tricot, interlocks, jerseys, light sweater knits, stretch terry, stretch velour	Double-stitched, straight and zigzag, narrow zigzag	11 (75), 14 (90), ballpoint	All-purpose: cotton/polyester, long-fiber polyester
Medium-weight	Wool flannel, linen types, crepe, gabardine, chino, poplin, chintz, corduroy, velvet, velveteen, velour, taffeta, double knits, fleece, sweatshirt knits, denim, quilted fabric	Welt, lapped, flat-fell, mock flat-fell, as well as plain seam with appropriate edge finish	11 (75), 14 (90), ballpoint for knits and fleece	All-purpose: cotton/polyester, long-fiber polyester
Medium- to heavyweight	Heavy wool flannel, fleece, fake fur, canvas, heavy denim, heavy cotton duck, coating	Welt, lapped, flat-fell, mock flat-fell, stitched-and-pinked	16/100, 18/100	Heavy-duty: cotton/polyester, long-fiber polyester, topstitching, and buttonhole twist
No grain (nonwoven)	Leather, suede (natural and man-made), buckskin, calfskin, reptile, plastic, felt	Welt, lapped, mock flat-fell, topstitched, plain seam	11/75, 14/90, 16/100	All-purpose: cotton-wrapped, polyester, long-fiber polyester, Leather: avoid cotton-wrapped, polyester

Classic Fabric Textures and Designs

Whether or not you have had much sewing experience, this group of fabrics probably looks familiar because it includes fabrics that are always in fashion. Some require out-of-the-ordinary sewing techniques, and some need special handling because they have unique surface textures. Others rate extra attention because they have woven, knitted, or printed designs that affect pattern layout.

a **Loose weaves** have coarse or uneven textures and tend to fray. The primary sewing challenge with loosely woven fabrics is to control raveling.

b **Plaids** require careful pattern layout. Study the fabric before pattern layout to decide which bars are dominant, where to position them on the pattern pieces, and whether the design has a one-way direction. Arrange the pattern pieces so the fabric design matches at the most noticeable seams. Careful pinning or basting ensures against mismatches.

c **Stripes** require handling similar to that of plaids. Careful layout and basting is necessary to match stripes attractively.

d **Large prints** are among the most dramatic types of fabric designs. Print repeats can be as large as 24" (61 cm). With prints this size, position the print motifs for pleasing balance.

e **Diagonal fabrics** are woven, knitted, or printed designs that cross the straight fabric grain on a slant. To sew diagonals, it is necessary to adapt patterns for special layouts so the diagonal lines flow around the body in the same direction.

f **Gabardine** is a firmly woven fabric with a twill weave. Characteristic of this weave are the fine diagonal ribs on the right side. The surface is hard and long wearing. This texture needs a "with nap" pattern layout for uniform color shading in the completed garment.

(g) **Velvet** is similar to velveteen because the pile covers the entire surface, but it is made a different way. A velvet pile is formed from warp (lengthwise)—yarns woven into the base. This creates a deep, straight, erect pile. Velvet is handled the same way as corduroy and velveteen.

(h) **Velveteen** is made by shearing pile loops, but unlike corduroy, the loops cover the entire surface. Velveteen requires techniques for layout, stitching, and pressing similar to those for corduroy.

(i) **Corduroy** has a ribbed pile, formed by sheared rows of loops or ribs that contrast with the flat base of the fabric. Use a "with nap" layout and sewing techniques that keep the fabric from shifting while it is being stitched. Special pressing techniques are also necessary.

LOOSE WEAVES

Loosely woven fabrics are often made from yarns that are thick and lightly spun to preserve irregularities and create a hand-loomed look. Two considerations are to control the raveling and to maintain the soft, loose hand of the fabric.

The loosely woven basketweave (a) has two or more yarns woven together in a basket effect. Heavy raw silk (b) is ravel-prone because of the thick and thin crosswise yarns. Gauze fabrics (c), lightweight and crinkly, should be handled with sewing techniques for sheer fabrics. The homespun look (d) is achieved with lightly spun yarns that ravel easily. A pulled thread look (e) creates a novelty windowpane effect.

Pattern Selection

Choose a pattern that has the potential for omitting linings, facings, and interfacings, as well as closures such as buttons and zippers. Many jacket, blouse, and skirt patterns, especially pullover or wrap styles, can be adapted this way. The less stable the fabric, the more loosely fitted the pattern should be. Simple styles are the best. Test the stability of loosely woven fabrics by draping the fabric over your hand and letting a length hang freely. See how much it stretches and whether it drapes softly.

Gently tug on the true bias grain to get a feeling for the amount the fabric gives in this direction.

Fabric Preparation

Preshrink all loose weaves, using the care method planned for the finished garment. To prevent excessive raveling, zigzag crosswise cut ends or bind them with sheer bias tricot binding before washing. To wash, treat loose weaves like delicate fabrics. Air dry to prevent shrinkage from the heat of a dryer. Roll the fabric in towels to remove excess moisture. Spread on a flat surface, and straighten the grain.

Layout, Cutting, and Marking

It is important to arrange the fabric straight and on-grain for pattern layout. Any wavy grainlines will show clearly on the finished garment. When the fabric texture comes from nubby, irregular yarns, use a "with nap" layout. Space pins closely to anchor the pattern pieces securely to the fabric.

If you are working with a fabric that frays readily, cut out the pattern with 1" (2.5 cm) seam allowances. Wider seam allowances are easier to handle for special seam and edge finishes, and they provide ample fabric for clean cuts on raw edges that must be trimmed. Transfer pattern markings with marking pen or thread basting.

Special Seam Techniques

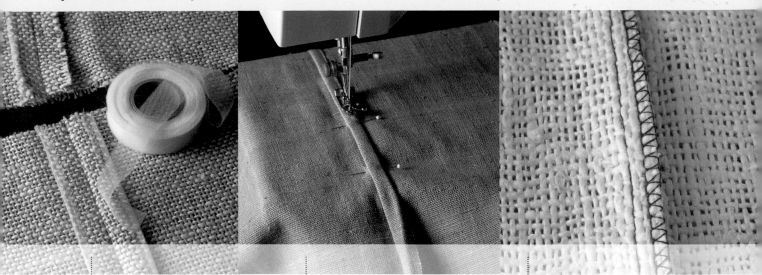

(a) **Plain seam** with raw edges enclosed in sheer tricot bias binding is quick, neat treatment. Use zigzag, 3-step zigzag, or long straight stitches, 10 to 12 per inch (2.5 cm).

(b) **Flat-fell seam**, formed on right side of garment, makes reversible seam which is ideal for roll-up sleeves or other areas showing both faces of seams.

(c) **Overlocked seam**, sewn on 4-thread overlock machine or 3-thread machine with a row of straight stitches, covers raw edges with thread.

Special Hem Techniques

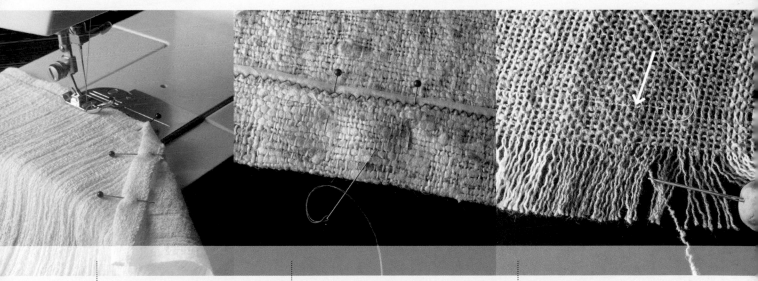

(d) **Topstitch** to stabilize hem edges. This method is fast and attractive. Finish raw edge before hemming; use a zigzag stitch or a 2-thread or 3-thread overlock stitch.

(e) **Bind** edge with sheer tricot bias binding. Hand hem with blind catch-stitch or blind hem, worked loosely between garment and hem.

(f) **Fringe edge.** Pull a thread at desired depth of fringe. Stitch on thread-pulled line (arrow); then one by one remove fabric yarns below stitching.

CORDUROY AND VELVETEEN

Corduroy, made from cotton or a blend of cotton/polyester fibers, comes in many forms. Corduroys are usually named according to the size and style of the ribs (wales).

(a) **Pinwale** corduroy, also named baby wale or fine wale corduroy, is lightweight and has 16 ribs per inch (2.5 cm).

(b) **Midwale** corduroy is heavier than pinwale and has fewer ribs.

(c) **Wide wale**, also called jumbo wale, is a heavyweight corduroy with as few as three ribs per inch (2.5 cm).

(d) **Thick and thin** corduroy is one of the many novelty variations with alternating sizes of ribs.

(e) **Ribless corduroy** resembles the allover plush pile of velveteen.

Traditionally, corduroy is used for casual sports clothes and children's wear because it is durable and washable. Select patterns according to the form you wish to use.

The heavier the fabric and the bulkier the wales, the simpler the pattern style should be. Lightweight corduroys drape softly and can be used for more detailed styles, including those with gathered sections or ruffles. Midweight corduroys are often used for tailored jackets.

(f) **Velveteen**, like corduroy, may be all-cotton or a cotton/polyester blend, but the texture is shorter and thicker than that of corduroy. Velveteen is a medium-weight fabric used whenever the look of velvet is desired. Velveteen is easier to sew and more durable than velvet.

Fabric Preparation

Preshrink corduroy and velveteen to prepare them for pattern layout. Tumble dry to fluff up the pile. This is especially important for all-cotton types, even though prewashing fades strong colors and can make the fabric look worn sooner. Poly-ester/cotton types shrink less, are less likely to fade, and shed wrinkles better than those made of all-cotton.

Stitching Tips

Pile fabrics such as corduroy and velveteen tend to shift as you stitch. An Even Feed foot or roller foot helps to prevent this. It is helpful to pin seams at close intervals and to practice taut sewing, holding the fabric under tension in front of and behind the presser foot. Stitch in the direction of the nap to keep the pile fabric texture smooth.

Some sewing machine adjustments may be needed for a smooth, bal-anced stitch. Use a long stitch, 10 to 12 per inch (2.5 cm), on most corduroys and velveteens. On thick, bulky corduroy, decrease pressure on the presser foot.

The raw edges of corduroy and velveteen ravel easily, so finish them with binding or overlocking. Grade enclosed seams to reduce bulk, but do not trim too closely. Enclosed raw edges can ravel unless topstitched or treated with liquid fray preventer.

Hem bulky or heavy corduroys and velveteen by hand. Or face the hem to reduce bulk. Use purchased hem facing, or cut 2" (5 cm)-wide bias strips of polyester/cotton broadcloth.

Sewing Techniques for Corduroy and Velveteen

(1) **Decide** which color shading you prefer before pattern layout. When nap feels smoother running up toward top of garment, color looks darker. When nap feels smoother running down toward garment hem, color looks lighter with slight sheen. Corduroy wears longer when nap runs down.

(2) **Mark** cutout pattern sections with chalk and pins or marking pen; mark only on wrong side of fabric layers. Do not use tracing wheel and dressmaker's carbon paper without testing; tracing wheel can mar plush textures.

(3) **Press** plush textures gently. Place self-fabric scrap, right side up, on pressing surface and place garment, right side down, on top. Press gently to avoid flattening pile. To prevent imprints on right side, use paper strips under seam allowances, or press seams open on a seam roll.

(4) **Finish** all raw edges to prevent raveling. Use a zigzag stitch (a), bias binding (b), or either 2-thread or 3-thread (c) overlock using extra-fine thread.

(5) **Grade** enclosed seam allowances to reduce bulk. Optional topstitching may be placed far enough in from edge to enclose raw edges of graded seam. This prevents raveling and strengthens garment edges.

(6) **Hem** with catchstitch. Bind, zigzag, or overlock raw hem edge to prevent raveling. Work blind catchstitch between hem and garment, using loose stitches to prevent hem imprint.

KNITS

A knit is a fabric made from interlocking looped stitches. Because of this construction, knits shed wrinkles well, are comfortable to wear, and are easy to sew because they do not ravel. Knits can be grouped into five general categories.

Firm, stable knits do not stretch significantly and are handled similarly to woven fabrics. In this group are double knits (a), which have fine lengthwise ribs on both sides. It is difficult to tell the right and wrong side of a double knit unless the right side has a decorative design. Raschel knit (b) is a lacy or open knit texture that does not stretch because lengthwise threads are locked into some of the knitted loops.

Lightweight single knits have fine ribs running lengthwise on the right side and loops running crosswise on the wrong side. Pull the crosswise edge of a single knit and it will roll to the right side. Single knits such as jersey (c), tricot (d), and interlock (e) do not stretch lengthwise, but they do have crosswise give.

Textured knits may be single or double knits, which are distinguished by a surface texture, usually on the right side. Knitted terry (f) and velour (g) are pile knits that look like their woven namesakes; however, they usually have a great deal of crosswise stretch. Another textured knit is the sweater knit (h). Patterned sweater knits have floats on the wrong side where colored yarns are carried from one motif to another. This limits their crosswise stretch. Comfortable sweatshirt fleece (i) looks like a single knit on the right side; the wrong side has a soft, brushed surface. It is usually stable with little stretch.

Two-way stretch knits have a great degree of stretch crosswise and lengthwise and a high percentage of resilient spandex fibers. Absorbent cotton/spandex and cotton/polyester/spandex knits (j) are favored for active sportswear such as leotards, body suits, and aerobic exercise outfits. Strong nylon/spandex knits (k) are resilient, even when wet, and are usually selected for swimwear.

Ribbing is a very stretchy knit that can be used for tops and for finishing knit garments at wrists, ankles, neck, and waist. One type is tubular ribbing (l), which is sold by the inch (2.5 cm) and must be cut open along one lengthwise rib for sewing. Another type is rib trim (m), which is color coordinated with sweater knits; one edge is prefinished, and the other is sewn to the garment.

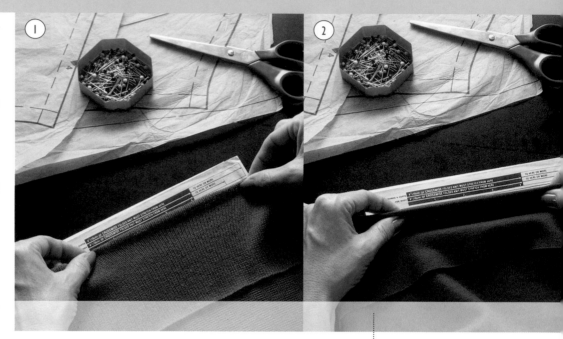

Techniques for Knits

Patterns for knits depend on the stretch characteristics and weight of the knit. The list of suggested fabrics on the back of a pattern envelope usually includes a combination of knit and woven fabrics. If a knit is soft and lightweight, such as jersey, it is suitable for patterns that have gathers, draping, and similar features. If it is firm, such as double knit, a pattern with tailoring or a shaped, fitted silhouette is suitable. If it is bulky or textured, such as a sweater knit, a pattern with few seams and details works best to show off the knit texture.

Certain patterns, however, require knits that stretch. These are closely fitted pattern styles, such as swimsuits and leotards, which would be too small to wear if made from a fabric without elasticity, or tops and pants that use the knit for a comfortable close-to-the-body fit. Most patterns designed for knits have a stretch gauge printed on the back of the envelope. Test the knit that you have selected against the ruler gauge.

When the pattern specifies "two-way stretch knit," test the crosswise and lengthwise stretchability of the knit.

Patterns designed for knits often have ¼" (6 mm) seam allowances. If the pattern you have selected has ⅝" (1.5 cm) seam allowances, trim them to ¼" (6 mm) when using knit sewing techniques.

Fabric Preparation

For best results, preshrink knits. Wash and dry them if they will be washed as part of their routine care. Use a bulk dry-cleaner if the finished garment will be dry-cleaned. It is not necessary to preshrink ribbing unless using a dark-colored ribbing on a light-colored garment.

If, after preshrinking, a knit still has a crease where it was folded on the bolt, steam the crease. If the crease cannot be removed by steaming, it is permanent. Refold the knit for pattern layout to prevent the crease from showing on the garment.

To straighten the ends of knits, draw a chalk line across the cut crosswise edges at right angles to the ribs. Cut the fabric on the chalk line.

How to Use a Stretch Knit Gauge

(1) **Correct** knit for pattern stretches easily to right-hand side of the gauge printed on pattern envelope. To test, fold crosswise edge of knit over 3" to 4" (7.5 to 10 cm), and test fold against gauge. Knit that stretches even more than gauge requirements may still be used for pattern.

(2) **Wrong** knit for pattern is forced beyond reasonable limits to satisfy gauge printed on pattern envelope. Ribs of knit are distorted, and stretched edge folds over on itself because of too much stress on fabric. Knit does not have enough natural elasticity for this pattern style.

Pressing

Press knits on the lengthwise ribs by lifting and lowering the iron. Use a low iron temperature setting, and raise the temperature as needed. Do not press across the ribs or handle the fabric until it is completely cooled. Either action can stretch knits out of shape.

Block sweater knits instead of pressing. To block, pat the fabric or the garment into shape on a flat surface. Steam with a hand steamer, or hold a steam iron above the knit surface. Allow the fabric to dry and cool completely before further handling.

Pattern Layout

Always use a "with nap" pattern layout on knits. Because of knit construction, they have a directional quality that shows up as a difference in color shading in the completed garment.

Stretch both crosswise edges of a knit before pattern layout to see if the knit runs. If so, the runs will occur more readily along one edge than the other. When you lay out the pattern, position the run-

prone edge at the garment hemline. The hem is subject to less stress, so the knit will be less likely to run after the garment is sewn.

When laying out and cutting a knit fabric, do not let it hang off the work surface. The weight of the fabric can distort the portion on the work surface, pulling it off grain.

On bulky or textured knits, it is easier to lay out the pattern on a single layer of fabric. Position the textured side down; pin and mark on the smoother, wrong side of the knit. Use weights instead of pins on knits with open or lacy textures.

Interfacings

Interface knits stabilize details, such as buttonholes, plackets, and patch pockets, and to support shaped areas such as collars. Select a supple interfacing that does not change the character of the knit. Two types of interfacings especially suitable for knits are fusible tricot and stretch nonwoven.

Tips for Interfacing Knits

① **Fusible tricot interfacing** adds support and body to fashion knits without adding stiffness. It also allows for some crosswise stretch. Use tricot to stabilize detail areas such as cuffs, pockets, and plackets.

② **Stretch nonwoven interfacing** stabilizes knit lengthwise but allows knit to stretch crosswise. Use this interfacing for flexible shaping in collars, necklines, facings, tabs, and zipper openings.

SHEER AND SILKY FABRICS

Sheer fabrics can have a soft or crisp hand; crisp sheers are easier to cut and sew. Soft sheers are batiste (a), chiffon (b), China silk (c), and georgette (d). Crisp sheers include fabrics such as organza (e), voile (f), and organdy (g).

The major consideration with sheer fabrics is their transparent quality. The stitches on the inside of a sheer garment show from the outside. Whether revealed clearly or as mere shadows, details such as seams, facings, and hems must be neat and narrow to look well made.

Silky fabrics are made from natural silk fibers or synthetic fibers that look like silk, such as polyester, nylon, rayon, and acetate. The polyester types are popular because they are less costly than silk fabrics. Most synthetic silk-like fabrics do not shrink or fade, and can be washed and dried by machine. This group of fabrics includes charmeuse (h), crepe de chine (i), lightweight jacquard weaves (j), lightweight satin-backed crepe (k), and tissue faille (l).

Even when silk and synthetic silk-like fabrics do not have the see-through character of sheers, they do have similar fine weaves and light weights. Inner construction can show as ridges on the outside of silky garments. That is why many of the same sewing supplies and techniques are suggested for both kinds of fabrics. An additional consideration with silk-like fabrics is their smooth, slick texture, which makes them slippery to handle. You will need to take special steps when laying out and cutting the pattern pieces to control these fabrics.

Guide to Sewing Sheer and Silky Fabrics

Equipment and Techniques	Soft Sheers Batiste, chiffon, China silk, georgette **Crisp Sheers** Organdy, organza, voile	Lightweight Silks Charmeuse, crepe de chine, jacquard weaves, satin-backed crepe, tissue faille
Machine Needles	Size 8 (60), 9 (65), or 11 (75)	
Stitch Length	12 to 16 per inch (2.5 cm)	
Millimeter Stitch Setting	2.5 to 2	
Thread	Extra-fine long staple polyester; silk or mercerized cotton. These threads are often sold as notions for lingerie, machine embroidery, or quilting. Use finest thread possible.	
Hand Needles	Betweens, sizes 8–12	Betweens, sizes 8–12
Interfacings	Sheer nonwoven fusible or sew-in, self-fabric, organza	Fusible tricot, sheer nonwoven fusible or sew-in, batiste, self-fabric, lining fabric, organza, organdy
Special Seams	French, hairline, overlocked, double-stitched	French, overlocked, double-stitched
Special Hems	Overlocked, rolled overlocked, hand-rolled, tricot-bound, hairline, narrow topstitched	

Techniques for Sheer and Silky Fabrics

Keep in mind the delicate nature of sheer and silky fabrics when choosing patterns. The most suitable pattern designs are those that fit loosely and have graceful, flowing lines. Look for soft details such as gathers, ruffles, shirring, or draping. Crisp sheers, however, can be sewn from patterns with tailored, shirt-style details. Bias-cut pattern sections can be difficult to handle on silk and synthetic silk fabrics, which stretch a great deal as well as slip and slide.

For sheers, the fewer seams, darts, facings, and other details to sew, the less inside construction will show through to the right side. Also, the less time you will spend with special finishing techniques. Avoid patterns that require zippers, and omit in-seam pockets because zippers and pockets are bulky and can create an unattractive show-through on the outside of the garment.

Fabric Preparation

For best results, wash and dry sheer and silky fabrics before you begin working with them if they will be washed as part of their routine care. This preshrinks the fabric and removes resins, which can cause skipped stitches and make stitching difficult on synthetic fabrics. Follow the care instructions provided by the fabric manufacturer. Typical care instructions are to machine wash in a gentle cycle and tumble dry at a low temperature setting. Before washing, stitch along cut edges of the fabric to prevent excessive fraying.

Pure silk and silk/synthetic blend fabrics require special consideration. Silk fabrics can be dry cleaned, but hand washing may be preferred. Warm water releases a natural substance from within the silk fibers, which renews the fabric and gives it a refreshed look. Prewashing also frees you from worry about water spotting. The dyes in some silk fabrics may run. Hand washing is not recommended for strong colors and prints. Use a sample of your fabric as a test to see how it reacts to hand

washing; then prepare the entire length of fabric accordingly.

Also preshrink other fabrics, such as interfacings and linings. Even a tiny amount of shrinkage on these inner fabrics will show up as puckers or bubbles on thin, lightweight outer fabrics.

If you dry-clean your silk garment, prepare the fabric for sewing by steam pressing on the wrong side. Use a press cloth to protect the fabric. Set the iron at the lowest end of the steam setting.

Pressing

The best approach to pressing sheer and silky fabrics is to work with fabric scraps first. Determine the optimum temperature setting on your iron, beginning with a low setting and raising it as needed. Fabrics made from rayon or polyester fibers scorch easily and require a cool iron temperature. Use a press cloth to protect fragile fabrics and fibers, or use a soleplate cover on your iron. Avoid a metal-coated ironing board cover because it reflects too much heat into the fabric.

Most pure silk fabrics can be pressed at a low steam setting, but test to see if steaming leaves spots. This is a hazard especially on pure silk fabrics that have not been prewashed before pattern layout and on lustrous fabrics such as charmeuse.

Avoid overpressing. Thin, lightweight fabrics are quickly penetrated by heat and need less pressing effort than heavier fabrics. A light touch is all that is necessary. Use a hand steamer on finished garments.

Layout and Cutting

Fine, lightweight fabrics are easier to handle during pattern layout if you cover the cutting surface with a sheet, other matte-surfaced fabric, or flannel-backed vinyl tablecloth with the flannel side up. Cardboard cutting boards and padded work surfaces also help to make slippery fabrics more controllable.

To pin patterns in position, use superfine pins (0.5 mm diameter). They penetrate the fabric weave without marring it. Prepare new pins by wiping off the manufacturer's oil coating to prevent leaving spots, or use the pins first on dark fabric. In spite of their name, silk pins are too coarse for these fabrics and should be reserved for use with heavier fabrics such as raw silk.

The fastest way to cut out fine fabrics is with a rotary cutter. The blade cuts fabric edges neatly and does not shift the fabric as you work. Another good cutting tool are bent-handled dressmaker's shears. The shape of the handle allows you to rest one cutting blade on the work surface for accurate strokes that barely disturb the fabric layers. Serrated-edge shears can also be helpful. The special blades firmly grip thin and slippery fabrics, a benefit not only for initial cutting but also for trimming raw edges. Whichever tool you use, be sure it is sharp; blades of shears should be in good alignment. Also, synthetic fabrics cause a fuzz buildup, which dulls the cutting blades; wipe this off with a soft cloth.

Use a "with nap" layout for all fabrics that have luster or shine. This one-way pattern layout guarantees uniform color shading in the finished garment. Some fabrics look lighter or brighter in one direction than the other; study the fabric before pattern layout and decide which shading you prefer.

How to Hand Wash Silks

(1) **Swish** fabric gently in lukewarm water. Use mild detergent, mild soap, or natural shampoo such as castile. Rinse in cool water.

(2) **Roll** fabric in towel to remove excess moisture. Do not wring or twist; this causes wrinkles, which are difficult to remove.

(3) **Press** on wrong side of fabric while it is wet. Use dry iron at cool temperature, such as synthetic setting, keeping grainlines true.

Layout Techniques for Slippery Fabrics

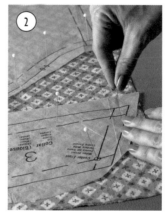

(1) **Fold** fabric right side out, so less-slick wrong sides face each other. Pick up fabric along folded edge, and let fabric fall naturally to ensure accuracy of crosswise grain.

(2) **Push** pins straight down through pattern seam allowance, fabric, and padded or cork-covered work surface to secure slippery layers. If using cardboard cutting board, avoid using superfine pins because cardboard dulls them quickly.

(3) **Sandwich** extremely slippery or thin fabrics between two layers of tissue paper for better control. Place tissue paper on cutting board; place fabric and pattern on tissue; pin through all layers. Pin only in seam allowances.

LUSTROUS FABRICS

The lustrous surface of special occasion fabrics can come from the weave of the fabric, as is true for satin, or from fibers with sheen, such as silk and acetate. Special finishes also create surface luster, or metallic yarns or sequins can be added to give an ordinary fabric glamorous sparkle.

(a) **Satin** is a weave that produces a shiny surface texture from floating yarns. The combination of fibers such as silk, rayon, or polyester with the distinctive weave makes the fabric likely to water-spot; protect the fabric with a press cloth, and use a dry iron when pressing. Use superfine pins to avoid snagging surface yarns.

(b) **Crepe-backed satin** is also called satin-backed crepe because the fabric is reversible; one face has the matte, pebbly texture of crepe, and the other face has the smooth, shiny texture of satin. One side may be used as a binding or trim for the other.

(c) **Satin peau** is a satin with a firm twill weave on the right side. Some peaus are double faced, with fine crosswise ribs on both sides. Because pins and ripped-out stitches can leave marks, pin only in seam allowance; test-fit to avoid ripping stitches.

(d) **Taffeta** has a crisp hand and drapes stiffly. Test sewing techniques on scraps, because pins and ripped-out stitches can leave marks. When the fiber content includes acetate, steam can leave spots.

(e) **Moiré taffeta** is passed between heated rollers to give it a watermarked surface texture.

(f) **Brocade** comes in all weights, from light to heavy, and has raised tapestry-style motifs. The motifs should be balanced on major garment sections and matched at prominent seams. Most brocades are woven, but some are knit. Careful pressing on a padded surface preserves the surface texture. When brocades have shiny metallic threads, set the iron at a low temperature for pressing. To make metallic brocades more comfortable, underline with batiste.

(g) **Metallic fabrics** have metallic yarns woven or knit into them. Most metallics are sensitive to heat and discolor when steam is used. Finger press seams with a thimble or blunt end of a point turner, or use a cool, dry iron.

(h) **Lamé** is a smooth, shiny metallic fabric, either knit or woven. Knit metallics drape and ease better than the wovens. Besides traditional gold, silver, and copper tones, lame is available in iridescent colors.

(i) **Sequined fabrics** have a knit or sheer woven base. A simple pattern style is especially important for these fabrics. Or use sequined fabric for only a part of the garment, such as the bodice.

Techniques for Lustrous Fabrics

Many fabrics fit into the lustrous category, and some have unique sewing requirements. However, all of these fabrics are alike in two ways: A "with nap" pattern layout is used for uniform color shading in the finished gar-ment, and the less handling, the better. Keep handling to a minimum by choosing patterns in simple styles with few seams and darts. Avoid buttoned closings and details such as shaped collars and welt pockets. Use a simple pinked finish on plain seams, or treat raw edges with liquid fray preventer instead of using elaborate dressmaker techniques. Take special care when pressing, using a light touch and covering the press-ing surface with a scrap of self-fabric so nap faces nap. To prevent ridges when press-ing seams, press over a seam roll or place strips of heavy brown paper between seam allowance and garment.

Guide to Sewing Lustrous Fabrics

Equipment and Techniques	Medium-weight Crepe-backed satin, lamé, satin, satin peau, silk, taffeta, moiré	Heavily Textured Brocade, sequined fabrics
Machine Needles	Size 11 (75)	Size 14 (90) or 16 (100)
Stitch Length	8 to 12 per inch (2.5 cm)	8 to 12 per inch (2.5 cm)
Millimeter Stitch Setting	3.5 to 2.5	3.5 to 2.5
Thread	All-purpose cotton or cotton/polyester, silk for silk fabric	All-purpose cotton or cotton/polyester
Hand Needles	Betweens, size 7 or 8	Betweens, size 7 or 8
Interfacings	Sew-in nonwoven or woven	Sew-in nonwoven or woven
Special Seams	Plain seam: pinked, overedge, three-step zigzag, or liquid fray preventer finish	Plain seam or lined to edge
Special Hems	Catchstitched, topstitched, horsehair braid, faced	Faced

Tips for Handling Lustrous Fabrics

(1) **Layout.** Pin only in seam allowances to prevent pin marks. Use extra-fine silk pins for finely woven fabrics such as satin and taffeta. Shears must be sharp or strokes will chew raw edges of fabric. Cut directionally for smoothest edges. Always use "with nap" layout for fabrics with luster.

(2) **Seams.** Use plain seams with a simple edge finish. Raw edges can be pinked, overlocked, or finished with three-step zigzag. If fabric frays easily, apply thin coat of liquid fray preventer to raw edges. Slip envelopes be-tween seam allowances and garment to protect garment from stray drops.

LACE AND EMBROIDERED FABRICS

Laces look fragile and delicate but are actually easy to sew. True laces have a net or mesh background, which has no grainline and does not ravel. You can cut into the fabric freely for creative pattern layouts, seams need no time-consuming edge finishes, and hemming requires little more than trimming close to the edges of prominent motifs.

The openwork designs of lace fabrics have rich histories. Some laces still bear the names of the European localities where they were once made by hand from silk, cotton, or linen fibers. Today, many laces are made by machine from easy-care cotton blends, polyester, acrylic, or nylon.

(a) **Alençon** lace has filled-in motifs outlined by soft satin cord on a sheer net background. One or both lengthwise edges usually have a finished border.

(b) **Chantilly** lace has delicate floral motifs worked on a fine net background and outlined with silky threads.

A popular bridal fabric, Chantilly lace usually has an allover pattern.

(c) **Eyelet** is a finely woven cotton or polyester/cotton fabric embroidered with a satin-stitched openwork design. Even though eyelet embroideries are not true laces, they require pattern layout and pressing techniques similar to those for laces.

(d) **Peau d'ange** is a form of Chantilly lace made with a flossy yarn to give it a soft texture.

(e) **Venice** lace is made from heavy yarns and unique stitches that give it a three-

dimensional texture. Picot bridges join the motifs. Venice lace does not have the net background that is typical of most laces.

(f) **Point d'esprit** has an open net or fine tulle background with a pattern of embroidered dots.

(g) **Cluny** lace is made from heavy cotton-like yarns and looks hand-crocheted. It usually has paddle or wheel motifs and may have raised knots as part of the design.

(h) **Schiffli** is an embroidered sheer or semi-sheer fabric decorated on a Schiffli machine, which imitates hand embroidery stitches.

Guide to Sewing Laces

Equipment and Techniques	Delicate Chantilly, peau d'ange, point d'esprit	Embroidered Eyelet, Schiffli	Textured Alençon, Cluny, Venice
Machine Needles	Size 8 (60) or 9 (65)	Size 9 (65) or 11 (75)	Size 11 (75)
Stitch Length	12 to 16 per inch (2.5 cm)	10 to 12 per inch (2.5 cm)	10 to 12 per inch (2.5 cm)
Millimeter Stitch Setting	2.5 to 2	3 to 2.5	3 to 2.5
Thread	Extra-fine	All-purpose	All-purpose
Hand Needles	Betweens, size 7 or 8	Betweens, size 7 or 8	Betweens, size 7 or 8
Interfacings	Omit	Omit	Omit
Special Seams	Lapped, overlocked, double-stitched	Overlocked, double-stitched	Lapped, double-stitched
Special Hems	Self-hem, appliquéd	Self-hem	Self-hem, appliquéd, horsehair braid

Techniques for Sewing Lace and Embroidered Fabrics

Select a pattern that suits the texture and weight of the lace fabric. Patterns for bridal and evening gowns that are illustrated in lace fabrics may require specific forms of lace, such as edgings of specific widths or a wide allover lace. Check the back of the pattern envelope for the pattern requirements.

When considering a pattern that is not illustrated in laces, select a pattern with sections sized to fit the fabric width. If planning to use a bordered lace on sleeves, you may have to use a short-sleeved pattern if the lace is not wide enough for long sleeves, or place the lace at the lower edge of an organza sleeve. Because lace has no grainline, it is possible to turn the pattern pieces to use an edge or border as a finished edge.

Fabric Preparation

Lace rarely requires any preparation for sewing. Most laces must be dry cleaned. Although shrinkage is rare, if the care label on a lace fabric indicates it is washable, and you are combining it with other fabrics and trims to make a washable garment, then you should preshrink the lace. Add it to the other components of the garment as you preshrink them.

Facings, Interfacings, and Underlinings

Facings and interfacings are not used on lace garments. Finish outer edges with lace trim, lace borders, or sheer tricot bias or French binding. Cut collars and cuffs as single layers, and finish the outer edges with lace trim or appliqué. Use a narrow seam to join them to the garment.

If you need to add body or support to lace, underline the lace with tulle netting. The tulle netting adds strength without showing through or changing the character of the lace.

Layout and Cutting

Pattern layout is an important preliminary step for lace fabrics. Begin by studying the details of the lace design. Unfold the fabric fully on the work surface, laying contrasting fabric underneath if necessary to make the design easier to read.

Note the placement of prominent motifs, the spacing of the repeats, and the depth of any borders. The most noticeable motifs should be matched at the seams and centered or otherwise balanced on major garment sections, just like large fabric prints. If the design has one-way motifs, use a "with nap" pattern layout.

Plan how to use the motifs creatively. Some laces have large primary motifs and smaller secondary motifs or borders that can be cut out and used as appliqués. To use borders as hems, determine the finished skirt and sleeve lengths before pattern layout. If you plan to trim the border from the fabric and sew it to the garment as a decorative edging, you do not need to determine lengths in advance so precisely.

Before cutting, decide which seam treatment you will be using. Allover laces can be sewn like sheer fabrics, with narrow seams. However, if you are working with a re-embroidered lace or a special heirloom lace with a large motif, lapped seams may be better. They will not interrupt the flow of the lace design around the garment because the seam is nearly invisible. With this method, pattern sections must be pinned in place and cut out one by one in sequence. You may use a combination of seams in one garment, with lapped seams at shoulder and side seams and narrow zigzag or double-stitched seams for set-in sleeves.

Once lace is cut, there is little margin for fitting changes. Fit the pattern before layout to avoid ripping out stitches later.

Pressing

Avoid overhandling lace with pressing. If a light touch-up is needed, press with right side down on a well-padded surface to avoid flattening the lace texture. Use a press cloth to prevent the tip of the iron from catching or tearing the net background. If you are working with lace made from synthetic fibers, such as polyester or nylon, use a low temperature setting on the iron. Finger press seams, darts, and other construction details. Wear a thimble and press firmly. If further pressing is necessary, steam lightly, then finger press.

Lace Appliqués

Lace appliqués, either purchased as single medallions or cut from lace fabric, make elegant trims on special-occasion garments. These trims are often used as accents on bridal and evening gown bodices when the skirt is cut from lace fabric. They can also be used as details on silky lingerie and blouses.

To stitch appliqués in place, use either the hand or machine method. Another quick technique is securing appliqués with fusible web. This method is suitable for laces and background fabrics that are not sensitive to heat and steam.

Attaching Lace Appliqués

① **Use lace fabric.** Clip around lace motif. Leave one or two rows of net around edges to give motif definition and to keep re-embroidered lace cordings from raveling. You can also purchase lace appliqué.

② **Hand-stitch.** Use short running stitches ¼" (6 mm) from appliqué edges. Keep stitches loose so background fabric stays smooth and appliqué is not flattened. (Contrasting thread is used to show detail.)

③ **Machine-stitch.** Use a narrow zigzag or short straight stitch ¼" (6 mm) inside edges. Under the motif, trim fabric close to zigzag stitching for sheer effect. (Contrasting thread is used to show detail.)

④ **Fuse.** Position garment, right side up, on covered pressing surface. Place appliqué on garment. Slip circles of fusible web under appliqué. Cover with paper towels or absorbent press cloth. Fuse, following manufacturer's directions.

SYNTHETIC FUR, SUEDE, AND LEATHER

Synthetic fur has a deep pile texture on the right side, which can imitate the coloring and texture of natural pelts, such as mink (a), seal (b), fox (c), or sheepskin (d). Or a synthetic fur fabric can have a novelty texture (e) that looks man-made. Synthetic furs are usually made from modacrylic or polyester fibers and can be washed and dried by machine. Most have a knitted backing.

Synthetic suede is a nonwoven, softly napped polyester/polyurethane fabric that closely resembles genuine sueded leather. Unlike real leather, it is an easy-care fabric that can be washed and dried by machine. The main difference between synthetic suedes is weight. Lightweight synthetic suedes (f) drape softly and do not require special patterns. Medium-weight types (g) are more like real suede.

With conventional sewing methods, you may need to take extra finishing steps, such as fusing the seam allowances and topstitching the edges because suedes are difficult to press flat with conventional pressing techniques. Or you can use flat construction techniques, such as lapped seams and faced hems. Besides solid colors, the synthetic suedes can be embossed (h) or printed (i) to add textural interest.

Synthetic leather/vinyl fabrics can be smooth (j) or textured (k). Like suedes, vinyls have different weights. Lightweight, supple vinyls have a knitted or woven backing. When handling vinyls, use many of the same methods used for synthetic suedes, except vinyls are damaged by heat and steam so they cannot be pressed.

Guide to Sewing Synthetic Fur, Suede, and Leather

Equipment and Techniques	Synthetic Fur	Synthetic Suede	Synthetic Leather/ Vinyl
Machine Needles	Size 14 (90) or 16 (100)	Size 11 (75); 16 (100) for topstitching	Size 11 (75)
Stitch Length	10 to 12 per inch (2.5 cm)	8 to 10 per inch (2.5 cm)	8 to 10 per inch (2.5 cm)
Millimeter Stitch Setting	3 to 2.5	3.5 to 3	3.5 to 3
Thread	All-purpose polyester or polyester/cotton; topstitching/two strands of all-purpose for topstitching		
Interfacings	Omit	Fusible	Sew-in
Special Seams	Butted	Lapped, topstitched, welt	Topstitched, welt
Special Hems	Faced or lined to the edge	Topstitched, faced, fused	Topstitched

INTERFACING

Interfacing plays a supporting role in almost every garment. It is the inner layer of fabric used to shape and support details such as collars, cuffs, waistbands, pockets, lapels, and buttonholes. Even simple styles often need interfacing to add stability to necklines, facings, or hems.

Interfacings come in many different fibers and weights. The pattern may require more than one kind. Choose interfacing according to the weight of the fashion fabric, the kind of shaping required and the way the garment will be cleaned. Generally, interfacing should be the same weight or lighter than the fashion fabric. Drape two layers of the fabric and the interfacing together to see if they hang well. Areas such as collars and cuffs usually need stiffer interfacing. For sheer fabrics, another piece of the fashion fabric may be the best interfacing.

Interfacings are available in woven or nonwoven fabrics. Woven interfacing has a lengthwise and crosswise grain. It must be cut with the same grain as the part of the garment to be interfaced. Nonwoven interfacing has no grain. Stable nonwovens can be cut in any

direction and will not ravel. Stretch nonwovens have crosswise stretch, most effective for knits.

Both woven and nonwoven interfacings are available in sew-in and fusible versions. Sew-in interfacing must be held in place by machine stitching. Fusibles have a coating on one side which, when steam-pressed, melts and fuses the interfacing to the wrong side of the fabric. Fusibles come in plastic wrappers which have directions for applying. Follow them precisely, since each fusible is different.

Choosing between fusible and sew-in interfacing is usually a matter of personal preference. Sew-ins require more hand work. Fusibles are quick and easy, and give more rigidity to the garment. However, some delicate fabrics cannot take the heat that fusing requires. Textured fabrics such as seersucker cannot be fused because the texture would be lost.

Interfacings are made in weights from sheer to heavy and usually come in white, gray, beige, or black. There are special timesaving interfacings for waistbands, cuffs, and plackets. These have pre-marked stitching lines to keep edges even.

Another interfacing aid is fusible web, available in strips of various widths. It bonds two layers of fabric together, making it possible to bond a sew-in interfacing to the fashion fabric.

Guide to Interfacings

Fusible woven interfacings are available in different weights and crispness. Cut them on the same grain as the garment piece, or on the bias for softer shaping.

Fusible nonwoven interfacings come in all weights, from sheer to heavyweight. Stable nonwovens have little give in any direction and can be cut on any grain.

Fusible knit interfacings made of nylon tricot are stable in the lengthwise direction and stretch on the crosswise grain to be compatible with lightweight knit und woven tabrics.

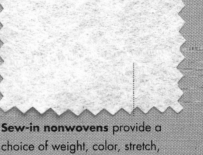

Sew-in woven interfacings preserve the shape and qualities of the fabric, and should be used with woven fabrics. Weights range from sheer organza and batiste to heavyweight hair canvas.

Sew-in nonwovens provide a choice of weight, color, stretch, stable, or all-bias combinations. They are appropriate for knits and stretch fabrics as well as for wovens.

Fusible web is a bonding agent used to join two layers of fabric without stitching. It can be used to bond a sew-in interfacing to the fashion fabric.

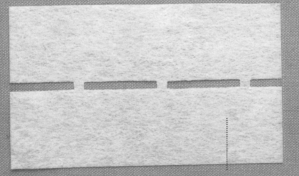

Nonwoven fusible waistbanding is precut in widths or strips to be used for extra firm, crisp edges such as waistbands, cuffs, plackets, and straight facings. It has premarked stitching or foldlines.

Nonwoven sew-in waistbanding is a heavyweight, very firm finished strip for stiff, stable waistbands or belts. It is available in several widths. It can be sewn to the back or facing of a wristband, but is too stiff to sew into a waistband seam.

How to Apply Fusible Interfacing

① **Position** interfacing on warm fabric, resin side down; smooth into place. Lightly mist interfacing with water, or steam shrink. Position press cloth and dampen with liberal misting, even when using steam iron.

② **Start** at center of large or long pieces of interfacing, and work toward each end to fuse. Do not slide iron from one position to the next. To ensure complete coverage, overlap fused areas with iron.

③ **Use** two-handed pressure, and lean on iron; fuse for recommended time, 10 to 15 seconds for most fusible interfacings. Otherwise, bond will not be permanent and will eventually separate from fabric.

④ **Press** the fused area from right side of fabric for better bonding. Use a press cloth or iron soleplate guard to protect fabric surface. Cool and dry fused fabrics before moving them; interfacing is easily reshaped or distorted while warm.

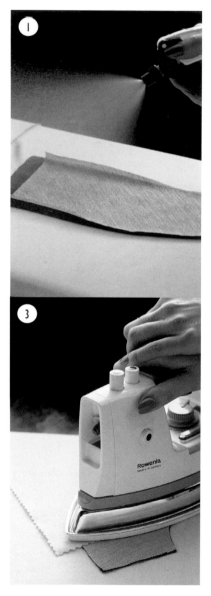

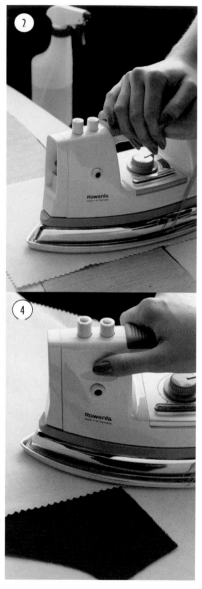

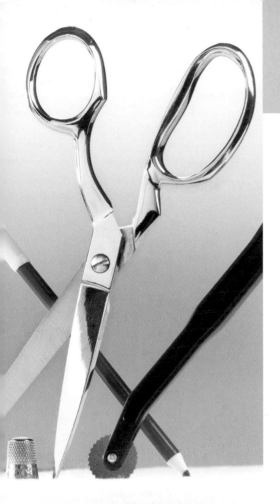

Layout, Cutting, and Marking

Once you have chosen the pattern and fabric and assembled the proper equipment, you're ready to start creating your garment. Before you cut, make sure the fabric is properly prepared and the pattern correctly laid out.

Much of fabric preparation and layout has to do with the fabric grain. Grain is the direction in which the fabric threads run.

Woven fabrics consist of lengthwise threads intersecting crosswise threads. When these threads cross one another at perfect right angles, the fabric is on-grain. If the intersection of lengthwise and crosswise threads does not form right angles, the fabric is off-grain. It is essential that your fabric be on-grain before cutting. If fabric is cut off-grain, the garment will never hang or fit correctly.

The direction of the lengthwise threads is called the lengthwise grain (a). This grainline runs parallel to the selvage, a narrow, tightly woven border which runs along both lengthwise sides of the fabric. Because lengthwise threads are stronger and more stable than crosswise threads, most garments are cut so the lengthwise grain runs vertically. The crosswise threads form the crosswise grain (b), which runs at right angles to the selvage. In most fabrics, it has a slight amount of give. Fabrics with border prints are often cut on the crosswise grain so the border will run horizontally across the garment.

Any diagonal line intersecting the lengthwise and crosswise grains is called a bias. Fabric cut on the bias has more stretch than fabric cut on the grainline. A true bias (c) is formed when the diagonal line is at a 45-degree angle to any straight edge. Strips cut on the true bias are often used to finish curved edges such as necklines and armholes. Plaids and stripes can be cut on the bias for an interesting effect. Garments cut on the true bias usually drape softly.

Knit fabrics are formed by interlocking loops of yarn called ribs (d). The ribs run parallel to the lengthwise sides of the fabric. Their direction can be compared to the lengthwise grain of woven fabrics. The rows of loops at right angles to the ribs are called courses (e) and are comparable to the woven crosswise grain. Knits have no bias and no selvage. Some flat knits have perforated lengthwise edges that look like a selvage, but do not represent true lengthwise grain. Others are made in a tubular shape; these can be cut open along a lengthwise rib if a single thickness is needed for layout. Knits have the most stretch in the crosswise direction, and are cut with the crosswise grain running horizontally around the body for maximum comfort.

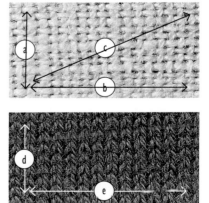

PREPARING THE FABRIC

Before laying out the pattern, take the necessary steps to prepare the fabric for cutting. The label on the bolt tells whether the fabric is washable or dry-cleanable and how much, if any, the fabric will shrink. If the fabric has not been preshrunk by the manufacturer, or if the label says it will shrink more than one per cent, you must preshrink the fabric before cutting. It is often advisable to preshrink knits, since this removes the sizing that sometimes causes skipped stitches. Zippers and trims may also need preshrinking. Dry-cleanable fabrics can be preshrunk by steam pressing or by a professional dry cleaner. This is especially important if you plan to use fusible interfacing, which requires more steam than normal pressing and may cause shrinkage. To make sure the fabric is on grain, begin by straightening the crosswise ends of your fabric. This may be done by pulling a crosswise thread, or cutting along a woven design or crosswise rib of a knit. Next, fold the fabric lengthwise, matching selvages and crosswise ends. If the fabric bubbles, it is off-grain. Fabric that is slightly off grain can be straightened by steam pressing. Pin along selvages and both ends, matching edges. Press from the selvages to the fold. Fabric that is very much off grain must be straightened by pulling fabric in the opposite direction from the way the ends slant. Permanent-finish fabrics cannot be straightened.

How to Preshrink Fabric

Preshrink washable fabric by laundering and drying it in the same manner you will use for the finished garment.

Steam press to preshrink dry-cleanable fabrics. Steam evenly, moving iron horizontally or vertically (not diagonally) across the grain. After steaming, let fabric dry on smooth, flat surface for four to six hours, or until thoroughly dry.

How to Straighten Crosswise Ends of Fabric

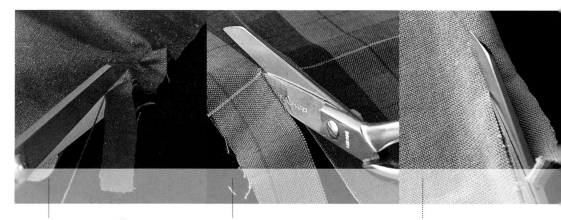

1 **Pull threads** to straighten woven fabric. Clip one selvage and gently pull one or two crosswise threads. Push fabric along threads with your other hand until you reach opposite selvage. Cut fabric along pulled thread.

2 **Cut on a line** to straighten a stripe, plaid, check, or other woven design. Simply cut along a prominent crosswise line. Do not use this method for printed designs, because they may be printed off grain.

3 **Cut on a course** (a crosswise rib) to straighten ends of a knit. It may be easier to follow along the course if you first baste-mark it with contrasting thread, or mark with marking pencil or chalk.

LAYING OUT THE PATTERN

Get ready to lay out the pattern by preparing a large work area such as a table topped with a cutting board, or other large flat surface. Assemble all the pattern pieces for the view you are making and press them with a warm, dry iron to remove wrinkles.

Locate the correct layout diagram on the pattern direction sheet. Pattern layouts are reliable guides for laying out the pattern quickly and efficiently. Find the layout for the view, fabric width and pattern size you are using. When working with a napped or other directional fabric (page 77), choose a "with nap" layout. Circle the layout with a colored pen to make sure you refer to the correct layout each time.

Fold the fabric as indicated on the layout. Most fabrics are cut with the right side folded in. This makes it easier to mark and faster to stitch, since some pieces will be in position to sew. Cottons and linens are usually folded right side out on the bolt;

wools, wrong side out. The right side of the fabric may appear shinier or flatter, or have a more pronounced weave. Selvages look more finished on the right side. If you cannot tell which is the right side, simply pick the side you like best and consistently use that as the right side. A slight difference in shading that is not apparent as you cut may be noticeable in the finished garment if two different sides are used.

The layout diagram indicates the placement of the selvages and fold. Most garments are cut with the fabric folded along the lengthwise grain. If the fabric is to be cut folded on the crosswise grain, the fold is labeled "crosswise fold" on the layout. The crosswise fold should not be used on napped or other directional fabrics.

Place the pattern pieces on the fabric as indicated in the layout. The symbols and markings used in layout diagrams are standardized for all major pattern companies. A white pattern piece indicates that this piece is to be cut with the printing facing up. A shaded piece should be cut with the printing facing down. A dotted line indicates that a pattern piece should be cut a second time.

When a pattern piece is shown half white and half shaded, it should be cut from folded fabric. Cut the other pieces first and refold the fabric to cut this piece. A pattern piece shown extending beyond the fold is cut from a single layer rather than the usual double layer of fabric. After cutting the other pieces, open the fabric right side up and position this piece by aligning the grainline arrow with the straight grain of the fabric.

After all pattern pieces are in place, pin them to the fabric according to the directions at right. Do not begin cutting until all pattern pieces are in place.

How to Pin Pattern Pieces in Place

(1) **Position** pattern pieces to be cut on the fold first. Place each directly on folded edge of fabric. Pin corners of pattern diagonally. Continue pinning in the seam allowance, placing pins parallel to the cutting line. Space pins about 3" (7.5 cm) apart, closer together on curves or on slippery fabrics.

(2) **Place** straight-grain pattern pieces on fabric with grainline arrow parallel to the selvage of woven fabrics, parallel to a rib for knits. Measure from each end of the arrow to the selvage or rib, shifting the pattern until the distances are equal. Pin both ends of the grainline so pattern will not shift. Continue pinning as directed in step 1.

LAYING OUT PLAIDS AND STRIPES

Select simple styles for plaids and stripes. Complicated fashions can detract from or distort the fabric design. Avoid diagonal bustline darts, long horizontal darts, and patterns designated "not suitable for plaids and stripes."

Always buy extra yardage to allow for matching the design at the seams. The extra amount needed depends on the size of the repeat (the four-sided area in which the pattern and color of the design are complete) and the number and lengths of major pattern pieces. Usually an extra ¼ to ½ yd. (0.25 to 0.5 m) is sufficient.

It is easier to work with even plaids and balanced stripes than uneven plaids and unbalanced stripes. Even plaids have the same arrangement of colors and stripes in both lengthwise and crosswise directions. The area of repeat is perfectly square. In uneven plaids, the color and stripes form a different arrangement in the lengthwise or crosswise direction, or both. Balanced stripes repeat in the same order in both directions; unbalanced stripes do not. To avoid having to match two layers of yardage it is recommended that each pattern piece be layed out in a single layer.

Before cutting and layout, decide the placement of plaid design lines within the garment and where they will fall on the body. Avoid placing a dominant horizontal line or block of lines at the bustline and waistline if possible. Experiment with the fabric draped from shoulder to hem. Some plaid garments look more balanced when the hemline falls at the bottom of a dominant crosswise line. If you wish to draw the eye away from the hemline, place the hemline between two dominant lines. When laying out plaids and stripes, match stitching lines, not cutting lines.

To match at the seams, lay out each piece in a single layer beginning with garment front. Place dominant vertical lines at the center front and center back, or position the pattern so the center front is halfway between two dominant vertical lines. Position the sleeve in the same way, using the shoulder dot as the guide for centering the sleeve on or between the dominant vertical lines.

Although it is not always possible to match the design at every seam, try to match: crosswise bars at vertical seams such as center front and back, and side seams; set-in sleeves to the bodice front at armhole notches; lengthwise stripes where possible; and pockets, flaps, and other details to the area of the garment they will cover. The plaid may not match at the shoulder seams or the back notch in the armhole of a set-in sleeve.

Identifying even and uneven plaids. An even plaid has lengthwise and crosswise color bars that match when the repeat is folded diagonally through the center (a). An uneven plaid may have differing color bars in one or more directions (b). Or an uneven plaid may have matching color bars but not form a mirror image when folded diagonally because the repeat is not square (c). This type of uneven plaid is the most difficult to identify.

Tips for Laying Out Plaid Fabrics

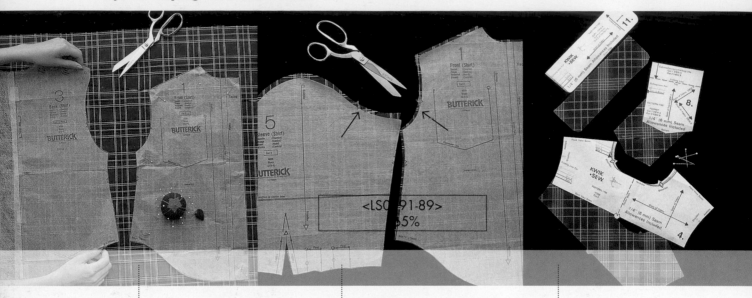

1. **Lay out** each piece in a single layer, beginning with front pattern piece. Use dominant part of design for center front and center back. Match notches at side seams of front and back.

2. **Center** sleeve at same dominant part of design as center front. The design should match at the notches (arrows) of the sleeve front and armhole of garment front; notches at back may not match.

3. **Position** pockets, cuffs, yokes, and separate front bands on the true bias to avoid time-consuming matching. Center a dominant design block in each pattern piece.

How to Lay Out Uneven Plaids

Lay out pattern on single layer of fabric, flipping pattern pieces over to cut right and left halves. Place most dominant color bar at center front and center back or position the pattern so the center front is halfway between two dominant vertical lines. Place pattern pieces in one direction only, using "with nap" layout. Plaid will repeat around the garment instead of forming a mirror image on each side of the center front and center back seams.

LAYING OUT DIRECTIONAL FABRICS

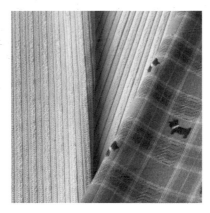

Directional fabrics include napped fabrics such as corduroy, velveteen, and flannel; plush fabrics such as fake fur; shiny fabrics such as taffeta and satin; and print fabrics which have one-way designs. Other fabrics which can be directional include some twill weave fabrics such as denim and gabardine, and knits such as jersey, single, or double knits which appear lighter or darker depending on the direction of the grain.

To prevent the garment from having a two-toned look or having its design running in two different directions, all pattern pieces must be laid out with their tops facing the same direction. Napped fabrics can be cut with the nap running either up or down. Nap running up gives a darker, richer look. Nap running down looks lighter and usually wears better. Plush fabrics look best with the nap running down. Shiny fabrics can be cut in whichever direction you prefer. One-way designs should be cut so that the design will be right side up when the garment is completed.

How to Lay Out Directional Fabrics

Choose the direction your fabric will run, then lay out the pattern pieces according to the "with nap" layout on the pattern direction sheet. To ensure proper placement, mark each pattern piece with an arrow pointing to the top of the piece. Sometimes the pattern calls for a crosswise fold. In this case, fold the fabric as the layout indicates, then cut along the foldline. Turn the top layer of fabric around so the nap runs in the same direction as the nap of the lower layer of fabric, and cut both layers at the same time.

CUTTING TIPS

Arrange your cutting table so you can move around it to get at the pattern from all angles. If your cutting surface is not this accessible, cut groups of pattern pieces apart from the rest of the fabric so you can turn these smaller pieces around.

Accuracy is important, since a mistake in cutting cannot always be corrected. Before cutting, double check placement of pattern pieces and alterations. Before cutting plaids, one-way designs or directional fabrics, make sure the fabric is folded and laid out correctly. Basting tape (page 30) may be helpful to keep fabric from shifting. Heavy or bulky fabric can be cut more accurately one layer at a time. Slippery fabric is easier to cut if you cover the table with a sheet, blanket or other nonslip material.

Choose sharp, plain or serrated blade, bent-handled shears, 7" or 8" (18 or 20.5 cm) in length. Take long, firm strokes, cutting directly on the dark cutting line. Use shorter strokes for curved areas. Keep one hand on the pattern near the cutting line to prevent the pattern from shifting and to provide better control.

The rotary cutter (page 28) is especially useful for cutting leather, slippery fabrics or several layers of fabric. The rotary cutter can be used by either right or left-handed sewers. Use a cutting mat to protect the cutting surface.

Notches can be cut outward from the notch markings, or with short snips into the seam allowance (page 83). Be careful not to snip beyond the seamline. Use snips to mark the foldlines and stitching lines of darts and pleats, and the center front and center back lines at the top and bottom. Mark the top of the sleeve cap above the large dot on the pattern with a snip. On bulky or loosely woven fabric where snips cannot be easily seen, cut pattern notches out into the margin. Cut double or triple notches as one unit, not separately.

After you finish cutting, save scraps to test stitching or pressing techniques, make trial buttonholes, or cover buttons. For accurate marking and easy identification, leave each pattern piece pinned in place until you are ready to sew that piece.

Your pattern may call for bias strips of fabric to enclose raw edges such as necklines or armholes. Ideally, these are cut from a piece of fabric long enough to fit the area to be enclosed. Bias strips may also be pieced together to form a strip of the correct length.

How to Cut and Join Bias Strips

(1) **Fold** fabric diagonally so that a straight edge on the crosswise grain is parallel to the selvage or lengthwise grain. The foldline is the true bias. Cut fabric along the foldline to mark the first bias line.

(2) **Mark** successive bias lines with a marking pencil or chalk, and yardstick or see-through ruler. Cut along marked lines. When a bound finish is called for in a pattern, the pattern will specify the length and width of bias strips needed.

(3) **Join** bias strips if piecing is necessary. With right sides together, pin strips together with shorter edges aligned. Strips will form a "V." Stitch a ¼" (6 mm) seam. Press seam open. Trim points of seams even with edge of bias strip.

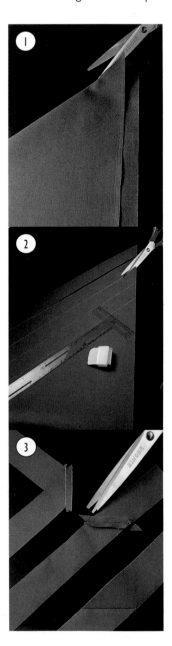

MARKING TIPS

In marking, key pattern symbols are transferred to the fabric after cutting and before the pattern is removed. These markings become reference points to help you through all stages of garment construction. Pattern symbols that should be marked include construction symbols and position marks for placement of details.

Marking is usually done on the wrong side of the fabric. Some symbols, such as pocket placement and buttonholes, should be transferred from the wrong side to the right side of the fabric (not marked on the right side).

There are several ways to transfer markings, each suitable for different fabrics. Choose whichever gives you the fastest, most accurate marking.

Pins are a quick way to transfer markings. They should not be used on fine fabrics or those on which pin marks would be permanent, such as silk or synthetic leathers. Use pin marking only when you plan to sew immediately, since pins may fall out of loose weaves or knits.

Tailor's chalk or dressmaker's pencil, used with pins, are suitable for most fabrics.

Tracing wheel and tracing paper work best on plain, flat-surfaced fabrics. The wheel may damage some fabrics, so test on a scrap first. Before marking, place a piece of cardboard under the fabric to protect the table. On most fabrics, both layers can be marked at once.

Liquid markers are felt-tip pens designed especially for fabric. The marker transfers through the pattern tissue onto the fabric. The ink rinses out with water or disappears on its own, so liquid markers can be used on the right side of most fabrics.

Machine basting transfers markings from the wrong side of the fabric to the right side. It can also be used to mark intricate matching points or pivot points. After marking on the wrong side, machine-stitch through the marking. Use a long stitch length or speed-basting stitch, with contrasting color thread in the bobbin. The bobbin thread marks the right side. To mark a pivot point, stitch on the seamline with regular-length stitching and matching thread. Leave the stitching in place as a reinforcement.

Snips or clips can be used on most fabrics except loosely woven tweeds and bulky wools. With the point of scissors, snip about ⅛" to ¼" (3 to 6 mm) into the seam allowance.

Pressing can be used to mark foldlines, tucks, or pleats. It is a suitable method for any fabric that holds a crease.

How to Mark with Chalk, Pencil, or Liquid Marker

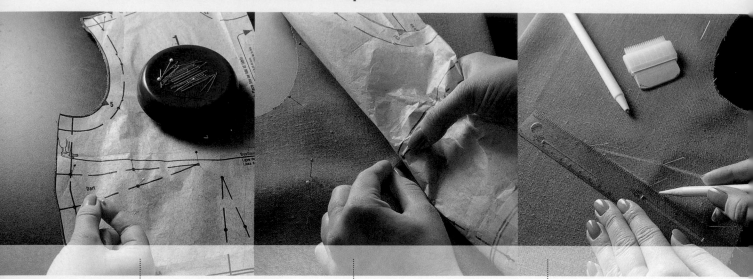

1) **Insert** pins straight down through pattern and both layers of fabric at marking symbols.

2) **Remove** pattern carefully by pulling over pin heads. Mark top layer with chalk, pencil, or marker at pinpoints on wrong side.

3) **Turn** fabric over and mark other layer at pinpoints. Remove pins and separate layers.

How to Mark with Basting or Pressing

1) **Hand-baste** with long and short stitches to mark one layer of fabric. Stitch through pattern and fabric along a solid line, using short stitches on the tissue side and long stitches through fabric. Carefully pull pattern tissue away.

2) **Machine-baste** to transfer pencil, chalk, or tracing paper markings from the wrong side to the right side. Use contrasting thread in the bobbin, longest stitch on machine. Do not use machine basting on fabrics which mar. Do not press over machine basting.

3) **Press** to mark foldlines, tucks, and pleats. Pin pattern to a single layer of fabric. Fold pattern and fabric along marking line. Press along the fold with a dry iron.

How to Mark with Tracing Wheel and Tracing Paper

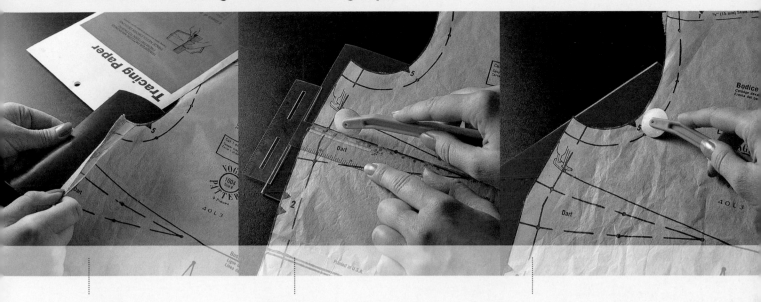

1) **Place** tracing paper under pattern, with carbon sides facing the wrong side of each fabric layer.

2) **Roll** tracing wheel over lines to be marked, including center foldlines of darts, using a ruler to help draw straight lines.

3) **Mark** dots and other large symbols with short lines perpendicular to the stitching line, or an "X." Use short lines to mark the ends of darts or pleats.

Timesaving Marking Techniques

Snips can be used to mark notches, ends of darts, foldlines, or center front and back locations. Make tiny snips, ⅛" (3 mm) deep, into seam allowance. Snip through pattern and both fabric layers with point of scissors.

Pins can mark darts, dots, or foldlines without the help of marking pencil. Insert pins through pattern and fabric. Pull pattern carefully over heads. Mark bottom layer with second set of pins. Secure first set of pins to mark top layer.

Tailor tacker has tailor's chalk inserted in two holders. One side has a pin which is inserted through pattern marking to meet chalk on the other side. Twist both sides of tacker so chalk marks two fabric layers in one timesaving step.

SEWING TECHNIQUES

General Guidelines for Pattern Adjustments

Pattern adjustments change the measurement and shape of standard pattern pieces to fit your figure. To streamline the entire fitting process, make as many fitting changes as you can before you cut. Step-by-step instructions for specific adjustments are given on the following pages. The basic guidelines that follow apply to most changes you are likely to make.

Press pattern pieces with a warm, dry iron before you start. It's hard to be accurate when working with wrinkled tissue pieces.

Pin-fit the pattern to preview how well the fashion style fits your figure. Adjust the pattern on your body, or decide how extensively you need pattern adjustments. If you need many adjustments, reconsider your choice of pattern style. Another style may fit your figure with fewer adjustments. Also, pin-fit after making pattern adjustments as a fast check of their accuracy.

Work in a logical order, completing lengthening or shortening pattern adjustments first. Then work from the top of the pattern down to make additional adjustments to fit body width and contours.

Watch for chain reactions. Adjustments on one pattern piece usually require matching adjustments on adjoining pattern sections. If you change the neckline seam, for example, you must change the neck facing to match. Sometimes a compensating rather than a matching adjustment is necessary. For example, if you lower the shoulder seams to fit sloping shoulders, you must also lower the underarm seam to retain the armhole size.

Maintain the original grainline as printed on the pattern pieces, so the finished garment hangs properly. Extend the grainline from one edge of the pattern piece to the other before cutting. This helps preserve grainline as you make adjustments.

Blend the adjusted stitching and cutting lines back into the original lines. When adjustments are blended correctly, the original shape of the pattern piece will not be distorted.

To blend a seam, draw a continuous line where one has become broken during pattern adjustment. To blend a straight line, use a ruler or straight edge, connecting the beginning and end of the new line. To blend a curved line, use a curved ruler to reconstruct the original curve of the pattern, blending to each end from a point halfway between the broken seamline.

Blend the seamline first, then the cutting line. On multiple-sized patterns where no seamlines are marked, blend the cutting line only, and stitch the specified seam allowance, usually 5/8" (1.5 cm).

When there is a dart in the seamline, fold the dart out before blending the line. Be sure to mark all notches and darts on the new blended seamline.

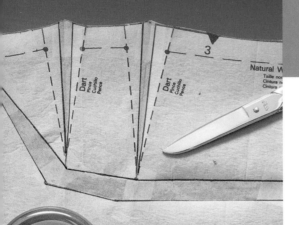

CHOOSING AN ADJUSTMENT METHOD

Wherever possible, two methods are given for the most common pattern adjustments: the minor, or in-seam, method and the major, or cut-and-slide, method. Choose one method or the other, depending on how much of an adjustment you need to make.

Minor in-seam pattern adjustments are quick and easy, because you can mark them directly on the printed pattern within the seam allowance or on the pattern tissue margin. In-seam methods have narrow limitations. Usually you can add or subtract no more than ⅜" to ½" (1 to 1.3 cm).

In the photos, to clarify where an addition would normally be marked on the margin of the tissue pattern, the margin has been trimmed and a contrasting tissue placed under the pattern. This procedure is not necessary on patterns that have not been used previously, because they have generous tissue margins around them.

Major cut-and-slide pattern adjustments allow you to add or subtract greater amounts than in-seam methods and to make adjustments exactly where they are needed to fit your figure. Cut-and-slide methods also have limits, usually to a maximum of 2" (5 cm). The specific amount is stated with the step-by-step instructions. Do not attempt to adjust beyond the stated maximums or you will distort the shape of the pattern pieces and cause the finished garment to hang off-grain. It will also be more difficult to make matching or compensating adjustments on adjoining pattern sections.

If you need a greater adjustment than cut-and-slide methods allow, consider working with another pattern size. Or distribute the adjustment over additional pattern seams and details instead of concentrating the adjustment in one area.

BASIC LENGTH ADJUSTMENTS

Before making any other pattern adjustments, adjust the length of pattern pieces to fit your personal length proportions. If your figure is close to average, basic length adjustments may be the only changes needed.

Basic length adjustments are made in two areas: above and below the waist. Use your back waist length measurement to determine the correct pattern length above the waist. To determine the correct pattern length below the waist, measure from the waist in back to the proposed hemline. Make these length adjustments using the adjustment lines printed on the pattern pieces.

Adjustments for Special Figures

If your bust point does not match the placement on the pattern it may be necessary to adjust the length above the bust or to adjust the darts so that they point to the fullest part of the bust. If you have a full bust, adjust the front pattern length above the waist, as on page 93.

For petite figure types, reduce the pattern length proportionately, by dividing the total adjustment into smaller amounts. Shorten the pattern

at the chest and sleeve cap and at the hip adjustment line, in addition to using the printed adjustment lines above the bust and waist. Length may also be adjusted at the hemline.

Standard pattern shortening adjustments for petite are remove ¼" (6 mm) at chest, ¾" (2 cm) above waist, 1" (2.5 cm) at hip adjustment line, and 1" (2.5 cm) at hem to shorten pattern by 3" (7.5 cm). Standard adjustments for women's petite are similar, but the chest adjustment is omitted because armhole size does not need to be reduced. Customize standard length adjustments to suit your own proportions.

How to Determine Length Adjustments

(1) **Above the waist.** Measure back waist length from prominent bone at back of neck to natural waistline. Compare with back waist length measurement for your pattern size given on pattern envelope to determine how much to adjust bodice front and back patterns.

(2) **Below the waist.** Measure at center back from waist to proposed garment hemline, or use a garment of correct length to determine this measurement. Compare with finished garment length given on back of pattern envelope to determine how much to adjust skirt front and back patterns.

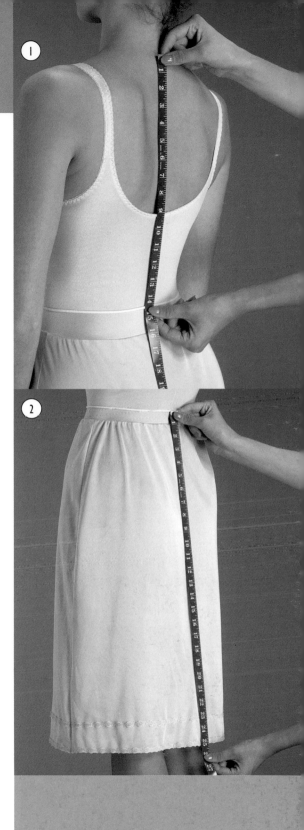

How to Shorten Patterns

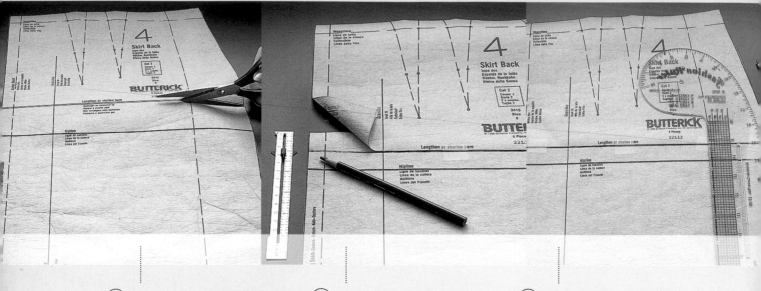

1. **Cut** pattern on the printed adjustment lines. If skirt pattern provides no adjustment lines, cut off excess length at bottom edge.

2. **Lap** cut sections. Overlap equals total amount pattern must be shortened. Tape sections together, keeping grainline straight.

3. **Blend** stitching and cutting lines. Make matching adjustments on back and front pattern pieces.

How to Lengthen Patterns

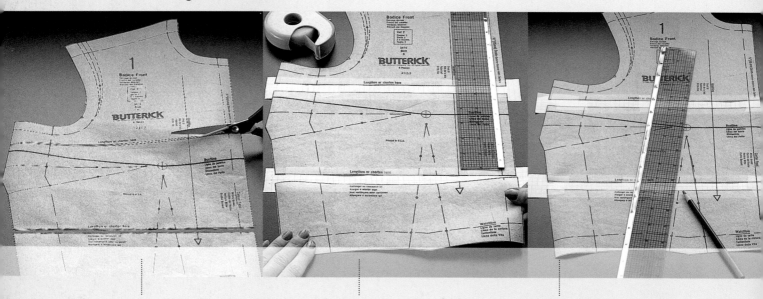

1. **Cut** pattern on the printed adjustment lines.

2. **Spread** cut sections the amount needed. Place paper underneath to bridge gap. Tape sections in place, keeping grainline straight.

3. **Blend** stitching and cutting lines. Make matching adjustments on back and front patterns.

How to Shorten Patterns for Petites

1) **Pin-fit** or measure pattern to determine how much length to remove across chest above armhole notches, at adjustment line above waist, at hipline, and at adjustment line below waist.

2) **Draw** adjustment lines on front and back, midway between armhole and shoulder seam notches. Draw similar line across sleeve cap. Draw hip adjustment line 5" (12.5 cm) below waist on skirt front and back.

3) **Cut** pattern pieces on each adjustment line; lap to shorten. Shorten back and front patterns equally. Shorten sleeve cap by same amount removed from bodice at chest.

FITTING THE BUST

When fitted correctly, the bodice of a garment drapes smoothly over the bust without pulling, and the waistline of the garment lies at natural waistline and is parallel to the floor. Adjust bodice back length according to back waist length measurement. Make similar adjustments on bodice front. In addition, front bodice seams or darts may need to be adjusted to fit your bust size and shape.

If your bust is fuller than standard, you may need to add additional length and width to the bodice front pattern. Keep in mind that bodice front and back side seam lengths must match. If you have selected a pattern featuring loose or oversized fit, you can use some of the design ease in the pattern to fit a full bust and make a lesser adjustment.

For an average or small bust, pin-fitting, see opposite, will determine whether it is necessary to raise or lower darts. Repositioning the darts may be all that is needed to improve pattern fit.

Minimum Ease

Garment	Minimum Bust Ease
Blouse, dress, jumpsuit	2½" to 3" (6.5 to 7.5 cm)
Unlined jacket	3" to 4" (7.5 to 10 cm)
Lined jacket	3½" to 4½" (9 to 11.5 cm)
Coat	3½" to 4½" (9 to 11.5 cm)

If you make bust adjustments on the pattern beyond simply raising or lowering darts, you may want to test your adjustments by making a bodice fitting shell from the adjusted pattern. Many fitting solutions are easier to visualize in fabric, and this extra step can save time in the long run.

Ease, or extra room, is necessary for comfort at the bustline. Add the minimum amount of ease to your bust measurement, as shown on the chart above, before comparing with the pattern to judge whether pattern adjustments are needed.

The ease amounts given on the chart are general guidelines. At times you may want to fit with more or less ease. For example, thick fabrics require more ease than lightweight ones. Knits require less ease than wovens, and very stretchy knits require no ease at all or even negative ease for formfitting garments.

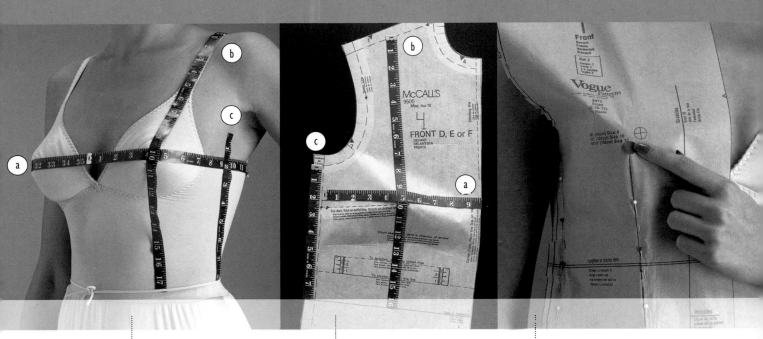

How to Determine Pattern Adjustments

Measure bust (a) at fullest part, keeping tape measure parallel to floor. Add minimum ease to bust measurement. Measure the front waist length (b) from midpoint of shoulder, over bust point, straight down to waist. Measure the side length (c) from 1" (2.5 cm) below underarm to waist. Use two fingers under arm to determine distance.

Measure pattern front and back at bustline (a). Measure bodice front pattern from midpoint of shoulder, over bust point, to waist (b). Note any differences to decide if pattern length must be adjusted above waist or bust (pages 88 and 89). Measure side seam of bodice front pattern from underarm to waist (c). Note any differences to decide if pattern length must be adjusted.

Pin-fit pattern to mark the bust point. Note if bust shaping or darts on the pattern should be raised or lowered for good fit. Compare pattern measurement with body measurement plus minimum ease to determine how much width to add for full bust or how much to remove for small bust.

High Bust

Poor fit, when the bust is higher than average, shows in pulls across the fullest part of the bust and in wrinkles under the bust. Dart does not point to fullest part of curve. Underarm dart must be raised; dart from the waistline (if any) needs to be lengthened.

Low Bust

Poor fit, when the bust is lower than average, shows in pulls across the fullest part of the bust and in wrinkles above the bust. Darts are too high and need to be lowered and shortened.

How to Raise or Lower Darts

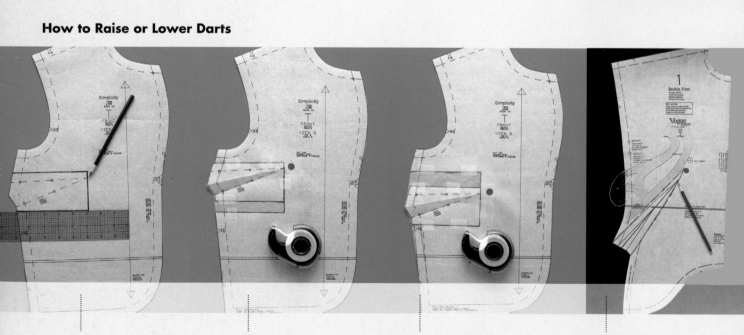

(1) **Draw** horizontal lines on the pattern ½" (1.3 cm) above and below the underarm dart, at right angle to grainline. Connect the lines with a vertical line through dart point. Cut out dart on marked lines.

(2) **Raise** dart the amount needed for a high bust. Position dart so that it points to the bust point (dot) or fullest part of figure. Place paper under pattern. Tape cut edges in place, keeping edges even. Redraw side seam.

(3) **Lower** dart the amount needed for a low bust. Position dart so that it points to the bust point (dot) or fullest part of figure. Place paper under pattern. Tape cut edges in place, keeping edges even. Redraw side seam.

(4) **Diagonal dart** requires change in direction so that it points to bust point. Mark new dart point on pattern. Redraw dart, connecting side seam ends of the dart and new dart point.

How to Fit a Full Bust without Darts

Accommodate full bust on less closely fitted pattern styles by making an adjustment that does not create a dart. This method can be used to increase the pattern a limited amount. Exceeding the maximum adjustment distorts the fabric grain at the lower edge of the garment. This adjustment is not appropriate on plaids, checks, or stripes.

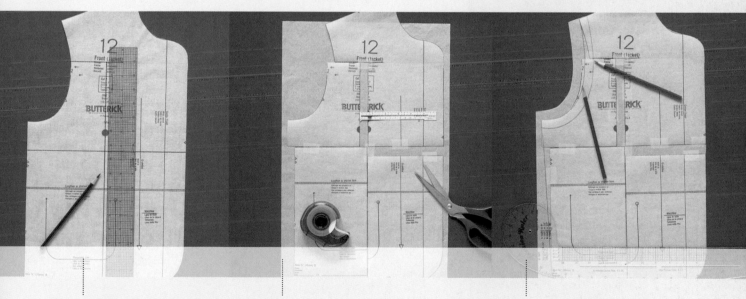

1) **Draw** line across bodice front midway between armhole notch and shoulder seam, at right angle to grainline. Draw second line 2" to 4" (5 to 10 cm) below armhole, at right angle to grainline. Draw third line through bust point, parallel to grainline to connect first two lines; extend line to lower edge.

2) **Cut** pattern on adjustment lines. Slide armhole portion out a maximum of ¾" (2 cm) to add total of 1½" (3.8 cm) to bodice width. Slide center front waist section down no more than 2" (5 cm) to add bodice length. Tape to paper.

3) **Blend** stitching and cutting lines at armhole and side seams. Use curved ruler to blend lower cutting line from the center front, tapering back to the original side seam.

FITTING THE WAIST AND ABDOMEN

Although a waistband or waistline should fit snugly, it must be slightly larger than your waist for good fit. For wearing comfort, a finished waistband should be from ½" to 1" (1.3 to 2.5 cm) larger than your actual measurement. In addition, allow ½" (1.3 cm) of ease from pattern waist measurement to waistband. Apply the same fitting guidelines to garments with faced waistlines. If garment has a waistline seam and no band, allow the total amount, 1" to 1½" (2.5 cm to 3.8 cm), for basic ease.

One indication of good waist fit is the way the side seams hang. They should hang straight, visually bisecting the body, without being pulled to the front or the back. Figure and posture variations may cause distortion of the side seams and require separate adjustment of skirt front and back. For example, a body with a full abdomen will need additional width and length in front, while a person with swaybacked posture may need to shorten the skirt pattern at center back. Adjustments for full abdomen and swayback should be determined and made at the same time that the waist width adjustment is made.

How to Determine Pattern Adjustments

① **Measure** your waist. Compare with the waist measurement for your pattern size. Minimum wearing ease is included in the pattern, so adjust the pattern accordingly, enlarging or reducing as needed.

② **Pin out** waistline darts, tucks, or pleats to measure pattern to compare with body measurements plus ease. Measure at the waistline seam; on a garment without a waistline seam, measure at the waistline mark at the narrowest part of the waistline area. Double the pattern measurement to compare with your waist measurement.

Small Waist

Poor fit has waistline or waistband that is too large, although garment fits at hips and bust. A dress with a waistline seam is baggy, with loose vertical folds at the waist. On a skirt or pants, waistband stands away from waist and tends to slide down.

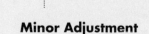

Minor Adjustment

Remove one-fourth the amount needed at each seam—maximum of ⅜" (1 cm) per seam from sizes smaller than 16; ⅝" (1.5 cm) from size 16 and larger. Blend stitching and cutting lines, using curved ruler. On dart-fitted skirts or pants, do not make darts deeper to reduce waistline unless additional garment contouring is needed to fit broad curvy hips or full round seat. Adjust width on adjoining pattern pieces.

Major Adjustment

(1) **Draw** a line 5" (12.5 cm) long, parallel to lengthwise grainline, between side seam and dart. Draw a second line from bottom of first line to side seam, at right angle to grainline.

(2) **Slide** section in to remove up to 1" (2.5 cm) from waist seam. Tape paper underneath. Blend stitching and cutting lines. Make matching adjustment on back, removing up to 2" (5 cm) from each seam for a total reduction of 4" (10 cm).

(3) **Pin-fit** pattern to check position of waistline darts. It may be necessary to reshape or move the darts closer to center front and back for good fit. Make a corresponding width adjustment to adjoining waistband, facing, or bodice pattern.

Large Waist

Poor fit is indicated by horizontal wrinkles near the waist, which cause the waistline of a dress to rise. A waistband on skirt or on pants creases from strain. Wrinkles fan out from waist or form horizontal folds below waistband.

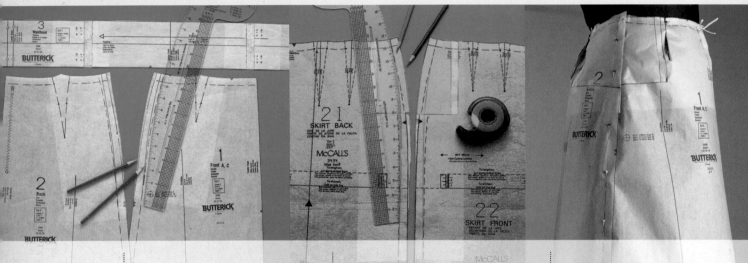

Minor Adjustment

Add one-fourth the amount needed at each seam, adding up to ⅜" (1 cm) per seam allowance for total of ¾" (2 cm) per seam. On dart-fitted skirts, each dart can be reduced up to ¼" (6 mm) to enlarge waistline. Blend stitching and cutting lines, using curved ruler. Make corresponding width adjustment to adjoining waistband, facing, or bodice patterns.

Major Adjustment

1) **Draw** adjustment lines and cut pattern as in step 1 for small waist (page 95). Slide section out up to 1" (2.5 cm). Tape paper underneath. Blend stitching and cutting lines to waist, using curved ruler, and to hem, using straightedge. Make matching adjustment on back pattern, adding up to 2" (5 cm) per seam for total of 4" (10 cm).

2) **Pin-fit** pattern to check position of waistline darts. It may be necessary to reshape darts or move them closer to the side seams for a better fit. Make a corresponding width adjustment to adjoining waistband, facing, or bodice sections.

Prominent Abdomen

Poor fit is indicated by horizontal wrinkles across the front below the waistline. Diagonal wrinkles from abdomen to sides pull side seams forward. Waistline and hemline may ride up. Extra length and width are needed at center front.

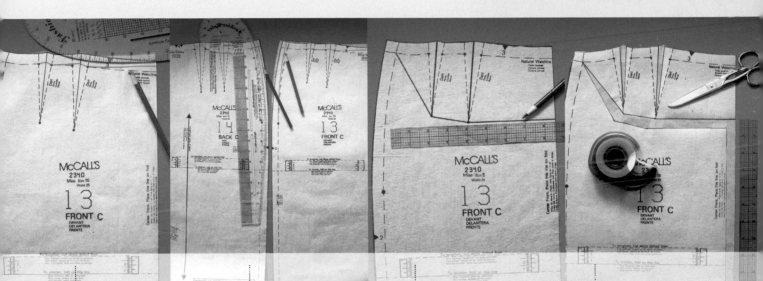

Minor Adjustment

① **Raise** waist stitching line on front skirt or pants pattern up to ⅜" (1 cm) at center front to add more length. Fold out darts, and blend stitching and cutting lines, using curved ruler.

② **Add** up to ½" (1.3 cm) at side seam of the front pattern piece. Remove same amount from back pattern piece to maintain the waist circumference. To further improve fit, convert front darts to gathers or unpressed pleats.

Major Adjustment

① **Draw** diagonal adjustment lines on pattern from intersection of side seam and waistline seam through dart points, extending at right angle to center front. Cut on line. Cut on dart foldline to, but not through, dart point.

② **Slide** center section up the amount needed and out half the amount needed, opening darts and diagonal slash. Extend center front line from new position to hemline. Darts can also be converted to gathers or unpressed pleats. Blend stitching and cutting lines at waistline.

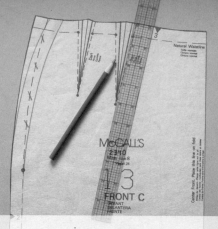

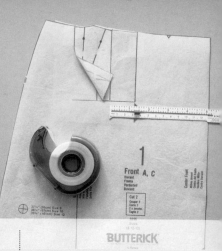

Flat Abdomen

Poor fit is indicated by vertical wrinkles and excess fabric at center front. Hipbones may protrude. Darts are poorly located and too deep for flat abdomen contour.

Adjustments for Flat Abdomen

(1) **Redraw** shallower darts by removing an equal amount on each side of dart foldline. To restore the original waistline measurement, remove the same amount from side seam, blending from a point on waist-line seam to hipline with curved ruler.

(2) **Move** darts closer to side seam for prominent hipbones. Cut out dart as for raising or lowering bust dart (page 92), and slide it to correct position after pin-fitting pattern. Fold out dart, and blend waistline stitching and cutting lines, using curved ruler.

Swayback

Poor fit is caused by posture variation; area directly beneath waist in back does not fit smoothly, or skirt bags in seat area, indicating that garment is too long at center back. Diagonal wrinkles form, indicating that dart width or length is wrong for body shape. Pin out excess to determine amount to shorten at center back.

Adjustment for Swayback

Adjust darts, if necessary, to accommodate protrusion of seat. If dart width is changed, make corresponding width adjustment at side seam to maintain waist size. Lower the waist stitching line on the back skirt pattern the amount needed. Fold darts toward center and blend stitching and cutting lines, using curved ruler.

FITTING HIPS

When garments fit well at the hipline, they feel comfortable whether you are standing or sitting. They also look smooth, without strained wrinkles or excess fabric folds.

Before adjusting for width, make any basic lengthening or shortening adjustments below the waistline. Length adjustments may eliminate the need for adjusting pattern hip circumference. If you have one hip higher than the other, it may be necessary to make a copy of the pattern and adjust a separate pattern piece for each side of the body If your hips are fuller or slimmer than the average, adjust the pattern to include the right amount of ease. For wearing comfort, there must be a minimum of 2" (5 cm) ease, or extra room, at the hipline of the garment for sizes smaller than 16. For size 16 or larger, there must be at least 2½" (6.5 cm) of ease. You may need more than minimum ease for good fit if you have full hips or are using a thick fabric. You may need less if you are working with a knit.

How to Determine Pattern Adjustments

(1) **Measure** hips, as viewed from the side, where seat protrudes most, keeping tape measure parallel to floor. Determine where hipline falls by measuring at side seam from waist to fullest part of hips. Add 2" to 2½" (5 to 6.5 cm) minimum ease to measurement.

(2) **Mark** pattern side seam at point where fullest part of hipline falls. Lap the back and front pattern pieces at mark. Measure hipline from center front to center back at this position. Double this measurement to arrive at total finished circumference. Compare with hip measurement plus ease to determine if adjustment is needed.

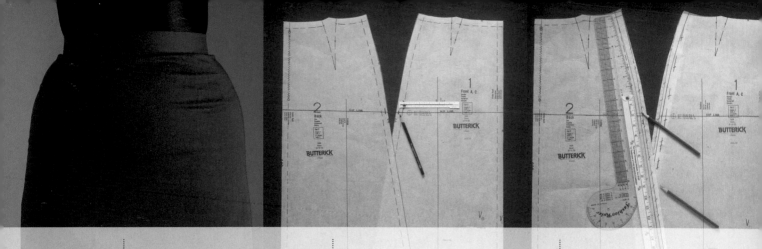

Full Hips

Poor fit causes horizontal wrinkles across hips. Skirt cups under seat in back. Skirt tends to ride up, because there is not enough width at hip level to fit full hips. Pattern needs enlarging at hipline.

Minor Adjustment

(1) **Mark** hipline at side seam of back and front patterns. Add one-fourth the amount needed at each side seam, next to mark. Add maximum of ⅜" (1 cm) per seam allowance for total of ¾" (2 cm) per seam.

(2) **Blend** stitching and cutting lines from hip to waist with curved ruler. Mark new stitching and cutting lines from hip to hem with straightedge.

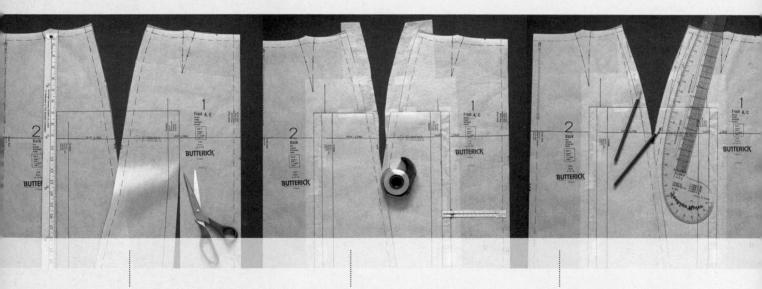

Major Adjustment

(1) **Draw** a line parallel to the hipline approximately 5" (12.5 cm) below the waistline. Draw a second line parallel to lengthwise grainline from end of first line to hem. Cut on lines.

(2) **Slide** section out to add one-fourth the amount needed. Add maximum of 1" (2.5 cm) to sizes under 16 for total of 2" (5 cm) per seam, and 1½" (3.8 cm) to sizes 16 and above for total of 3" (7.5 cm) per seam.

(3) **Blend** stitching and cutting lines from hip to waist with curved ruler. Mark the hip area to the hem with a straightedge.

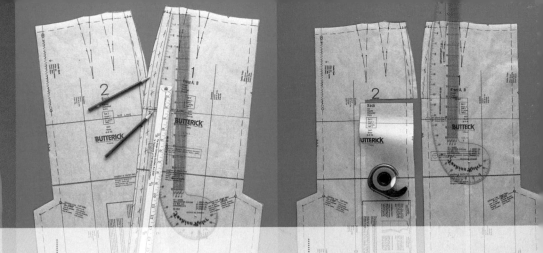

Small Hips

Poor fit causes excess fabric to drape in folds and look baggy. Skirt hipline is too broad for figure with slender hips. Pattern width needs reduction at hipline, and darts may have to be reduced. If darts are reduced, side waist seam must be decreased equal amount, as on page 95.

Minor Adjustment

1) **Mark** hipline at side seam on back and front patterns. Remove one-fourth the amount needed at each side seam, next to mark. Remove up to ⅜" (1 cm) per seam allowance for total of ¾" (2 cm) per seam. Mark new stitching and cutting lines as in step 2 (page 100, top).

Major Adjustment

2) **Reduce** dart size as needed. Make side waist adjustment (page 95). Draw adjustment line and cut as for major adjustment for full hips, step 1, opposite. Slide section in to remove one-fourth of the extra width at the hipline. Blend stitching and cutting lines from waist to hip area with curved ruler. Mark hip area to hem with straightedge.

Uneven Hips

Poor fit causes diagonal wrinkles on one side. Fabric is off grain in hip area. One hip may be fuller, slimmer, or higher than other hip. Make necessary width adjustments in darts and side seam.

How to Adjust Pattern for One High Hip

1) **Trace** front and back skirt pattern pieces. Label right and left sides. Draw adjustment line on poor fit side 5" (12.5 cm) long, parallel to lengthwise grainline, beginning midway between side seam and dart. Draw a second line at right angle from bottom of first line to side seam. Cut on adjustment lines.

2) **Slide** adjustment section up to add necessary length for fitting high hip. Tape paper underneath. Adjust skirt back and front to match. Fold darts or tucks as they will be pressed. Blend stitching and cutting lines at waist and side seams.

Seams

A seam is the basic element in all garment construction. It is created by stitching two pieces of fabric together, usually $\frac{5}{8}$" (1.5 cm) from the cut edge. Perfect seams are the most obvious sign of a well-made garment. Puckered, crooked, or uneven seams spoil the fit as well as the look.

In addition to holding a garment together, seams can be used as a design element. Seams placed in unusual locations or topstitched with contrasting thread add interest to a garment. Most plain seams require a seam finish to prevent raveling. A seam finish is a way of treating or enclosing the raw edges of seam allowances so they are more durable and do not ravel.

Variations of the plain seam include bound, encased, topstitched, and eased seams. Some, such as the flat-fell seam, add strength or shape. Others, such as French or bound seams, improve the appearance of the garment or make it longer wearing.

Techniques for Machine-Stitching Seams

(1) **Position** the bulk of the fabric to the left of the machine needle, with cut edges to the right. Support and guide fabric gently with both hands as you stitch.

(2) **Use** guidelines etched on the throat plate of the machine to help you sew straight seams. For extra help, use a seam guide or strip of masking tape placed the desired distance from the needle.

(3) **Use** the thread cutter located at the back of the presser bar assembly to cut threads after stitching. Or use a thread clipper to cut threads.

How to Sew a Plain Seam

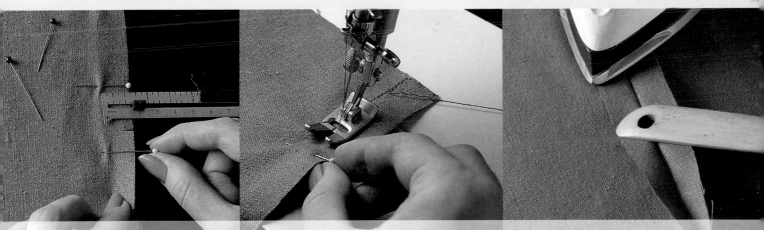

(1) **Pin** seam, right sides of fabric together, at regular intervals, matching notches and other markings precisely. Place pins at right angles to seamline, usually ⅝" (1.5 cm) from edge, with points just beyond seamline and heads toward cut edge for easy removal.

(2) **Secure** stitching with backstitching. Then stitch forward on seamline, removing pins as you come to them. Backstitch ½" (1.3 cm) at end to secure the stitching. Trim threads.

(3) **Press** over stitching line on wrong side to press seam flat. This blends stitches into fabric. Then press seam open. Use your fingers or the blunt end of a point turner to open seams as you press. If seam is curved, such as hip area of skirt or pants, press over curved area of a tailor's ham.

1 **Stitch** a line of reinforcement stitching just inside seamline of inner curve of center panel. Clip into seam allowance all the way to the stitching line at intervals along the curve.

2 **Pin** inner and outer curves, right sides together with clipped edge on top, spreading clipped inner curve to match all markings and fit outer curve.

3 **Stitch** on seamline with clipped seam on top, using shorter stitch than usual for the fabric and being careful to keep the lower layer of fabric smooth.

4 **Cut out** wedge-shaped notches in the seam allowance of outer curve by making small folds in seam allowance and cutting at slight angle. Be careful not to cut into stitching line.

5 **Press** seam flat to embed and smooth the stitches. Turn over and press on the other side.

6 **Press** seam open over curve of tailor's ham, using tip of iron only. Do not press into body of garment. If not pressed to contour, seam lines become distorted and look pulled out of shape.

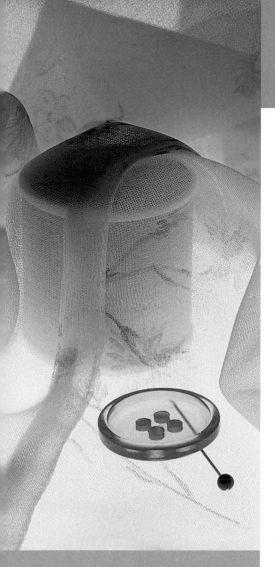

Encased seams differ from bound seams in that no additional fabric or binding is used. The cut edges of seam allowances are enclosed within the seam itself. Encased seams are best suited to lightweight fabrics, since the additional bulk created is not a problem. These seams are especially appropriate for sheer fabrics, because no raw or contrasting edges show through. Use a straight-stitch foot and needle plate (page 12) to keep sheer fabric from being pulled into the feed.

ENCASED SEAMS

Use encased seams for blouses, unlined jackets, lingerie, or sheer curtains. They are also an excellent choice for children's clothes, because they stand up to rugged wear and repeated laundering.

Self-bound seam begins with a plain seam. One seam allowance is then folded over the other and stitched again.

French seam looks like a plain seam on the right side and a narrow tuck on the wrong side. It begins by stitching the wrong sides of the fabric together. This seam is difficult to sew in curved areas, so is best used on straight seams.

Mock French seam begins with a plain seam. Seam allowances are trimmed, folded to the inside and stitched along the folds. The self-bound and mock French seams can be used in curved or straight areas.

How to Sew a Self-bound Seam

(1) **Stitch** a plain seam. Do not press open. Trim one seam allowance to ⅛" (3 mm).

(2) **Turn** under the untrimmed seam allowance ⅛" (3 mm). Then turn again, enclosing the narrow trimmed edge and bringing the folded edge to the seamline.

(3) **Stitch** on the folded edge, as close as possible to first line of stitching. Press seam to one side.

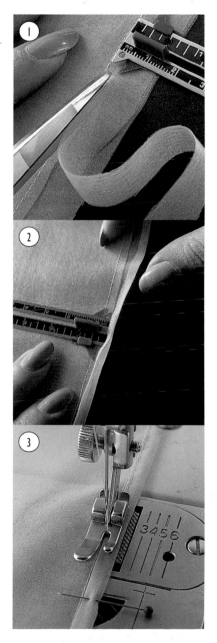

How to Sew a French Seam

① **Pin** wrong sides of fabric together. Stitch ⅜" (1 cm) from edges on right side of fabric.

② **Trim** seam allowance to ⅛" (3 mm). Fold right sides together, with stitching line exactly on fold. Press flat.

③ **Stitch** ¼" (6 mm) from fold. This step encases cut edges. Check right side to be sure no raveled threads are showing. Press seam to one side.

How to Sew a Mock French Seam

① **Stitch** a plain seam. Trim both seam allowances to ½" (1.3 cm). Press open.

② **Press** ¼" (6 mm) on each seam allowance toward inside of seam, so cut edges meet at stitching line.

③ **Stitch** edges together, stitching as close to folds as possible. Press seam to one side.

How to Sew a Flat-Fell Seam

(1) **Pin** fabric, wrong sides together, at seamline with pin heads toward raw edges. Stitch, taking the usual ⅝" (1.5 cm) seam allowance.

(2) **Press** seam allowances to one side. Trim the lower seam allowance to ⅛" (3 mm).

(3) **Turn** under ¼" (6 mm) on the upper seam allowance and press.

(4) **Pin** folded seam allowance to garment, concealing trimmed lower edge.

(5) **Edgestitch** on fold, removing pins as you come to them.

(6) **Finished seam** is a reversible flat seam with two visible rows of stitching on each side.

How to Sew a Mock Flat-fell Seam

① **Stitch** a plain seam. Press seam allowances to one side. Trim lower seam allowance to ¼" (6 mm).

② **Topstitch** on right side of garment, ¼" to ½" (6 mm to 1.3 cm) from the seamline. Edgestitch close to the seamline.

③ **Finished seam** looks like the flat-fell seam on the right side, but has one exposed seam allowance on wrong side.

STRETCH SEAMS

Stretch fabrics for casual or action wear include jersey, stretch terry, stretch velour, and other knits. Stretch woven fabrics include stretch denim, stretch poplin, and stretch corduroy. For swimwear and leotards, Lycra knits are available. Seams in these fabrics must stretch or "give" with the fabric. Some sewing machines have special knit stitches that incorporate stretch.

Test the seam or knit stitch on a scrap of fabric to determine its appropriateness to the weight and stretchiness of the fabric. Some of the special knit stitches are more difficult to rip than straight stitching, so be sure the garment fits before stitching. Because knits do not ravel, they usually do not require seam finishing.

Double-stitched seam gives an insurance row of stitching to a seam. Use this method if your machine does not zigzag.

Straight and zigzag seam combines a straight seam with the stretchiness of zigzag. This is a suitable finish for knits that tend to curl along the raw edges.

Narrow zigzag seam is used for knits that do not curl along edges. It is a fast, easy stretch seam.

Straight stretch stitch is formed by a forward/backward motion of reverse-action machines. It makes a strong, stretchy seam appropriate for stressed areas such as armholes.

Straight with overedge stitch has a special pattern which combines a straight stretch stitch with diagonal stitching. It joins and finishes the seam in one step.

Elastic stretch stitch is an excellent choice for swimwear and leotards. The stitch combines a narrow and wide zigzag pattern.

Taped seams are used in areas where you do not want stretch, such as shoulder seams.

How to Sew a Taped Seam

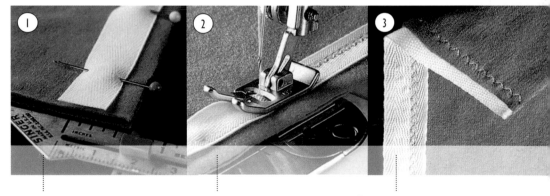

① **Pin** fabric, right sides together, so that twill tape or seam binding is pinned over seamline. Position seam binding so it laps 3/8" (1 cm) into the seam allowance.

② **Stitch**, using double-stitched, straight and zigzag, overedge, or narrow zigzag seam. Press seam open or to one side, depending on selected seam.

③ **Trim** seam allowance close to stitching, taking care not to cut into seam binding.

A seam finish lends a couture touch and improved appearance to any garment. Finish seams to prevent woven fabrics from raveling and knit seams from curling. Seam finishes also strengthen seams and help them stand up to repeated washings and wearing, making the garment look new longer.

SEAM FINISHES

Seams should be finished as they are stitched, before being crossed by another seam. A finish should not add bulk or show an obvious imprint on the right side of the garment after it is pressed. If you are not sure which seam finish to use, try several on a fabric scrap to see which works best.

The seam finishes shown here all begin with a plain seam. They can also be used as edge finishes for facings and hems.

Selvage finish requires no extra stitching. Appropriate for straight seams of woven fabrics, it requires adjusting the pattern layout so that the seam is cut on the selvage.

Stitched and pinked seam finish is suitable for firmly woven fabrics. It is a quick and easy finish that prevents raveling and curling.

Turned and stitched finish (also called clean-finished) is suitable for light- to medium-weight woven fabrics.

Zigzag seam finishes prevent raveling and are good for knits, because they have more give than straight-stitched finishes. These finishes use the built-in stitches on automatic zigzag machines.

Basic Seam Finishes

(a) **Selvage finish.** Adjust pattern layout so that edges of seam are cut on selvage. To prevent shrinking and puckering, clip diagonally into both selvages at 3" to 4" (7.5 to 10 cm) intervals after seam is stitched.

(b) **Stitched and pinked finish.** Stitch ¼" (6 mm) from edge of each seam allowance. Press seam open. Trim close to stitching with pinking or scalloping shears.

How to Sew a Turned and Stitched Finish

(1) **Stitch** ⅛" to ¼" (3 to 6 mm) from edge of each seam allowance. On straight edges, this stitching may not be necessary.

(2) **Turn under** seam allowance on stitching line. The stitching helps the edge turn under, especially on curves.

(3) **Stitch** close to edge of fold, through seam allowance only. Press seam open.

How to Sew a Zigzag Finish

(1) **Set** zigzag stitch for maximum width. Stitch near, but not over, edge of each seam allowance.

(2) **Trim** close to stitching, being careful not to cut into stitching.

Other Zigzag Finishes

Overedge zigzag finish. Trim seam edges evenly, if necessary. Adjust zigzag stitch length and width to suit fabric. Stitch close to edge of each seam allowance so that stitches go over the edge. If fabric puckers, loosen tension by turning to a lower number.

3-step zigzag finish. Use stitch that puts three short stitches in space of one zigzag width. Set machine for pattern stitch and adjust length and width to suit fabric. Stitch close to edge of seam allowance. On some machines, a serpentine stitch gives same results. Trim close to stitching line.

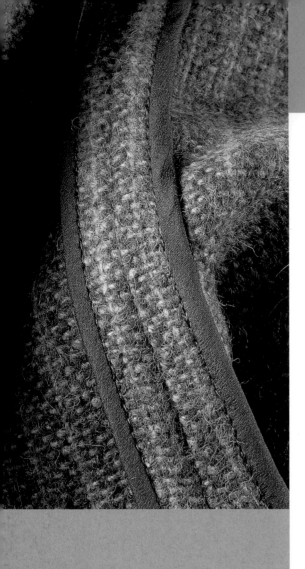

BOUND SEAM FINISHES

These finishes totally enclose the cut edge of seam allowances and prevent raveling. They also enhance the appearance of the inside of the garment. Bound seam finishes are a good choice for unlined jackets, especially those made of heavy fabrics or those which ravel easily.

The most commonly used bound finishes are the bias bound, tricot bound and Hong Kong finishes. Medium-weight fabrics such as chino, denim, linen, gabardine, and flannel, and heavyweight fabrics such as wools, velvet, velveteen, and corduroy can utilize any of the three. Begin each of these finishes by sewing a plain seam. Bound finishes can also be used on hem or facing edges.

Bias bound is the easiest bound finish. Use purchased double-fold bias tape, available in cotton, rayon or polyester, to match the fashion fabric.

Tricot bound is an inconspicuous finish for most fabrics. Precut sheer nylon strips are available in ⅝" (1.5 cm) or ¼" (3.2 cm) width. Use the narrower width for binding seams.

Hong Kong finish is a couture technique used on designer clothing, but because it is so easy and gives such a fine finish to the inside of a garment, it has become a favorite of many home sewers.

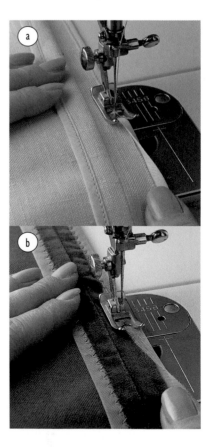

How to Sew a Hong Kong Finish

① **Cut** bias strips of lining fabric, 1¼" (3.2 cm) wide. Join strips as necessary (page 80) to form strips twice the length of the seams to be finished.

② **Align** bias strip on right side of seam allowance. Stitch ¼" (6 mm) from cut edge, stretching bias slightly as you stitch. Use edge of presser foot as stitching guide.

③ **Trim** seam allowance of heavy fabric to ⅛" (3 mm) to reduce bulk. Lightweight fabric does not need to be trimmed.

④ **Press** bias strip back over cut edge of seam allowance. Fold bias strip to the underside, enclosing the cut edge.

⑤ **Pin** bias strip in place through all layers. Cut edge of bias strip needs no finishing, since a bias cut does not ravel.

⑥ **Stitch** in the ditch (the groove where the bias strip and fabric were stitched together). This stitching is hidden on the right side and catches cut edge of bias strip underneath. Press lightly.

Serger Seams and Seam Finishes

Serged seams can be used on many garments. Your instruction manual may include suggestions for where stitches are used. Garment style, fabric selection, and personal preference will help you decide which seams to use. The serged seam alone is not always suitable for garment construction. Many seams are sewn using both the serger and the conventional machine. For example, pants, jackets, or garments requiring adjustable fit, or seams that will be subjected to a great amount of stress, should be sewn with a pressed-open conventional seam and over-edged seam allowances.

Types of Seams and Seam Finishes

Overlock seams (page 16) are appropriate for wovens and knits. Choose the 3-thread overlock for loosely fitted or nonstressed seams. The more secure 4-thread and 5-thread safety stitches are used primarily for wovens because the chainstitch may pop when stretched. The 3-thread and 4-thread mock safety stitches, designed for durable stretch seams, may also be used on wovens.

Overedge seam finish (page 116) for conventional seams is used when it is desirable to keep the entire ⅝" (1.5 cm) seam allowance. It is the best choice for tailored garments sewn from wools, linens, and silk suitings. It is also recommended whenever fit is uncertain to allow for letting out seams.

Reinforced seam (page 116) is recommended for seams that will be stressed.

French seam (page 116) is used for sheers and loosely woven fabrics. The seam will add bulk, so it is best used on full, gathered items such as skirts and curtains.

Rolled seam (page 117) may be used instead of French seams for sheers that are firmly woven and for laces.

Mock flat-fell seam (page 117) is used for denim and other heavy-weight woven fabrics.

Reversible lapped seam (page 117) is used for reversible garments or for thick, loosely woven fabrics to provide added strength.

Gathered seam (page 118) is finished in one easy step using differential feed and a shirring foot. An alternate method uses the conventional machine with the serger.

Mock flatlock seam (page 118) is used for a decorative effect, with decorative thread used in the upper looper.

Flatlock on a fold (page 119) is used for the decorative effect of a flatlock seam on fabric that has been folded and stitched.

Types of Stabilized Seams

There are several methods for stabilizing seams in serger garment construction. The type of fabric you are sewing and the desired effect will determine which method you choose.

Fusible stabilized seam (page 119) uses fusible interfacing strips to stabilize seams. Interfacing can also be used as a stable base for decorative edge finishes on stretchy knit or bias-cut fabrics.

Elastic stabilized seam (page 119) uses transparent elastic to allow full stretch and recovery in a serged seam, but prevents fabric from stretching out of shape.

Nonstretch stabilized seam (page 119) uses twill tape, seam tape, or ribbon to prevent stretching of the fabric at the seamline.

Slight-stretch stabilized seam (page 119) uses tricot bias binding to reinforce and stabilize a seam where slight stretch is desired. Use this method for stabilizing seams in sweater knits and T-shirt knits, which need support without completely restricting the stretch of the fabric.

Basic Seams and Seam Finishes

(1) **Overedge seam finish** for conventional seam. Stitch ⅝" (1.5 cm) seam, right sides together, using conventional machine. Stitch seam allowances, slightly trimming raw edge, using overedge or overlock stitch.

(2) **Reinforced seam.** Stitch ⅝" (1.5 cm) seam, right sides together, using conventional machine; use narrow zigzag on moderate-stretch knits. Serge seam allowances together ⅛" (3 mm) from seamline.

(3) **French seam.** Overedge seam, wrong sides together, with left needle positioned ¼" (6 mm) inside seam allowance. Fold fabric, right sides together, enclosing overedged fabric; press. Straight-stitch close to enclosed stitches, using zipper foot on the conventional machine.

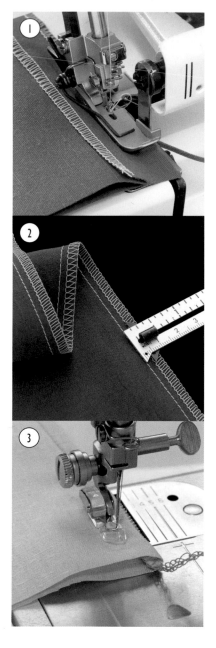

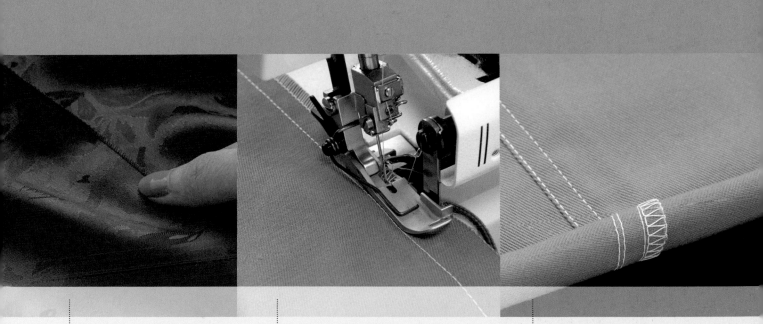

Rolled seam. Place fabric right sides together. Stitch seam, using a rolled hem stitch, with needle positioned on seamline; trim excess seam allowance. Press. Use tricot bias binding to stabilize lace edge, as shown on page 119, if desired.

How to Sew a Mock Flat-Fell Seam

(1) **Place** fabric right sides together. Stitch, using a conventional machine. Serge seam allowances together, trimming slightly.

(2) **Press** seam allowance toward one side; topstitch from right side next to seamline, using a conventional machine. Topstitch again, ¼" (6 mm) away, through all layers.

How to Sew a Reversible Lapped Seam

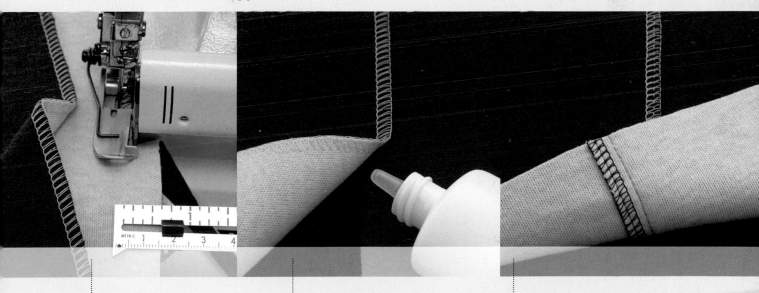

(1) **Stitch** each single-layer seam allowance, using overedge or overlock stitch and aligning needle to seamline.

(2) **Lap** garment sections so seamlines meet; glue-baste.

(3) **Straight-stitch** through all layers ⅛" (3 mm) from serged stitches, from both sides of garment, using conventional machine.

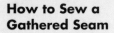

How to Sew a Gathered Seam

1. **Replace** regular presser foot with shirring foot; set differential feed to a larger number. Align edges of two fabric layers together; position layers so fabric to be gathered is on the bottom. Overlock the seam with needle positioned on the seamline.

Alternate Method

1. **Baste** in seam allowance near seamline, using conventional machine. Overedge seam allowance, slightly trimming raw edge. Align over-edged fabric to corresponding section, right sides together, matching as necessary; pin. Pull bobbin thread and serger needle thread, gathering fabric to fit.

2. **Stitch** seam, using conventional machine. Overedge seam allowances, using serger. Or, overlock seam, with left needle positioned on seamline, trimming away excess seam allowance; remove pins as they approach knives.

How to Sew a Mock Flatlock Seam

1. **Use** decorative thread in upper looper. Serge fabric, wrong sides together; press seam to one side with decorative thread on top.

2. **Topstitch** decorative serged seam through all layers, using conventional machine.

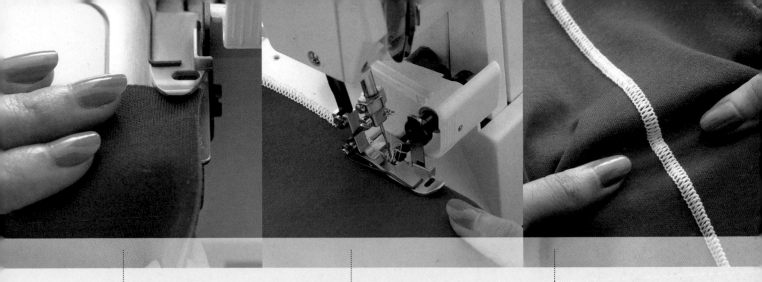

How to Flatlock on a Fold of Fabric

(1) **Mark** stitch placement line on right side of fabric. Fold, wrong sides together, on marked line. Adjust serger for flatlock stitch. Place fabric slightly to the left of knives.

(2) **Serge** seam without trimming fold of fabric. Position stitches half on and half off fabric.

(3) **Open** the fabric, and pull the stitches flat.

Stabilized Seams

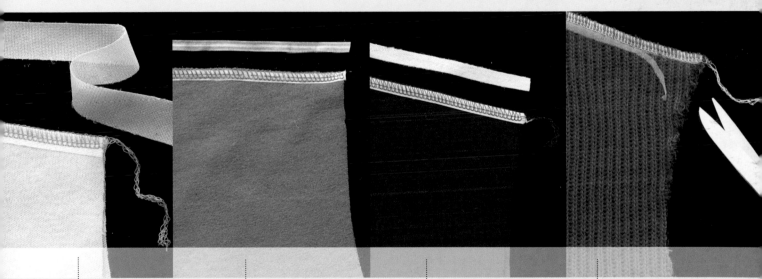

Fusible stabilized seam. Cut ¾" (2 cm) strip of fusible knit interfacing the length of the seam. Fuse to wrong side of garment. Stitch seam.

Elastic stabilized seam. Use elastic tape foot, if available, or use regular presser foot; adjust foot tension to drag slightly against elastic. Serge seam without trimming elastic; increase differential feed to ease fabric, if desired.

Nonstretch stabilized seam. Serge as in elastic stabilized seam, left; use twill tape, seam tape, or ribbon, and adjust foot tension so it does not drag on stabilizer. Decrease differential feed slightly, if desired, to prevent puckering of seam.

Slight-stretch stabilized seam. Cut a strip of tricot bias binding the length of the seam. Increase differential feed slightly, to ease fabric and prevent overstretching seam. Serge through relaxed strip; trim excess binding close to stitches.

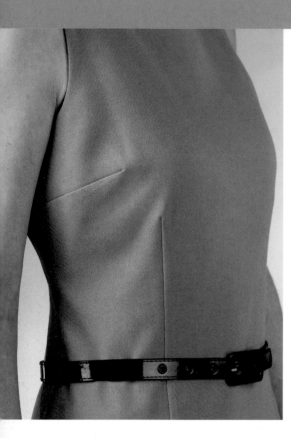

Darts

A dart is used to shape a flat piece of fabric to fit bust, waist, hip, or elbow curves. There are two types of darts. A single-pointed dart is wide at one end and pointed at the other. A shaped dart has points at both ends. It is usually used at the waistline, with the points extending to the bust and hips. Besides providing a closer fit, darts are also used to create special designer touches and unique styles. Perfect darts are straight and smooth, not puckered at the ends. The darts on the right and left sides of the garment should have the same placement and length.

Dart Techniques

Shaped darts are stitched in two steps, beginning at the waistline and stitching toward each point. Overlap stitching at waist about 1" (2.5 cm). Clip dart fold at waistline and midway along points, to within 1/8" to 1/4" (3 to 6 mm) of stitching to relieve strain and allow dart to curve smoothly.

Wide darts and darts in bulky fabrics should be slashed open on the foldline and trimmed to 5/8" (1.5 cm) or less. Slash to within 1/2" (1.3 cm) of point. Press dart open and press point flat.

Press darts over the curve of a tailor's ham to maintain the built-in curve. Vertical darts are usually pressed toward the center front or center back. Horizontal darts are usually pressed downward.

How to Sew a Dart

(1) **Mark** dart using appropriate marking method for fabric. Mark point of dart with horizontal line.

(2) **Fold** dart on center line, matching stitching lines and markings at the wide end, the point and in between. Pin in place, with heads of pins toward folded edge for easy removal as you stitch.

(3) **Stitch** from wide end to point of dart. Backstitch at beginning of stitching line, then continue stitching toward point, removing pins as you come to them.

(4) **Taper** to point of dart. When ½" (1.3 cm) remains, shorten stitch length to 12 to 16 stitches per inch (2.5 cm). Take last two or three stitches directly on fold. Do not backstitch at the point, because this may cause puckering. Continue stitching off edge of fabric.

(5) **Raise** presser foot and pull dart toward front. About 1" (2.5 cm) back from point of dart, lower presser foot and secure thread by stitching several times in fold of the dart with stitch length set at 0. Clip threads close to knot.

(6) **Press** folded edge of dart flat, being careful not to crease fabric beyond the point. Then place dart over curve of tailor's ham and press in proper direction (opposite). For a neat, flat finish, press darts before they are stitched into a seam.

Gathers

A soft, feminine garment line is often shaped with gathers. They may be found at waistlines, cuffs, yokes, necklines, or sleeve caps. Soft and sheer fabrics produce a draped look when gathered; crisp fabrics create a billowy effect.

Gathers start with two stitching lines on a long piece of fabric. The stitching lines are then pulled at each end to draw up the fabric. Finally, the gathered piece is sewn to a shorter length of fabric.

The stitch length for gathering is longer than for ordinary sewing. Use a stitch length of 6 to 8 stitches per inch (2.5 cm) for medium-weight fabrics. For soft or sheer fabrics, use 8 to 10 stitches per inch (2.5 cm). Experiment with the fabric to see which stitch length gathers best. A longer stitch helps to draw up the fabric, but a shorter stitch gives more control when adjusting gathers.

Before you stitch, loosen the upper thread tension. The bobbin stitching is pulled to draw up the gathers, and a looser tension makes this easier.

If the fabric is heavy or stiff, use heavy-duty thread in the bobbin. A contrasting color in the bobbin also helps distinguish it from the upper thread.

How to Sew Basic Gathers

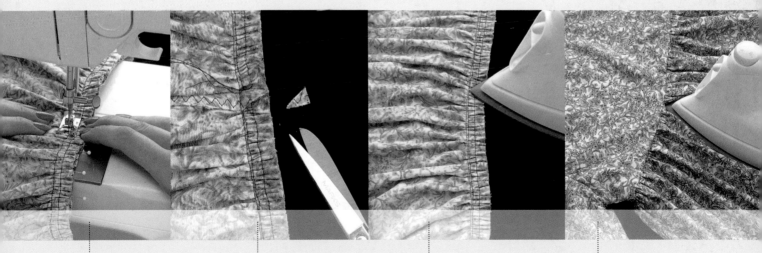

1) **Stitch** a scant ⅝" (1.5 cm) from raw edge on right side of fabric, starting and ending at seamline. Loosen upper tension and lengthen stitches appropriate to fabric. Stitch a second row in seam allowance, ¼" (6 mm) away from first row. This double row of stitching gives better control in gathering than a single row.

2) **Pin** stitched edge to corresponding garment section, right sides together, at seams, notches, center lines, and other markings. Fabric will droop between pins. If there are no markings to guide you, divide both edges into quarters and pin out fullness evenly.

3) **Pull** both bobbin threads from one end, sliding fabric along thread to gather. When half the gathered section fits the straight edge, secure bobbin threads by twisting in a figure eight around pin. Pull bobbin threads from other end to gather remaining half.

4) **Pin** gathers in place at frequent intervals. Distribute gathers evenly between pins. Reset stitch length and tension for regular sewing.

5) **Stitch**, gathered side up, just outside gathering lines. Adjust gathers between pins as you stitch. Hold gathers taut with fingers on both sides of needle to keep gathers even.

6) **Trim** seam allowances of any seams that have been sewn into the stitching line, trimming off corners at a diagonal.

7) **Press** seam allowance on wrong side, using tip of iron. Then open out garment and press seam in the desired direction: toward gathers for puffy look, toward garment for smoother look.

8) **Press** into gathers with point of iron on right side of garment, lifting iron as you reach seam. Do not press across gathers; this will flatten them.

Gathering with Elastic

Gathers formed with elastic offer comfortable and easy fit. This technique ensures uniform gathers and creates shape that is relaxed and not as close to the body as other shapebuilders.

Elastic can be stitched directly to the garment or inserted in a casing. A casing is a tunnel for elastic, created with a turned-under edge or with bias tape stitched to the fabric. Choose an elastic that is suitable to the sewing technique and area of the garment where it is used (page 33).

Elastic in a casing can be any width. Use a firm, braided, or non-roll elastic. Braided elastic has lengthwise ribs, and narrows when stretched.

Stitched elastic calls for woven or knitted elastics which are soft, strong, and comfortable to wear next to the skin. On short areas such as sleeve or leg edges, it is easiest to apply the elastic while the garment section is flat. At a waistline, overlap the ends of the elastic and stitch to form a circle before pinning to the garment.

Cut elastic the length recommended by the pattern. This length includes a seam allowance. To add elastic when the pattern does not call for it, cut the elastic slightly shorter than the body measurement plus seam allowance. Allow 1" (2.5 cm) extra for a stitched elastic seam, ½" (1.3 cm) extra for overlapping elastic in a casing.

How to Sew Stitched Elastic

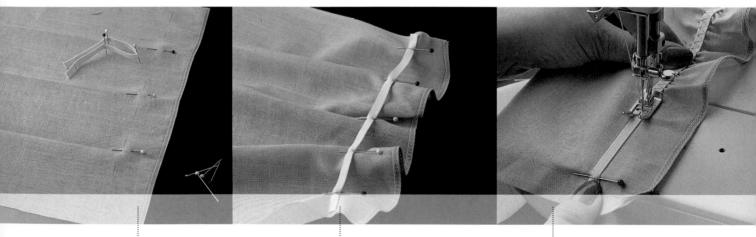

1. **Fold** elastic and fabric into fourths. Mark foldlines of elastic and garment with pins.

2. **Pin** elastic to wrong side of garment, matching marking pins. Leave ½" (1.3 cm) seam allowance at each end of elastic.

3. **Stitch** elastic to fabric, stretching elastic between pins, with one hand behind needle and other hand at next pin. Apply with a zigzag, multi-stitch zigzag, or two rows of straight stitching, one along each edge.

How to Sew Elastic in Casing (waistline seam)

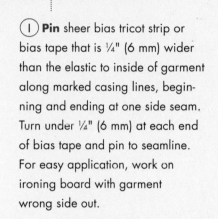

(1) **Pin** sheer bias tricot strip or bias tape that is ¼" (6 mm) wider than the elastic to inside of garment along marked casing lines, beginning and ending at one side seam. Turn under ¼" (6 mm) at each end of bias tape and pin to seamline. For easy application, work on ironing board with garment wrong side out.

(2) **Stitch** tape close to edges, leaving opening at seam to insert elastic. Do not backstitch at ends of stitching, because this stitching shows on the right side of the garment. Instead, pull all four ends to inside and knot.

(3) **Insert** elastic through casing using a bodkin or safety pin, taking care not to twist elastic. Place a large safety pin across free end of elastic to prevent it from pulling through.

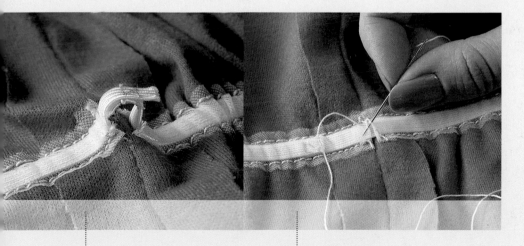

(4) **Lap** ends of elastic ½" (1.3 cm) and sew together with straight or zigzag stitches, stitching forward, backstitching, and forward again. Clip thread ends. Ease elastic back into casing.

(5) **Slipstitch** ends of casing together. Distribute gathers evenly along the elastic.

Sleeves

Whether short or long, all sleeves are one of three basic styles: set-in, kimono, or raglan.

Set-in sleeves have a rounded cap that is larger than the corresponding part of the armhole. The cap must be eased to fit smoothly into place. As a softer fashion detail, set-in sleeves may also have gathers or pleats in the sleeve cap. The traditional method of setting in sleeves uses two rows of easestitching on the sleeve to fit the cap into place. The flat method, opposite, is used for a man-tailored shirt sleeve, which has less ease than classic set-in styles. The sleeve is inserted before the sleeve or garment side seams are stitched.

Kimono sleeves extend without seams from garment front and back sections. Shoulder shaping is rounded, as in raglan sleeves. Kimono sleeves are often loosely fitted and drape softly under the arms. Even loose-fitting kimono sleeves are subject to stress in the underarm area. Reinforce this curved seam with tape, two rows of stitching, shortened stitches, or a reinforcing stretch stitch.

Raglan sleeves have a slanted seam in the front and the back. Most raglan sleeves have a seam that curves over the shoulder and extends the length of the sleeve. This seam shapes the shoulder in a rounded way. In some patterns darts, instead of seams, shape the shoulders. For more comfort and better fit, stitch the sleeve and side seam before setting in the sleeve.

Shaping aids, such as sleeve puffs and shoulder pads, are needed to complete some sleeve treatments. Sleeve puffs are small pads that support gathered sleeve caps. Puffs lift gathers so the sleeve hangs straight and smooth.

Tips for Sewing Sleeves

Pattern markings such as notches, dots, and shoulder seam marks help to position set-in sleeve. More fabric must be eased at the back of the sleeve than at the front. No fabric should be eased into the armhole at the top of the sleeve cap for 1" (2.5 cm) at center dot.

Notches on pattern pieces tell which way sleeve and armhole edges should face. Double notches indicate the back of the sleeve and armhole. A single notch indicates the front. Mark notches with ¼" (6 mm) snips into the seam allowance.

How to Sew a Shirt Sleeve (flat method)

(1) **Pin** sleeve to armhole, right sides together, matching notches and small dots. Pin on garment side, easing sleeve cap to fit.

(2) **Stitch** sleeve to armhole with garment side up. Action of feed eases sleeve to fit armhole.

(3) **Press** seam away from sleeve. Trim garment seam allowance to ¼" (6 mm) for mock flat-fell seam.

(4) **Topstitch** sleeve seam on the right side of garment ¼" (6 mm) from the seamline.

(5) **Edgestitch** close to seamline.

(6) **Pin** side seam of garment and sleeve together. Stitch in one continuous seam. Reinforce underarm area with short stitches, or use mock flat-fell seam.

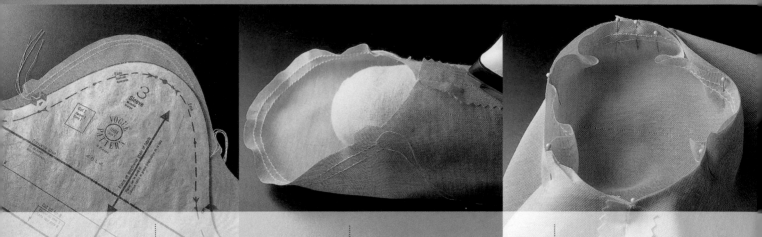

How to Sew a Set in Sleeve

(1) **Easestitch** cap of sleeve (the area between front and back notches) on right side, slightly inside seamline. Easestitch sleeve cap again, ⅜" (1 cm) from edge.

(2) **Stitch** underarm sleeve seam, right sides together. Press seam flat, then press seam open. Use sleeve board or seam roll to prevent impression of seam on top of sleeve.

(3) **Turn** sleeve right side out. Turn garment inside out. Insert sleeve into armhole, right sides together, matching notches, small dot markings, underarm seam, and shoulder line. Insert pins on seamline for best control of ease.

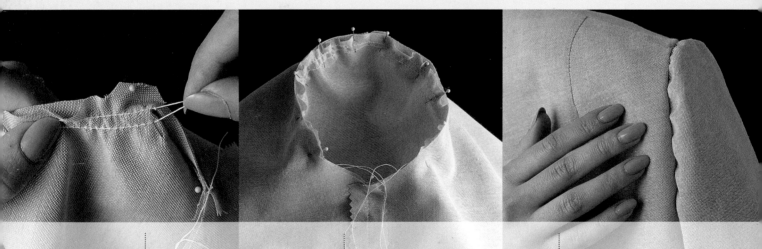

(4) **Draw up** bobbin threads of easestitching lines until cap fits armhole. Distribute fullness evenly, leaving 1" (2.5 cm) flat (uneased) at shoulder seam at top of sleeve cap.

(5) **Pin** sleeve to armhole at close intervals, using more pins in front and back where the bulk of the ease is located.

(6) **Check** sleeve from right side for smooth fit and correct drape. Adjust if necessary. There can be tiny pleats or puckers in seam allowance, but not in seamline.

7 **Secure** ends of easestitching thread by making a figure eight over each pin at front and back notches.

8 **Stitch** just outside easestitching line, sleeve side up, starting at one notch. Stitch around sleeve, past starting point, to other notch, reinforcing underarm with two rows of stitching. Remove pins as you come to them.

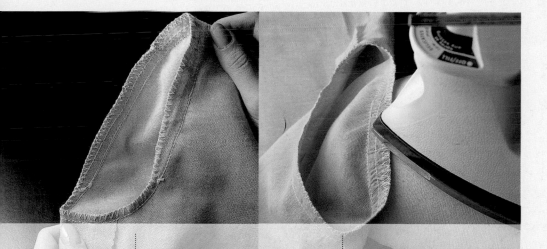

9 **Trim** seam allowance to ¼" (6 mm) between notches at underarm only. Do not trim seam allowance of sleeve cap. Zigzag seam allowances together.

10 **Press** seam allowance of sleeve cap only, using press mitt or end of sleeve board. Do not press into the sleeve.

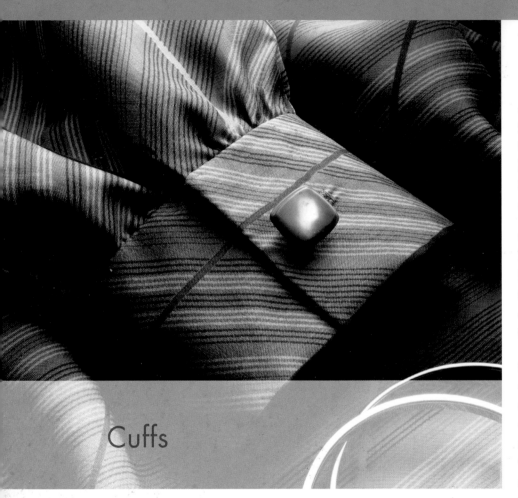

Cuffs

Long sleeves on shirts, blouses, and lightweight jackets often have cuffs with buttoned closings. In many ways, sewing cuffs is similar to sewing collars. The tips on pages 135 for trimming, interfacing, and pressing collars apply to cuffs, too.

Apply interfacing to half of a one-piece cuff. The interfaced half of the cuff shows on the outside of the finished sleeve. The half without interfacing is folded to the inside to form a self-facing. Interface one section of a two-piece cuff; this section belongs on the outside of the sleeve. The other cuff section forms the facing on the inside.

Apply cuffs, using either topstitching or hand finishing. Topstitching is usually faster, because it is done by machine. Cuffs without topstitching require hand finishing, but no stitches show on the outside.

Continuous bound placket is a slit bound with a strip of self-fabric. The binding strip is cut on the lengthwise fabric grain for stability. When the cuff is closed, this placket is hidden from view.

Shirt-style placket is a box-shaped sleeve opening finished with a shaped facing. The facing is folded and stitched so the edges of the placket overlap neatly. Adapted from menswear tailoring, this type of placket is found on patterns with traditional details. When the cuff is closed, the pointed portion of the facing shows on a shirt-style placket.

How to Sew a Continuous Bound Placket

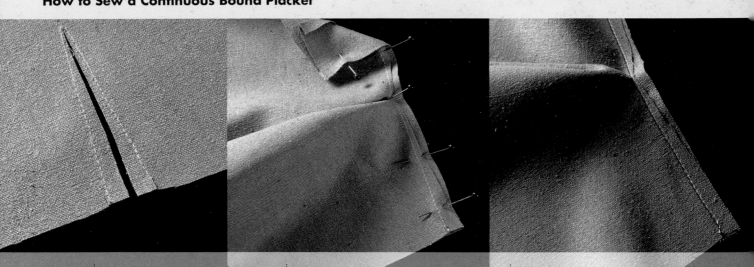

① **Staystitch** placket on seamline. Use short stitches on each side of placket point; take one stitch across point. Slash to stitch at point.

② **Press** one binding edge under ¼" (6 mm). Hold slash straight to pin other binding edge to placket, right side of binding to wrong side of sleeve.

③ **Stitch** next to sleeve staystitching with ¼" (6 mm) seam allowance on placket; use presser foot as guide. Raw edges line up evenly only at seam ends.

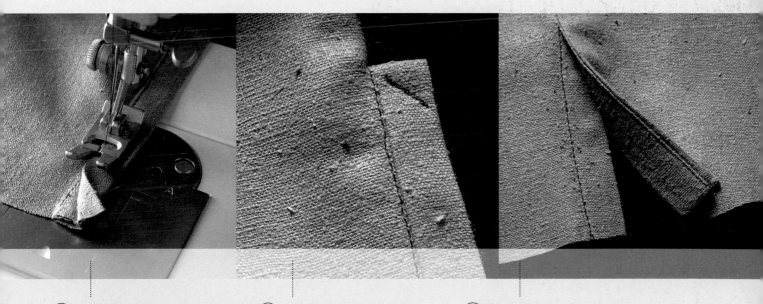

④ **Bring** folded binding edge over seam. Fold should barely cover seam. Edgestitch fold through all layers of fabric; press.

⑤ **Line up** edges of binding on wrong side of sleeve; stitch diagonally from top of binding to keep binding inside sleeve when cuff is finished.

⑥ **Press** binding flat on underlapping back placket edge. Press binding under on overlapping front placket edge. Attach cuff (page 133).

How to Sew a Shirt-style Placket

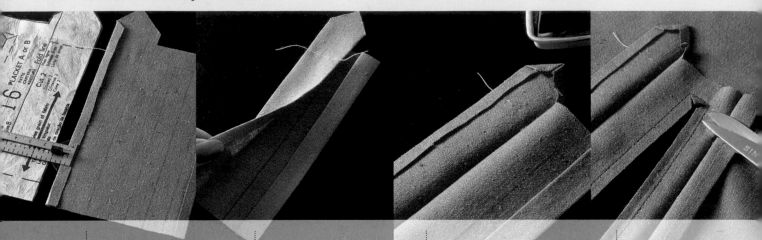

1. **Press** under ¼" (6 mm) seam allowances on sides of placket facing. Baste-mark across top of placket opening.

2. **Press** facing sides on foldlines. Facing edges should line up with marking for placket opening.

3. **Press** under seam allowances on point. Miter angled corners by folding seam allowance across point before folding side edges.

4. **Match** markings on facing and sleeve placket opening, right side of facing against wrong side of sleeve; stitch. Slash to ¼" (6 mm) from top, then clip to corners.

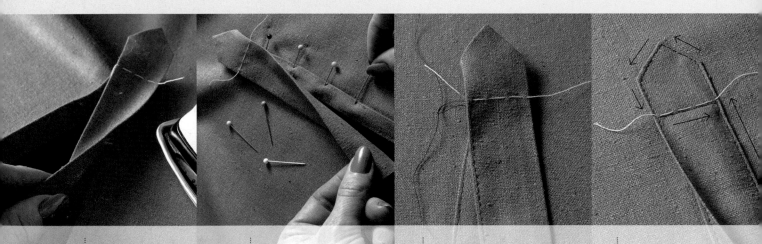

5. **Pull** facing through opening to right side of sleeve. Press seams toward placket opening. Press up triangle at top of placket.

6. **Pin** narrow facing edge to cover placket stitching; edgestitch inner fold of facing through all layers.

7. **Fold** other side of facing to cover placket stitching; pin. Edgestitch outer fold of overlap facing to top of opening. Pull threads to underside and tie.

8. **Arrange** overlap so edges are flat and even. Edgestitch in direction of arrows, starting at lower edge, up around point, and across placket. Secure stitching. Attach cuff (opposite).

How to Attach a Cuff

1. **Fold** cuff pattern in half and cut fusible interfacing from folded pattern, eliminating seam allowances. Fuse interfacing to upper cuff.

2. **Press** under seam allowance on interfaced edge. Fold cuff in half lengthwise, right sides together; stitch ends, opening out pressed seam allowance. Trim and grade seams. Press seams open. Turn cuff right side out.

3. **Pin** and stitch wrong side of sleeve to non-interfaced side of cuff, matching markings. Be sure ends of cuff are even with finished placket edges. Do not trim seam allowances.

4. **Wrap** free cuff section around placket opening to front of sleeve as far as it will go. The right side of cuff is on right side of sleeve. Pin about 1" (2.5 cm) from placket opening.

5. **Stitch** pinned area at each end of cuff exactly on first stitching so first row will not show on outside. Trim seam close to stitching to eliminate bulk.

6. **Turn** cuff right side out; press. Right side of cuff edge is stitched to sleeve for about 1" (2.5 cm) next to placket opening.

7. **Edgestitch** folded edge of cuff over seam. Topstitch ¼" (6 mm) from edge of cuff. For a cuff that is not top-stitched, attach to right side of sleeve, turn to inside, and slipstitch in place.

Collars

Collars are important details worthy of careful sewing. A well-made collar circles your neck without rippling or pulling and keeps its neat appearance through repeated cleanings. Pointed tips should match. Edges should be smooth and flat.

Interfacing, usually cut from the collar pattern piece, adds shape, support, and stability. Most collar styles benefit from the slightly firm finish provided by fusible interfacings. Select the special crisp type of fusible interfacing suitable for men's shirts if you are working with classic shirting fabrics such as oxford cloth or broadcloth. If your fabric is soft or delicate, like challis or crepe de chine, choose a lightweight fusible that bonds at low iron temperatures.

Convertible collar looks similar to the notched collar and lapels on a tailored blazer. The front facings fold back to form the lapels. This collar can be worn open or closed. The top button is usually omitted on casual wear.

Shirt collar with a stand comes from menswear traditions. There are two separate sections: the collar, and the stand between collar and neckline. In some patterns the stand is an extension of the collar section. This eliminates one seam and is faster to sew, but the sewing methods for both versions are similar. For a professional look, topstitch collar edges and stand seams close to the edge.

Standing collar may be shaped or cut double depth and folded along its length to form a self-facing.

Tips for Sewing Collars

Trim outer edges of undercollar a scant ⅛" (3 mm) so the seam rolls toward the underside of the collar when stitched and turned. Pin right sides of collar and undercollar together with outer edges even.

Press collar seam open on a point presser; turn collar right side out. Gently push collar points out with a point turner. Press collar flat, allowing the seam to roll slightly toward the undercollar.

Roll collar into its finished position and pin. If necessary, trim raw edge of undercollar so it is even with upper collar edge. This makes the collar roll properly when it is sewn in place.

How to Sew a Pointed Collar (nonfusible interfacing)

1) **Trim** corners of interfacing diagonally just inside seamline. Machine-baste interfacing to wrong side of upper collar, ½" (1.3 cm) from edge. Trim interfacing close to stitching.

2) **Trim** a scant ⅛" (3 mm) from outer edges of undercollar. This keeps undercollar from rolling to right side after collar is stitched to the neckline. Pin right sides of collar and undercollar together with outer edges even.

3) **Stitch** on seamline, taking one or two short stitches diagonally across each corner instead of making a sharp pivot. This makes a neater point when the collar is turned.

4) **Trim** corners, first across the point, close to stitching, then at an angle to the seam on each side of the point.

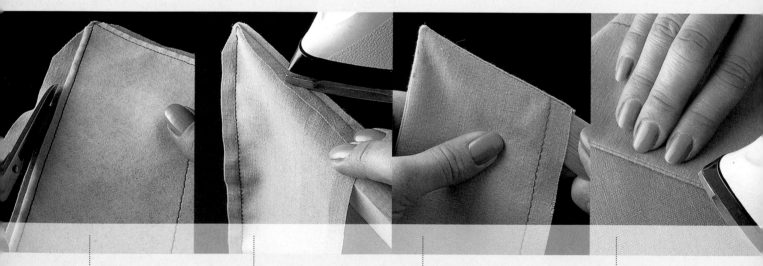

5) **Grade** seam allowances by trimming undercollar seam allowance to ⅛" (3 mm) and collar to ¼" (6 mm).

6) **Press** seam open on a point presser. Turn collar right side out.

7) **Push** points out gently with a point turner.

8) **Press** collar flat, rolling seam slightly to the underside so it will not show on finished collar.

How to Sew a Round Collar (fusible interfacing)

1) **Trim** seam allowances from fusible interfacing and fuse to wrong side of upper collar, following manufacturer's instructions on package.

2) **Trim** scant ⅛" (3 mm) from outside edge of undercollar, as for pointed collar (opposite). Stitch right sides of collar and facing together, using shorter stitches on curves.

3) **Trim** seam allowances close to stitching line, using pinking shears. Or, grade and clip seam allowances. Press seam open, even though seam is enclosed. This flattens stitching line and makes collar easier to turn.

How to Line a Facing with Interfacing

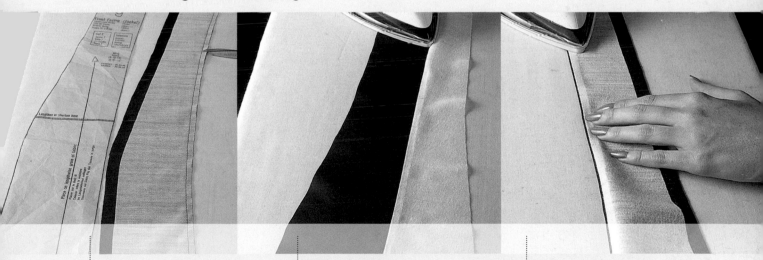

1) **Stitch** fusible interfacing to facing, right sides together, using ¼" (6 mm) seam allowance; nonadhesive side of interfacing is right side. Clip curves.

2) **Press** seam away from facing. To prevent interfacing from fusing to ironing board, be careful that the edge of the iron does not go beyond the seam allowance.

3) **Fold** interfacing on seamline. Finger-press fold, and position interfacing on wrong side of facing. Fuse interfacing to facing. Attach facing to garment.

How to Attach a Convertible Collar

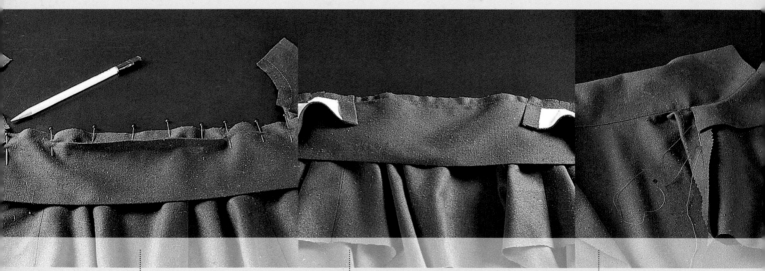

① **Staystitch** upper collar neck seam before stitching to undercollar. Clip collar seam allowance to stay-stitching at shoulder marks. Press seam allowance to wrong side between clips.

② **Interface** front facings up to foldline, using lined facing technique (page 133) or finishing facing edges with finish appropriate to fabric. Turn under facing seam allowances at shoulder seams; press.

③ **Stitch** shoulder seams. Staystitch garment neck edge on seamline. Clip seam allowance at frequent intervals, stopping short of staystitching. Stitch upper and undercollars. Turn right side out, and press.

④ **Pin** undercollar only to garment between shoulder seams. Keep collar neck edge free. Pin upper collar and undercollar to front neck edge, matching markings.

⑤ **Fold** front facings over collar. Pin through all layers. Stitch neckline seam, right side of garment up; do not catch folded edge of collar in stitching. Trim across corners, and grade seam; turn facings right side out.

⑥ **Bring** folded edge of upper collar over neck seam, and edgestitch or slipstitch in place. Slipstitch facings to shoulder seam allowances.

How to Attach a Shirt Collar with a Stand

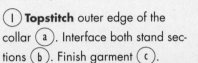
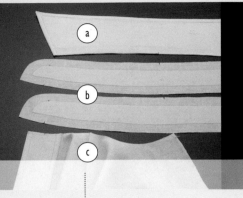
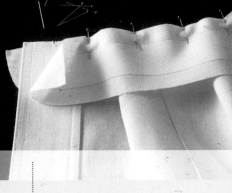

(1) **Topstitch** outer edge of the collar (a). Interface both stand sections (b). Finish garment (c).

(2) **Pin** the stand sections, right sides together, with shirt sandwiched between layers.

(3) **Stitch** stand to neck seam. Stop 5/8" (1.5 cm) from stand edges (arrow). Trim and grade seam.

(4) **Roll** shirt fronts out of the way. Stitch curve from neck seam to collar placement mark.

(5) **Clip** to seamline at marking. Trim curve; clip seams.

(6) **Turn** stand right side out.

(7) **Stitch** collar to right side of outside stand, with undercollar next to stand. Trim and grade seam; press seam toward stand.

(8) **Press** under seam allowance of inside stand; trim to 1/4" (6 mm). Pin pressed edge of stand to cover stitching line.

(9) **Edgestitch** around stand through all fabric layers.

Waistbands

Because a waistband supports the entire garment, it must be a strong and sturdy outer edge finish. A basic waistband for skirts and pants is cut on the lengthwise grain of the fabric where there is the least amount of stretch. The waistband is stabilized with interfacing, doubled and sewn to the waistline edge, enclosing the seam allowance.

Most waistbands call for a turned-under edge as a finish on the inside. A faster, less bulky method requires changing the pattern layout so the waistband pattern is cut with one long edge on the selvage. Because the selvage does not ravel, a turned-under edge is not necessary. This method can be stitched entirely by machine. To further eliminate bulk, face waistbands of heavy fabrics with a lightweight fabric or grosgrain ribbon.

Cut a waistband long enough for adequate ease and overlap allowance. The length should equal your waist measurement plus 2¾" (7 cm). The extra amount includes ½" (1.3 cm) for ease, 1¼" (3.2 cm) for seam allowances, and 1" (2.5 cm) for overlap. The width should be twice the desired finished width plus 1¼" (3.2 cm) for seam allowances.

How to Sew a Waistband (selvage method)

① **Cut** waistband on the lengthwise grain, placing the cutting line of one long edge on the selvage.

② **Cut** length of purchased fusible waistband interfacing according to pattern, cutting off ends at stitching line so interfacing does not extend into seam allowances.

③ **Fuse** interfacing to waistband, with wider side of interfacing toward selvage edge. Interfacing should be placed so there is a ⅝" (1.5 cm) seam allowance on the notched edge (seam allowance on selvage edge will be narrower).

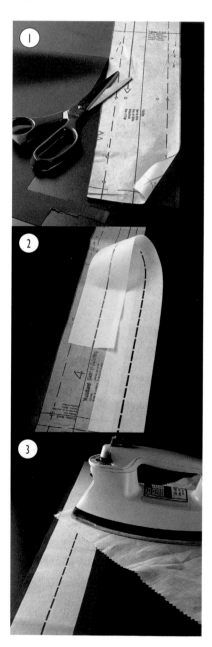

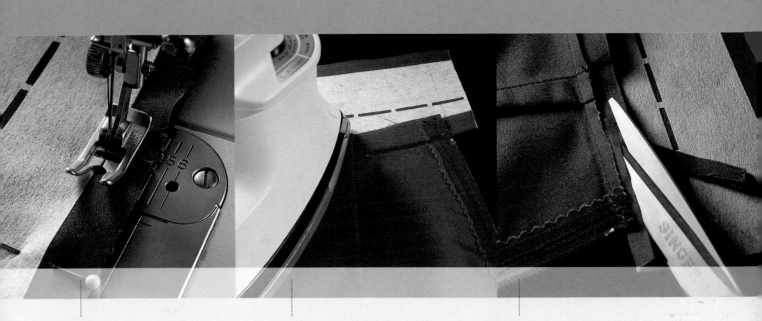

④ **Pin** right side of notched edge of waistband to right side of garment, matching notches. Stitch a ⅝" (1.5 cm) seam.

⑤ **Turn** waistband up. Press seam allowance toward waistband.

⑥ **Grade** the seam allowances to ¼" (6 mm) on the waistband and ⅛" (3 mm) on the garment to eliminate bulk.

⑦ **Fold** waistband on interfacing center foldline so waistband is wrong side out. Stitch ⅝" (1.5 cm) seam on each end. Trim seam allowances to ¼" (6 mm). Diagonally trim corners.

⑧ **Turn** waistband right side out. ⓐ On underlap side, diagonally clip from selvage edge to corner (arrow). ⓑ Tuck seam allowance, from edge of underlap to end of clip, up into waistband. Fold clipped corner under at an angle.

⑨ **Pin** selvage edge of waistband in place. From right side of garment, stitch in the ditch of waistline seam or topstitch ¼" (6 mm) above the seam, catching selvage edge in stitching. Edgestitch lower edge of underlap (arrow) when using stitch-in-ditch method.

Hems

Unless a hem is decorative, it should be virtually invisible from the right side. Use thread the same shade as, or slightly darker than, your fabric.

When hemming by hand, pick up only one or two threads from the outer fabric in each stitch. Do not pull the thread too tight during stitching. This causes the hem to look puckered or lumpy. Press carefully; overpressing creates a ridge along the edge of the hem.

The width of the hem is determined by the fabric and garment style. A hem allowance of up to 3" (7.5 cm) may be given for a straight garment; 1½" to 2" (3.8 to 5 cm) for a flared one. Sheer fabrics, no matter what the style, are usually finished with a narrow, rolled hem. A narrow hem on soft knits helps keep them from sagging. Machine-stitched and topstitched hems are fast and permanent.

Before hemming, let the garment hang for 24 hours, especially if it has a bias or circular hem. Try the garment on over the undergarments you will wear with it. Check to be sure it fits and hangs correctly. Wear shoes and a belt if the garment is to be belted.

Hemlines are usually marked with the help of a second person using a pin marker or yardstick. Mark the hemline with pins or chalk all around the garment, making sure the distance from the floor to the hemline remains equal. Stand in a normal position and have the helper move around the hem. Pin hem up, and try on the garment in front of a full-length mirror to double check that it is parallel to the floor.

Pants hems cannot be marked from the floor up, as skirts and dresses are. For standard-length pants, the bottom of the pants leg should rest on the shoe in front and slope down slightly toward the back. Pin up the hem on both legs, and try on in front of a mirror to check the length.

Before stitching, finish the raw edges of the hem to keep the fabric from raveling and to provide an anchor for the hemming stitch. Select the hem finish (opposite) and stitch that is appropriate to the fabric and the garment.

Blindstitching by machine makes a fast, sturdy hem on woven and knit fabrics. Many sewing machines have this built-in stitch. A special foot or stitching guide makes blindstitching easy.

Seam binding or lace provides a finish suitable for fabrics that ravel, such as wool, tweed, or linen. Lap seam binding ¼" (6 mm) over the hem edge on the right side of the fabric. Edgestitch the binding in place, overlapping ends at a seamline. Use woven seam binding for straight hems, stretch lace for curved hems and knits. Hem light-to medium-weight fabrics with the catchstitch, bulky fabrics with the blindstitch.

Hem Finishes and Stitches

Topstitched hem finishes the raw edge and hems the garment all in one step. Turn up hem 1½" (3.8 cm) and pin in place. For ravelly fabrics, pink or turn under raw edge. On right side, topstitch 1" (2.5 cm) from folded edge. Above, a second row of topstitching is applied as a design detail.

Twin-needle stitched hem is suitable for knits and casual styles. The twin needle produces two closely spaced parallel lines of stitching on the right side and a zigzag-type stitch on the wrong side. Turn hem up desired amount and stitch through both layers from right side, using seam guide. Trim excess hem allowance after stitching.

Zigzag finish is appropriate for knits and fabrics that ravel, because the stitch gives with the fabric. Stitch close to raw edge with zigzag stitch of medium width and length. Trim close to stitching. Hem with a blind-stitch, blind catchstitch, or machine blindstitch.

Turned and stitched finish is appropriate for woven lightweight fabrics. Turn raw edge under ¼" (6 mm). Stitch near the edge of the fold. Hem using slipstitch or blindstitch.

Bound hem finish is appropriate for heavy woolens and fabrics that ravel easily. Finish raw edge of hem in double-fold bias tape or Hong Kong finish (page 113). Hem with blind-stitch or blind catchstitch. Be careful not to pull hemming thread too tight or fabric will pucker.

Pinked and fused hem is a fast and easy finish for lightweight woven fabrics. Apply a fusible web strip between the hem and the garment. Steam press, following manufacturer's instructions.

How to Turn Up a Hem

① **Mark** garment an even distance from the floor using pins or chalk, and a yardstick or skirt marker. Have your helper move around you so you do not need to shift position or posture. Place marks every 2" (5 cm).

② **Trim** seam allowances in hem by half to reduce bulk. Trim seams from bottom of garment to hem stitching line only.

③ **Fold** hem up along marked line, inserting pins at right angles to the fold at regular intervals. Try on garment to check length.

④ **Hand-baste** ¼" (6 mm) from folded edge. Press edge lightly, easing hem to fit garment.

⑤ **Measure** and mark the desired hem depth, adding ¼" (6 mm) for edge finish. Work on ironing board or table, using a seam gauge to ensure even marking.

⑥ **Trim** excess hem allowance along markings. Finish raw edge according to fabric type (page 143). Pin finished edge to garment, matching seams and center lines.

How to Sew a Curved Hem

① **Prepare** hem as shown opposite, but do not finish raw edge. Curved hems have extra fullness which must be eased to fit garment. Loosen machine tension and ease-stitch ¼" (6 mm) from edge, stopping and starting at a seamline.

② **Draw** up bobbin thread by pulling up a loop with a pin at intervals, easing fullness to smoothly fit garment shape. Do not draw hem in too much, or it will pull against garment when finished. Press hem over a press mitt to smooth out some fullness.

③ **Finish** raw edge using zigzag stitching, bias tape, seam binding, or pinking. Pin hem edge to garment, matching seams and center lines. Hem using machine blindstitch or appropriate hand hemming stitch.

How to Machine Blindstitch

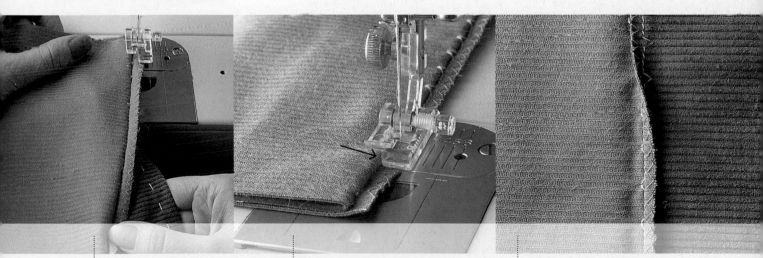

① **Prepare** hemline as shown, opposite. Hand-baste hem to garment, ¼" (6 mm) from raw edge. Adjust machine to blindstitch setting and attach blindstitch foot. Select zigzag width and stitch length, following guidelines in your machine manual.

② **Place** hem allowance face down over feed of machine. Fold bulk of garment back to basting line. The soft fold should rest against the right part of the foot (arrow). Some machines use a regular zigzag foot with a blindstitch hemming guide attached.

③ **Stitch** along hem close to the fold, catching garment only in zigzag stitch. While stitching, guide hem edge in a straight line and feed soft fold against the right part of the hemming foot or the edge of the guide. Open out hem and press flat.

Three Hems Using Serger with Conventional Machine

Overedged and blindstitched hem. Mark hem allowance, and grade seams in hem area. Serge hem edge. Fold hem as for blind hem, step 2, page 145. Pin hem into position, and blindstitch, using a conventional machine, or by hand.

Overedged and topstitched hem. Serge hem edge. Turn up hem; press. Topstitch from right side of garment, using conventional machine. Twin needle may be used for topstitching.

Eased hem. Ease hem fullness by pulling up needle thread. Or adjust differential feed, if available, to the ease setting. Pin hem into position; blindstitch, using a conventional machine, or by hand.

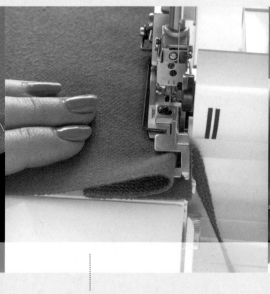

How to Overlock a Blind Hem

① **Adjust** machine for flatlock stitch; use blind hem foot, if available. Set stitch length at 4 mm. Fold up hem; press. On hem side of garment, place pins with the heads toward body of garment.

② **Fold** garment over hem allowance, with hem edge extending ¼" (6 mm) beyond fold. Stitch on extended hem edge, with needle barely catching fold; remove pins as you come to them.

③ **Open** hem, and pull fabric flat. Ladder of stitches shows on right side of lightweight fabrics, but is invisible on heavier textured fabrics.

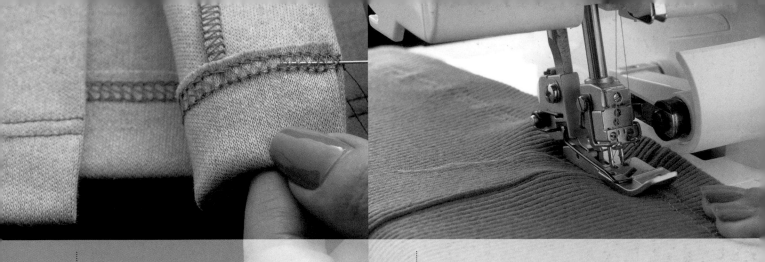

How to Sew a Cover Stitch Hem

Split hem. Adjust machine for cover stitch. Press up hem. Place fabric under raised presser foot, right side up, with fold aligned to desired needle plate guide line. Hold-ing threads, turn handwheel until needles enter fabric at beginning of hem. Stitch to fabric edge at end of hem; raise needles and presser foot. Holding stitches firmly, gently pull threads back. Cut threads, leaving tail; knot. Secure tails, using loop turner or needle.

Circular hem. Adjust machine and stitch hem as for split hem, left; start at back or side seam, and lap first stitches about 1" (2.5 cm). Raise needles and presser foot. Hold stitches behind foot firmly; gently pull fabric slightly back, and then to left.

Cut thread tails. Pull out loose threads; secure threads, using liquid fray preventer or knots as desired. Remove extra needle thread from surface of needle plate.

How to Flatlock a Sport Hem

① **Adjust** machine for flatlock stitch. Fold up hem, and press. Fold up, and press again, enclosing raw edge; flatlock on fold, taking care to catch hem edge in stitches.

② **Open** hem, and pull fabric flat. Lightly press. Decorative loops are on the right side of garment.

How to Flatlock a Fringed Hem

① **Mark** placement line, by pulling a thread or using a marking pen, to indicate depth of fringe. Press a crease on marked line. Adjust serger for flatlock stitch. Stitch on fold.

② **Cut** fabric up to stitches on grain every 3" (7.5 cm). Remove threads to create fringe. If flatlocking corners, apply liquid fray preventer to intersecting stitches, and use seam ripper to remove stitches in fringe area.

Easy Edges

A pullover blouse can be edge-finished quickly by machine. A bias neckline facing with overlapped ends makes a neat neckline finish, and narrow machine-stitched hems finish the sleeves and lower edges of the blouse.

To make the bias facing, cut a 1¼" (3.2 cm) bias strip about 2" (5 cm) longer than the neck opening, to allow for overlap.

A narrow machine-stitched hem is nonbulky, making it suitable for lightweight or silky fabrics. It can also be used for hems on garments made from satin, taffeta, or organza. Horsehair braid can be added to this narrow hem for extra body.

Before stitching the hem, trim hem allowance to ⅜" (1 cm).

How to Sew a Bias Neckline Facing

1) **Cut** bias facing, opposite. Fold strip in half lengthwise, wrong sides together; press. Trim garment seam allowance to ¼" (6 mm). Place strip on right side of garment, raw edges even, with end of strip 1" (2.5 cm) from center back.

2) **Taper** end of strip into seam allowance; stitch around neckline. Overlap ends, tapering other end into seam allowance.

3) **Trim** seam allowances. Press strip away from garment; then press it to inside of garment. Edgestitch around neckline from right side.

How to Sew a Narrow Hem

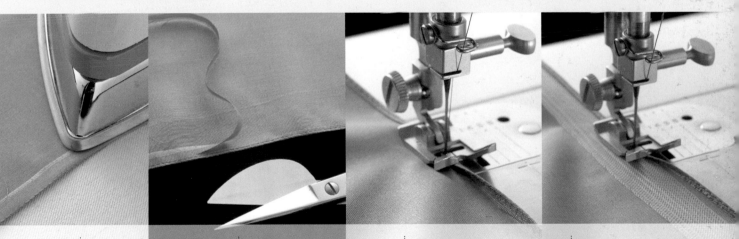

1) **Machine-stitch** ¼" (6 mm) from hem edge. Turn edge to wrong side on stitching line; press fold.

2) **Stitch**, using short stitch length, close to fold. Trim excess fabric close to stitching, using appliqué scissors. Press to remove fullness, if fabric has stretched.

3) **Turn** hem edge to wrong side, enclosing raw edge. Stitch an even distance from edge.

4) **Turn** hem edge to wrong side, enclosing raw edge. Slip horsehair braid into fold to add body to hem. Stitch an even distance from edge.

Pockets

Pockets vary in purpose from practical to decorative. Practical pockets usually are simple in style. Yet the shape, decorative trim, or position of a pocket can make it a fashion focus. To be useful, however, pockets should fall comfortably within hand's reach, even if this means adjusting the pattern.

Choose a sturdy, firmly woven fabric for hidden pocket sections of in-seam and slanted pocket styles. The pocket is less likely to wear out if cut from fabric such as cotton twill or drill cloth. Tailors use pocketing, a special lightweight twill, for pockets on pants and jackets. A durable lining fabric is also a good choice.

Patch pockets are sewn to the outside of a garment. Pocket edges should be neat, smooth, and securely applied. They may be interfaced for stability, lined, or self-lined on tailored lined garments.

In-seam pockets are hidden pockets. From the outside of a garment they look like an opening in a seam.

Slanted pockets open diagonally from the waist to the sides of pants and skirts.

Welt pockets are hidden pockets with a visible slit. They may have a single or double welt and are sometimes covered with a flap.

PATCH POCKETS

As outside details, patch pockets add fashion detail to a garment. Position them where they look best on your figure. Try pockets above, below, or beside the placement line on the pattern to find the most flattering position that will avoid calling attention to full bust or hips.

Once you've determined the position for pockets, double check the placement before attaching them. Measure carefully so pockets are precisely aligned. This step is especially important when pockets are symmetrical because a minor pattern adjustment can affect pocket alignment.

Patch pockets may be applied by hand or machine stitching. Choose the machine method for casual garments, as a time-saving technique, and for the most secure application. If you prefer a fine, invisible finish, sew the pockets in place by hand.

Interface patch pockets with a lightweight fusible interfacing for smooth shape and longer wear. Cut the interfacing to the hem fold at the pocket top and to the seamline at the sides and bottom of the pocket. Avoid a too-stiff pocket by cutting woven interfacings on the true bias grain.

Reinforce patch pockets at the upper corners. Stitch small triangles on man-tailored shirts and sportswear. Use fine zigzag stitches for bar tacks on children's clothes and rugged outdoor wear. Topstitching may be added for further reinforcement.

How to Sew a Patch Pocket with Square Corners

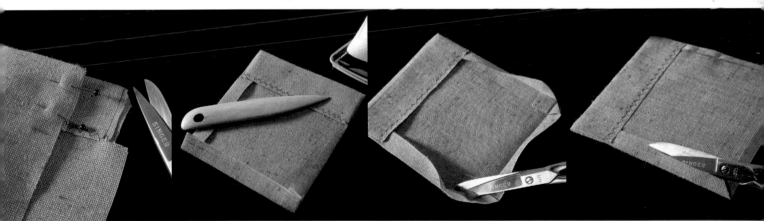

(1) **Finish** upper edge of pocket. Fold hem to outside. Pull hem edges ⅛" (3 mm) beyond pocket so seams will roll toward inside. Stitch on seamline. Trim corners diagonally; grade seams.

(2) **Turn** hem right side out, using point turner to push out corners. Press seam allowances under on sides and lower edges.

(3) **Fold** seam allowance diagonally across lower corners so pressed foldlines match. Press diagonal folds, then trim to ¼" (6 mm).

(4) **Press** seam allowance again to inside, forming miter at corners. Trim remaining seam allowances. Edgestitch or topstitch if desired.

How to Sew a Patch Pocket with Rounded Corners

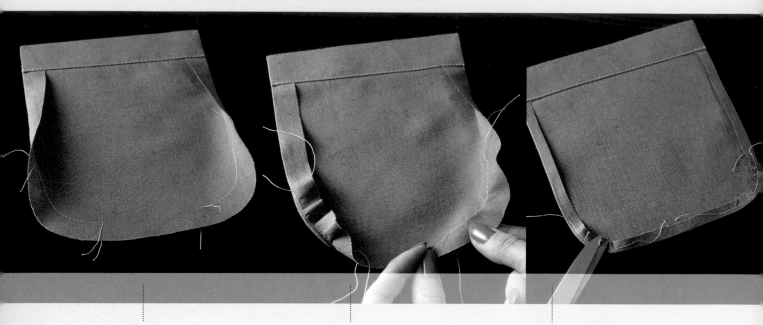

① **Stitch** upper hem as for patch pocket, page 151, step 1. Also easestitch around corners, just inside seamline.

② **Press** seam allowance to inside of pocket. Pull thread at corner stitches to ease in extra seam allowance evenly.

③ **Trim** entire seam allowance to ¼" (6 mm). If necessary, notch out fullness at corner curves to make seam allowance lie flat.

How to Sew a Self-lined Patch Pocket

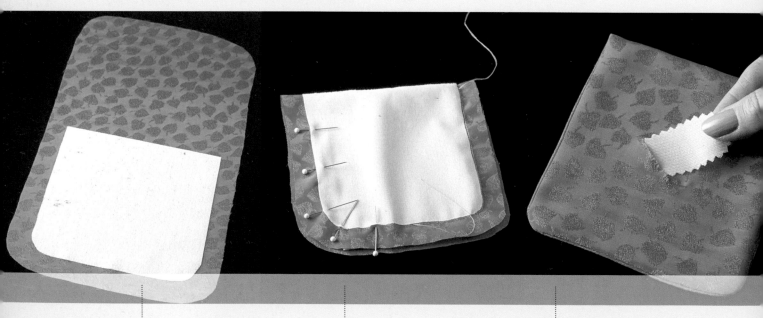

① **Fold** pocket pattern on hemline. Place pattern fold on fabric fold, and cut double pocket. Fuse interfacing on one half of pocket.

② **Pin** right sides together, pulling non-interfaced side ⅛" (3 mm) beyond edge. Stitch seam; trim and notch. Cut 1" (2.5 cm) bias slit on non-interfaced side of pocket.

③ **Turn** pocket to right side through slit. Press edges, rolling seam to side with slit in it. Close slit with fusible interfacing inserted adhesive side up.

How to Sew a Lined Patch Pocket

(1) **Fold** hem down on pocket pattern. Mark lining cutting line ½" (1.3 cm) from upper edge of pattern (arrow). Cut lining ⅛" (3 mm) smaller on sides and bottom.

(2) **Stitch** top of lining to top of pocket, right sides together, with ¼" (6 mm) seam. Leave opening for turning at center of seam (arrows). Press seam open.

(3) **Bring** lower edge of lining and pocket together. Stitch side and lower edges. Trim seams and corners; notch fullness from curves of rounded pockets.

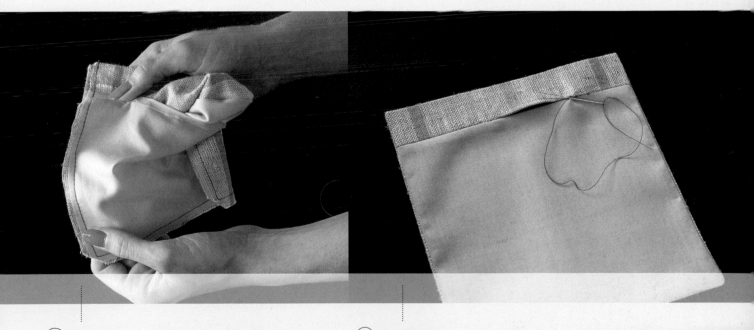

(4) **Turn** pocket right side out through opening in seam. Press pocket from lining side, rolling seam toward back of pocket.

(5) **Slipstitch** seam opening closed.

How to Apply a Patch Pocket by Machine

(1) **Transfer** pocket placement line to right side of garment with machine basting.

(2) **Use** basting tape, pins, or glue to hold pocket in place over the baste-marked line.

(3) **Edgestitch** pocket to garment. Reinforce upper corners with stitched triangles or bar tacks.

How to Apply a Patch Pocket by Hand

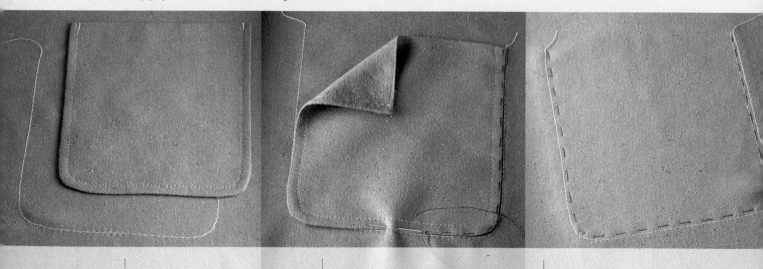

(1) **Topstitch** pocket before applying pocket to garment. Baste-mark pocket placement line as in machine method above, step 1.

(2) **Hand-baste** pocket in position, stitching along pocket edge to use as guideline on wrong side.

(3) **Backstitch** pocket in place, working from inside of garment. Stitching should not show from right side.

IN-SEAM POCKETS

There are three ways of cutting in-seam pockets: cutting the pocket as part of the garment, cutting a separate pocket, and cutting a garment extension plus a separate pocket.

Sewing an in-seam pocket that is part of the garment eliminates one seam but can create unwanted bulk unless the garment fabric is lightweight. Cutting a separate pocket reduces bulk because you can use a lining fabric. The third method, using an extension, reduces bulk and prevents the pocket lining from showing on the curve of the hip. To prevent the pocket opening from stretching when pockets are cut separately, stitch narrow twill or seam tape in the seam allowance of the front pocket.

Topstitching helps to hold the pocket in place and flattens any bulk at the seam, giving a slimmer line in the hip area.

How to Sew an In-Seam Pocket

① **Edgestitch** tape on wrong side in seam allowance of front pocket extension. Stitch pockets to front and back extensions. Trim seam to ¼" (6 mm). Zigzag edges together; press toward pocket.

② **Pin** garment front to garment back; machine-baste pocket opening closed. Stitch pocket and garment seam above and below pocket opening. Use short reinforcement stitches, and backstitch at opening.

③ **Stitch** around pocket, ending at side seam. Clip seam above and below extension on back garment section only, so seam can be pressed open.

④ **Press** garment seam open above and below clips. Press pocket toward garment front. Finish raw edges of pocket together. Remove basting stitches.

SLANTED POCKETS

Slanted pockets are formed
from two pattern pieces: the
pocket and the garment side
front. The side front fills in the
hip area of the garment above
the pocket opening and com-
pletes the inside of the pocket.
The pocket pattern can be cut
from lining fabric to minimize
bulk because the pocket is
hidden on the inside.

How to Sew a Slanted Pocket

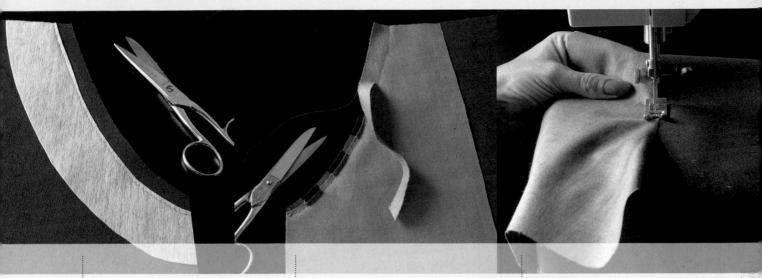

1. **Cut** 2" (5 cm) strip of sew-in interfacing to match shape of curved pocket edges. Stitch ½" (1.3 cm) from edge on wrong side. Trim interfacing. If edge is straight, instead of interfacing stitch seam tape over pocket seamline to stabilize bias grainline.

2. **Stitch** pocket to garment front, right sides together. Trim seam, grading so pocket seam allowance is narrower. Clip curves.

3. **Press** seam toward pocket. If pocket will not be topstitched, under-stitch seam on pocket side to prevent pocket from rolling to right side.

4. **Fold** pocket to inside. Press pocket edge, rolling seam toward pocket. Topstitch or edgestitch edge of pocket if it has not been understitched.

5. **Stitch** side front of garment to pocket. Finish raw edges with zig-zag stitches or another edge finish (pages 110 and 111).

6. **Baste** pocket to garment at side seam and at waist seam. Use pattern markings to line up fabric layers. Pocket should lie flat without ripples.

WELT POCKETS

Double welt pockets look like large bound buttonholes. A welt, which is a narrow, folded strip of garment fabric, finishes each edge of the pocket opening. The pocket, cut from a lining fabric, extends from the welts on the inside of the garment.

Making welt pockets is an expert tailoring technique that requires precise marking, cutting, and stitching. Before starting, carefully check the pocket position. Once you have started making the pocket, recheck the pocket position before slashing the welt. In the photos, the wrong side of the garment has been backed with fusible interfacing.

How to Cut and Prepare a Pocket Lining

(1) **Cut** the following pocket parts 7" x 3" (18 x 7.5 cm) for finished 5" (12.5 cm) welt: (a) pocket stay, from nonwoven sew-in interfacing; (b) welt and (c) pocket facing, from fashion fabric; (d) interfacing, from weft insertion fusible. Cut lining (e) 7" x 12" to 15" (18 x 30.5 to 38 cm).

(2) **Fuse** interfacing to wrong side of welt. Place welt (f), right side up, on one edge of pocket lining. Zigzag inner edge of welt to lining. Machine-baste outer edge of welt to lining. Stitch pocket facing (g) to other edge of lining as for welt. Upper interfaced part of lining will be welt. Lower non-interfaced part will be inside of pocket.

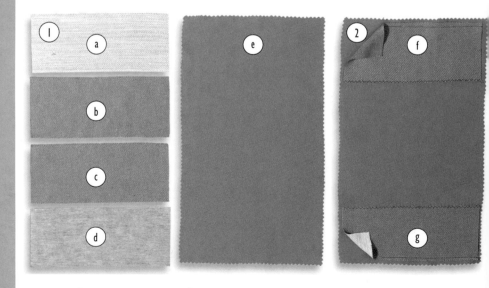

How to Sew a Welt Pocket

① **Mark** pocket placement line on wrong side of garment. Mark center of stay. Draw pocket stitching box with lines ¼" (6 mm) from center line. Mark ends with short vertical lines 5" (12.5 cm) apart, 1" (2.5 cm) from ends of stay.

② **Position** stay on wrong side at pocket placement marking. Sew around entire box, using small stitches and beginning on one long side. This transfers pocket stitching box to right side. Do not backstitch.

③ **Pin** right side of welt/pocket section to right side of garment, centering welt over baste-marked pocket stitching box.

④ **Stitch** long sides only of pocket stitching box, working from wrong side of garment. Stop exactly at end marks on box, backstitching to secure threads. (Presser foot has been removed to show where stitching ends.)

⑤ **Machine-baste** exactly ¼" (6 mm) from each long side of pocket stitching box, working from wrong side of garment. Use width of presser foot as stitching guide.

⑥ **Press** welt/pocket section up, working from right side of garment. Press firmly to create neat, flat fold. Pin. Lower line of machine basting is inside this fold.

(7) Stitch on lower long line of pocket stitching box from wrong side of garment. Stop exactly at end marks (arrow); backstitch to secure threads. This forms lower welt.

(8) Press welt/pocket section down. Upper line of machine basting is inside fold.

(9) Stitch on upper long line of pocket stitching box from wrong side of garment; backstitch to secure threads. This forms upper welt.

(10) Slash welt by cutting through center of welt between stitching rows. Do not cut into garment. Remove bastestitching from upper and lower welt.

(11) Cut through center of pocket stitching box from wrong side of garment. Stop ⅝" (1.5 cm) from each end, then cut diagonally to each corner, forming triangles. Be careful to cut garment fabric only.

(12) Turn welts and pocket to wrong side by pulling them through pocket opening. Make sure triangles are pulled through and folded flat between welts and pocket stay. Press.

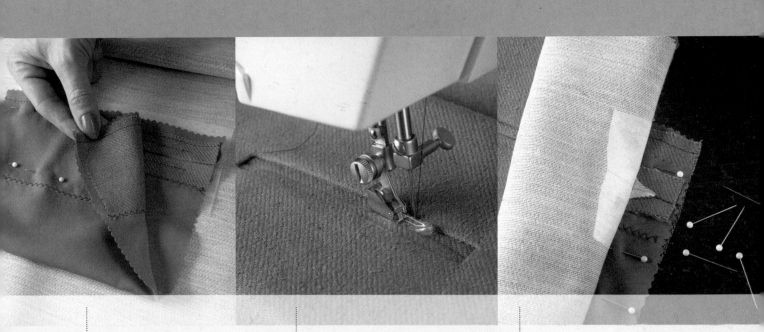

(13) **Fold** pocket up so pocket facing covers welts. Pin facing to top of welt.

(14) **Stitch** in the ditch of upper welt from right side of garment, using zipper foot. Stitch through all layers. This also secures pocket lining to welt.

(15) **Fold** garment back out of the way to prepare for stitching pocket side seams.

(16) **Stitch** pocket side seams, using zipper foot; stitch close to fold of triangles at ends of pocket opening.

(17) **Press** pocket lining so it lies flat.

(18) **Whipstitch** edges of upper and lower welts together to hold pocket opening in place while you sew the remainder of garment.

Closures

Zippers, buttons, snaps, and hooks and eyes are usually meant to be as inconspicuous as possible, but are sometimes used as decorative details. A stylish button, colorful separating zipper, or pearlized gripper snap can make a definite fashion statement.

Select the closure according to the style of garment and amount of strain that will be put on the opening. For example, a heavy-duty hook and eye closure (opposite) can better withstand the strain on a pants waistband than ordinary hooks and eyes. The back of the pattern envelope specifies the type and size of closures to purchase.

Because closures are under strain, it is important to reinforce the garment area where they are placed.

Seam allowances or facings provide light reinforcement. Other closure areas should be reinforced with interfacing.

For sewing on buttons, snaps, and hooks and eyes, use an all-purpose thread, and sharps or crewel needles. For heavyweight fabrics or for closures that are under considerable strain, use heavy-duty, or topstitching and buttonhole twist thread.

HOOKS AND EYES

Hooks and eyes are strong closures and come in several types. Regular, general-purpose hooks and eyes are available in sizes 0 (fine) to 3 (heavy), in black or nickel finishes. They have either straight or round eyes. Straight eyes are used where garment edges overlap, such as on a waistband. Round eyes are used where two edges meet, such as at the neckline above a centered zip-

per. Thread loops (opposite) can be used in place of round metal eyes on delicate fabrics or in locations where metal eyes would be too conspicuous. Button loops and belt carriers are made using the same technique, starting with longer foundation stitches.

Heavy-duty hooks and eyes are stronger than regular hooks and eyes, to withstand greater strain. Available in black or nickel finishes, they are used only for lapped areas. Large, plain, or covered hooks and eyes are available for coats and jackets. These are attractive enough to be visible and strong enough to hold heavy fabric.

How to Attach Waistband Hooks and Eyes

① **Position** heavy-duty hook on underside of waistband overlap, about ⅛" (3 mm) from inside edge. Tack hook in place with three or four stitches through each hole. Do not stitch through to right side of garment.

② **Lap** hook side over underlap to mark position of eye. Insert straight pins through holes to mark position. Tack in place with four stitches in each hole.

③ **Round hook and eye** is used for waistbands which do not overlap. Position hook as for heavy-duty hook. Tack through both holes and at end of hook. Position eye so it extends slightly over inside edge of fabric (garment's edges should butt together). Tack in place.

How to Make Thread Eyes

① **Insert** needle with double strand of thread at edge of fabric. Take two foundation stitches the desired length of the eye. These are the anchor on which blanket stitch is worked.

② **Work** blanket stitch by bringing eye of needle under foundation stitches and through the loop.

③ **Bring** needle through loop, pulling loop tight against foundation stitches. Work blanket stitch along entire length of foundation stitches.

④ **Secure** stitching by taking two small backstitches. Trim threads.

BUTTONHOLES

The standards of a well-made buttonhole are:

1. Width is appropriate to the weight of the fabric and size of the buttonhole.

2. Ends are bar-tacked to prevent buttonhole from tearing under stress.

3. Stitches are evenly spaced on each side of the buttonhole.

4. Buttonhole is ⅛" (3 mm) longer than the button.

5. Stitches on each side are far enough apart so that the buttonhole can be cut open without cutting the stitches.

6. Ends have not been cut open accidentally.

7. Interfacing supporting the buttonhole matches the fashion fabric and is not obvious on the cut edges.

8. Buttonhole is on-grain; vertical buttonholes are perfectly parallel to the garment edge, horizontal buttonholes are at perfect right angles to the edge.

Horizontal buttonholes are the most secure, because they are not as apt to let buttons slip out. These buttonholes also absorb any pull against the closure with little, if any, distortion. Horizontal buttonholes should extend ⅛" (3 mm) beyond the button placement line, toward the edge of the garment. Be sure that the space from the center line to the finished edge of the garment is at least three-fourths the diameter of the button. With this spacing, the button will not extend beyond the edge when the garment is buttoned.

Vertical buttonholes are used on plackets and shirt bands. These are usually used with more and smaller buttons to help keep the closure secure. Vertical buttonholes are placed directly on the center front or center back line.

When a garment is buttoned, the button placement lines and center lines of both sides must match perfectly. If the overlap is more or less than the pattern indicates, the garment may not fit properly.

Spaces between buttonholes are generally equal. You may have to change the pattern buttonhole spacing if you have made pattern alterations that change the length or alter the bustline. Respacing may also be necessary if you have chosen buttons that are larger or smaller than the pattern indicates. Buttonholes should be spaced so they occur in the areas of greatest stress. When they are incorrectly spaced, the closing gaps and spoils the garment's appearance.

For front openings, place buttonholes at the neck and the fullest part of the bust. Place a buttonhole at the waist for coats, overblouses and princess-seamed dresses or jackets. To reduce bulk, do not place a buttonhole at the waistline of a tucked-in blouse or belted dress. Buttons and buttonholes should end about 5" to 6" (12.5 to 15 cm) above the hemline of a dress, skirt, or coatdress.

To evenly respace buttonholes, mark the locations of the top and bottom buttons. Measure the distance between them. Divide that measurement by one less than the number of buttons to be used. The result is the distance between buttonholes. After marking, try on the garment, making sure the buttonholes are placed correctly. Adjust as necessary.

How to Determine Buttonhole Length

Measure width and height of button to be used. The sum of these measurements plus ⅛" (3 mm) for finishing the ends of the buttonhole is the correct length for a machine-worked buttonhole. The buttonhole must be large enough to button easily, yet snug enough so the garment stays closed.

Test proposed buttonhole. First, make a slash in a scrap of fabric the length of the buttonhole minus the extra ⅛" (3 mm). If button passes through easily, length is correct. Next, make a practice buttonhole with garment, facing, and interfacing. Check length, stitch width, density of stitching, and buttonhole cutting space.

How to Mark Buttonholes

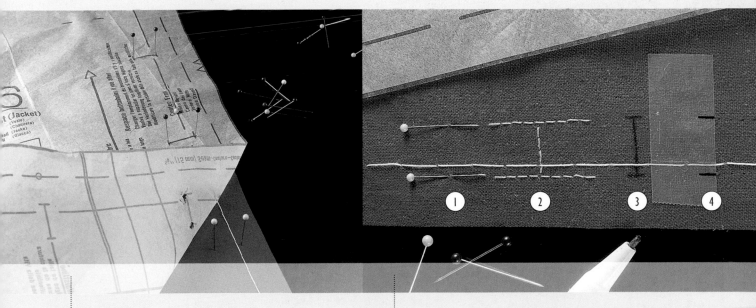

Place pattern tissue on top of garment, aligning pattern seamline with garment opening edge. Insert pins straight down through tissue and fabric at both ends of each buttonhole marking. Remove pattern carefully, pulling tissue over heads of pins.

Mark buttonholes using one of the following methods: (1) Secure pins. (2) Machine- or hand-baste between pins and along ends. (3) Use a water-soluble marking pen. (4) Place a piece of tape above the pins and mark buttonhole length with a pencil; test fabric first to be sure tape does not mar it.

Machine-made Buttonholes

Machine-made buttonholes are appropriate for most garments, especially those which are casual or tailored. There are four types: built-in (usually two- or four-step), overedge, one-step, and universal attachment. Always make a test buttonhole with appropriate interfacing before making the buttonholes on your garment. The test buttonhole also reminds you at which point your machine begins the buttonhole stitching, so you can position fabric correctly.

(a) **Built-in** buttonholes are made with a combination of zigzag stitching and bar tacks. Most zigzag machines have a built-in mechanism that stitches this type of buttonhole in two or four steps. The four steps are: zigzag forward, bar tack, zigzag in reverse, bar tack. A two-step buttonhole combines a forward or backward motion with a bar tack. Consult your machine manual for specific directions, because each machine varies. The advantage of this buttonhole is that it allows you to adjust the density of the zigzag

to suit the fabric and size of the buttonhole. Use spaced zigzag stitches on bulky or loosely woven fabrics, closer stitches on sheer or delicate fabrics.

(b) **Overedge** buttonholes are an adaptation of the built-in or one-step buttonhole. This buttonhole is stitched with a narrow zigzag, cut open and then stitched a second time, so the cut edge is overedged with zigzag stitches. The overedge buttonhole looks like a hand-worked buttonhole. It is a good choice when the interfacing is not a close color match to the fashion fabric.

(c) **One-step** buttonholes are stitched all in one step, using a special foot and a built-in stitch available on some machines. They can be stitched with a standard-width zigzag, or a narrow zigzag for lightweight fabrics. The button is placed in a carrier in back of the attachment and guides the stitching, so the buttonhole fits the button perfectly. A lever near the needle is pulled down and stops the foward motion of the

machine when the buttonhole reaches the correct length. All buttonholes are of uniform length, so placement is the only marking necessary.

(d) **Universal attachment** buttonholes are made with an attachment which will fit any machine, including a straight-stitch machine. The attachment has a template which determines the size of the buttonhole. This method also offers the advantage of uniform buttonhole length and adjustable zigzag width. The keyhole buttonhole, used on tailored garments or heavy fabrics, can be made using this attachment. The keyhole at one end of the buttonhole provides space for the shank.

If buttonholes do not have to be respaced because of pattern alterations, make the buttonholes after attaching and finishing the facings but before joining to another garment section. This way there is less bulk and weight to handle at the machine.

How to Make Buttonholes

Built-in buttonholes. Place fabric under buttonhole foot; align starting point with needle and center foot over mark. (Steps shown separately, but buttonhole is stitched con-tinuously, moving machine to new setting at each step.) (1) Set dial or lever selector at first step. Slowly stitch several stitches across end to form bar tack. (2) Stitch one side to marked end. (3) Stitch several stitches across end to form second bar tack. (4) Stitch other side to first bar tack to complete buttonhole. Return to starting position and make a few fastening stitches.

Overedge buttonhole. (1) Stitch buttonhole with narrow zigzag. Cut buttonhole open. (2) Reposition in exact position as first stitching. Adjust zigzag to wider stitch. Stitch second time over cut edge of buttonhole.

One-step buttonhole. Place button in attachment carrier. Check machine manual for proper stitch setting. Buttonhole is made the correct length and stitching will stop automatically.

Universal attachment buttonhole. Attach buttonhole attachment as instructed in manual. Select template of proper size to fit button. For sturdier reinforced buttonhole, stitch around the buttonhole a second time.

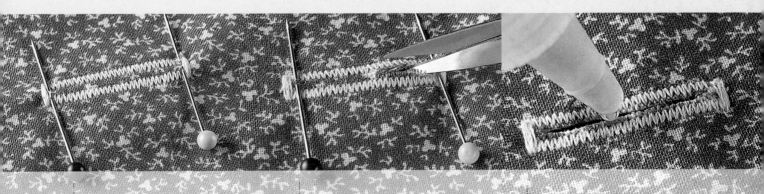

How to Open a Buttonhole

(1) **Insert** straight pins at each end of buttonhole in front of bar tacks to prevent cutting through ends.

(2) **Insert** point of small, sharp scissors or a seam ripper into center of buttonhole and carefully cut toward one end, then the other.

(3) **Strengthen** the cut edge and prevent raveling by applying liquid fray preventer to the edge. Test on a sample first.

BUTTONS

More than any other closure, buttons allow you to individualize your garment. Buttons can be decorative as well as functional. There are two basic kinds of buttons, sew-through and shank buttons, but the variations on these two types are endless.

Sew-through buttons are usually flat, with two or four holes. When they are merely decorative, they can be sewn so they lie directly against the garment. On all other applications, sew-through buttons need a thread shank. A shank raises the button from the garment surface, allowing space for the layers of fabric to fit smoothly when it is buttoned.

Shank buttons have their own shanks on the underside. Choose shank buttons for heavier fabrics, as well as when using button loops or thread loops.

When selecting buttons, consider color, style, weight, and care.

Color. The color of buttons is usually matched to the fabric, but interesting fashion looks can be achieved with coordinating or contrasting colors. If you are unable to find an appropriate color match, make your own fabric-covered buttons with a kit.

Style. Select small, delicate buttons for feminine garments; clean, classic styles for tailored clothes; novelty buttons for children's clothes. Rhinestone buttons add sparkle to a velvet garment. Try leather or metal buttons with corduroy and wool tweeds.

Weight. Match lightweight buttons to lightweight fabrics. Heavy buttons will pull and distort lightweight fabrics. Heavyweight fabrics need buttons that are bigger or look weightier.

Care. Choose buttons that can be cared for in the same manner as the garment, either washable or dry-cleanable.

The back of the pattern envelope tells you how many and what size buttons to purchase. Try not to go more than ⅛" (3 mm) smaller or larger than the pattern specifies. Buttons that are too small or too large may not be in proper proportion to the edge of the garment. Button sizes are listed in inches, millimeters, and lines. For example, a ½" button is also listed as 13 mm and line 20; a ¾" button, as 19 mm and line 30.

When shopping for buttons, bring a swatch of fabric with you to assure a good match. Cut a small slit in the fabric so a button on the card can be slipped through, giving you a better idea of how it will look when finished.

Sew on buttons with doubled all-purpose thread for lightweight fabrics, and heavy-duty or topstitch thread for heavier fabrics.

How to Mark Button Location

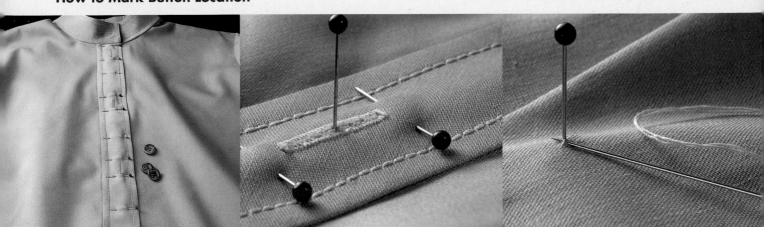

(1) **Mark** button placement by lapping the buttonhole side of garment over the button side, matching center lines. Pin garment closed between buttonholes.

(2) **Insert** pin straight through buttonhole and into bottom layer of fabric. For vertical buttonholes, insert pin in center of buttonhole. For horizontal buttonholes, insert pin at edge closest to outer edge of garment.

(3) **Carefully** lift buttonhole over pin. Insert threaded needle at point of pin to sew on button. Mark and sew buttons one at a time, buttoning previous buttons for accurate marking.

How to Sew on a Shank Button

(1) **Cut** a length of thread 30" (76 cm) long and run it through beeswax to strengthen it. Fold thread in half. Thread folded end through a crewel needle. Knot cut ends of thread. Position button at pin mark on the garment center line, placing shank hole parallel to the buttonhole.

(2) **Secure** thread on right side with small stitch under button. Bring needle through shank hole. Insert needle down into fabric and pull through. Repeat, taking four to six stitches through the shank.

(3) **Secure** thread in fabric under button by making a knot or taking several small stitches. Clip thread ends. If a shank button is used on a heavy fabric, it may also need a thread shank. Follow instructions for making a thread shank on a sew-through button, page 170.

How to Hand Sew a Sew-through Button

① **Thread** needle as for shank button (page 169) and position button at pin mark. Place holes in button so they line up parallel to buttonhole. Bring needle through fabric from underside and up through one hole in button. Insert needle into another hole and through the fabric layers.

② **Slip** a toothpick, match, or sewing machine needle between thread and button to form shank. Take three or four stitches through each pair of holes. Bring needle and thread to right side under button. Remove toothpick.

③ **Wind** thread two or three times around button stitches to form shank. Secure thread on right side under button by making a knot or taking several small stitches. Clip threads close to knot.

How to Machine Sew a Sew-through Button

① **Attach** button foot and special plate to cover feed, or drop feed. Button will be stitched with close zigzag stitching. Regulate stitch width and tension as directed in machine manual.

② **Position** button under foot. Lower needle into center of one button hole by turning handwheel toward you. Lower presser foot. Turn handwheel until needle rises out of button and is just above foot. Insert match or toothpick to form shank.

③ **Set** zigzag stitch width regulator so that stitch width equals the space between holes in button. Proceed slowly until you are sure you have the correct width. Take six or more zigzag stitches. Secure the stitching as directed in your machine manual.

SNAPS

Snaps are available as regular sew-on snaps, gripper-type snaps, or snap tape.

Sew-on snaps are suitable for areas where there is little strain, such as at the neckline or waistline to hold the facing edge flat when buttons are used, at the waistline of blouses, or at the pointed end of a waistband fastened with hooks and eyes. Sew-on snaps consist of two parts: a ball and a socket. Select a size that is strong enough to be secure, but not too heavy for the fabric.

Gripper-type snaps are attached with a special plier tool or a hammer. They have more holding power than a sew-in snap and will show on the right side of the garment. Gripper snaps can replace button and buttonhole closures in sportswear.

Snap tape consists of snaps attached to pieces of tape. The tape is stitched to the garment with a zipper foot. Snap tape is used in sportswear, home decorating, and for the inside seam of infant's and toddler's pants.

How to Attach Sew-on Snaps

1. **Position** ball half of snap on wrong side of overlap section, ⅛" to ¼" (3 to 6 mm) from the edge so it will not show on the right side. Stitch in place through each hole, using single strand of thread. Stitch through facing and interfacing only, not through to right side of garment. Secure thread with two tiny stitches.

2. **Mark** position of socket half of snap on right side of underlap section. Use one of the following methods: If there is a hole in center of ball half, insert pin from right side through hole and into underlap section. If there is no hole in ball, rub tailor's chalk on ball and press firmly against underlap.

3. **Position** center of socket half over marking. Stitch in place in same manner as ball half, except stitch through all layers of fabric.

ZIPPERS

Down the back, up the front, on sleeves, pockets, or pants legs—zippers provide closings on a variety of fashion features. Conventional zippers are most often used. They are closed at one end and sewn into a seam. Invisible, separating, and heavy-duty zippers are available for special uses.

The pattern specifies the type and length zipper to buy. When selecting a zipper, choose a color that closely matches your fabric. Also consider the weight of the zipper in relation to the weight of the fabric. Choose synthetic coil zippers for lightweight fabrics, because these zippers are lighter and more flexible than metal zippers. If you cannot find a zipper of the correct length, buy one that is slightly longer than you need and shorten it using the directions on the page 175.

There are several ways to insert a zipper. The one you choose depends on the type of garment and the location of the zipper in the garment. The following pages contain instructions for the lapped, centered, and fly-front applications for conventional zippers; two methods for inserting separating zippers; and instructions for inserting an invisible zipper. There are variations of each of these applications. Methods shown here are quick and easy, featuring timesaving tools such as fabric glue stick and transparent tape.

Close the zipper and press out the creases before inserting it in the garment. If the zipper has a cotton tape and will be applied in a washable garment, preshrink it in hot water before application. This will prevent the zipper from puckering when the garment is laundered. For best appearance, the final stitching on the outside of the garment should be straight and an even distance from the seamline. Stitch both sides of the zipper from bottom to top, and turn the pull tab up to make it easier to stitch past the slider.

Separating zippers in jackets and vests can be inserted with zipper teeth covered or exposed. A decorative sport zipper with plastic teeth is lightweight yet sturdy for active sportswear.

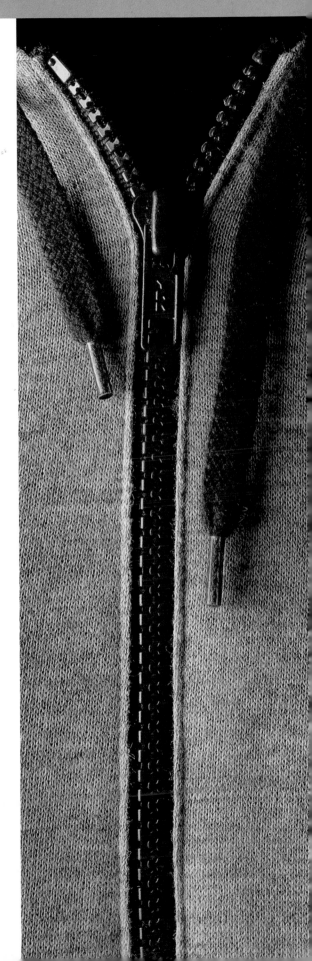

Parts of the Zipper

Top stop is the small metal bracket at the top that prevents the slider from running off the tape.

Slider and pull tab is the mechanism that operates the zipper. It locks the teeth together to close the zipper and unlocks the teeth to open the zipper.

Tape is the fabric strip on which the teeth or coil are fastened. The tape is sewn to the garment.

Teeth or coil is the part of the zipper that locks together when the slider runs along it. It may be made of nylon, polyester, or metal.

Bottom stop is the bracket at the bottom of the zipper where the slider rests when the zipper is open. Separating zippers have a bottom stop which splits into two parts to allow the zipper to be completely opened.

Applications for Conventional Zippers

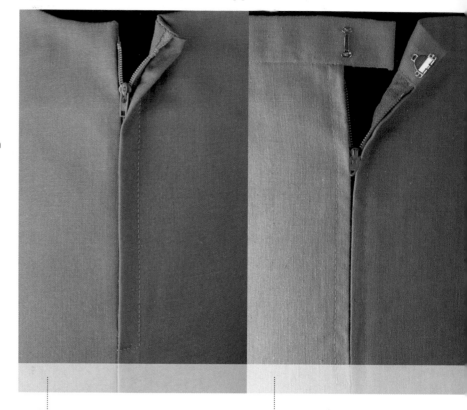

Lapped application totally conceals the zipper, making it a good choice for zippers that do not perfectly match the fabric color. It is most often used in side seam closings of dresses, skirts, and pants.

Centered application is most frequently used for center front and center back closings. Attach facings before inserting the zipper. Waistbands should be applied after the zipper is inserted.

Fly-front zipper is often found on pants and skirts, and occasionally on coats and jackets. Use the fly-front application only when the pattern calls for it, because it requires the wider underlap and facing included in the pattern.

Invisible zippers provide a garment closure that is inconspicuous, revealing only the pull tab. They are an excellent alternative to traditional zippers for center back or side installations. A special presser foot is required for inserting an invisible zipper. This foot unrolls the coil; after stitching, the coil and fabric roll to the inside, concealing the zipper. The presser foot is easily assembled to fit the shank length and needle slant of the sewing machine.

How to Shorten a Zipper

1) **Measure** desired length along the coil, beginning at top stop. Mark with pin.

2) **Machine** zigzag across the coil at pin to form new bottom stop.

3) **Cut** off excess zipper and tape. Insert zipper as usual, stitching slowly across coil at bottom.

How to Insert a Lapped Zipper

(1) **Turn** the garment to the wrong side. Check seam opening to make sure top edges are even. Length of opening should be equal to length of zipper coil plus 1" (2.5 cm). Pin seam from bottom of opening to top of garment.

(2) **Machine-baste** on seamline from bottom of the opening to top of the garment, removing pins as you stitch.

(3) **Clip** basting stitches every 2" (5 cm) to make basting easier to remove after zipper is inserted.

(4) **Press** seam open. If zipper is in side seam of skirt or pants, press seam over a press mitt or tailor's ham to retain shape of hipline.

(5) **Place** open zipper face down on right-hand side of seam allowance (top facing you). Position zipper coil directly on seamline with top stop 1" (2.5 cm) below cut edge. Turn pull tab up. Pin or glue right-hand side of zipper tape in place.

(6) **Replace** presser foot with zipper foot and adjust it to right side of needle. Machine-baste close to edge of coil, stitching from bottom to top of zipper with edge of zipper foot against coil. Remove pins as you stitch.

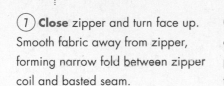

7 **Close** zipper and turn face up. Smooth fabric away from zipper, forming narrow fold between zipper coil and basted seam.

8 **Adjust** zipper foot to left side of needle. Starting at bottom of zipper tape, stitch near edge of fold, through folded seam allowance and zipper tape.

9 **Turn** zipper over so face side is flat against seam. Make sure pull tab is turned up to lessen bulk while stitching. Pin in place.

10 **Adjust** zipper foot to right side of needle. Starting at top of zipper, machine-baste through tape and seam allowance only. This holds seam allowance in place for the final stitching.

11 **Topstitch** ½" (1.3 cm) from seam on outside of garment. To aid straight stitching, use ½" (1.3 cm) transparent tape and stitch along edge. Starting at seamline, stitch across bottom of zipper, pivot at edge of tape and continue.

12 **Remove** tape. Pull thread at bottom of zipper to wrong side and knot. Remove machine basting in seam. Press, using a press cloth to protect fabric from shine. Trim zipper tape even with top edge of garment.

How to Insert a Centered Zipper (using glue stick)

① **Turn** garment to the wrong side. Check seam opening to make sure top edges are even. Length of opening should be equal to length of zipper coil plus 1" (2.5 cm).

② **Pin** seam from bottom of opening to top of garment.

③ **Machine-baste** on seamline from bottom of opening to top of garment. Clip basting stitches every 2" (5 cm) to make basting easier to remove.

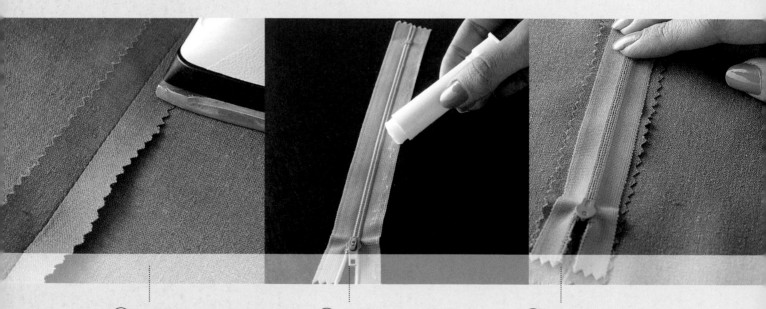

④ **Press** seam open. Finish raw edges if fabric ravels easily.

⑤ **Apply** glue stick lightly on face side of zipper.

⑥ **Place** zipper face down on seam, with zipper coil directly on seamline and top stop 1" (2.5 cm) below cut edge (keep pull tab up). Press with fingers to secure zipper. Let glue dry for a few minutes.

⑦ **Spread** garment flat, right side up. Mark bottom stop of zipper with pin. Use transparent or perforated marking tape, ½" (1.3 cm) wide and same length as zipper. Place down center of seamline. Do not use tape on napped or delicate fabrics.

⑧ **Replace** presser foot with zipper foot and adjust to left of needle. Topstitch zipper from right side, beginning at seam at bottom of tape. Stitch across bottom of zipper; pivot at edge of tape. Stitch up left side of zipper to top cut edge, using edge of tape as a guide.

⑨ **Adjust** the zipper foot to right side of needle. Begin at seam at bottom of tape and stitch across bottom. Pivot and stitch up right side of zipper, using edge of tape as a guide.

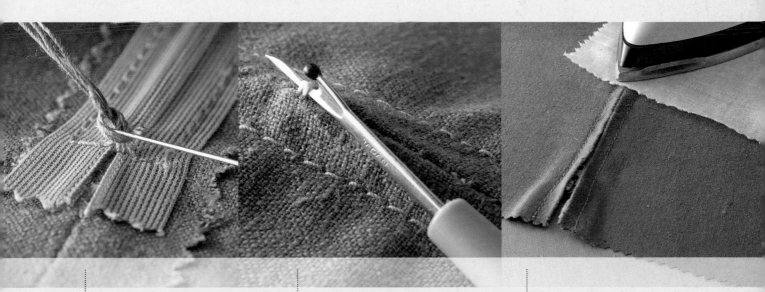

⑩ **Pull** both threads at bottom to wrong side. Tie all four threads, using pin to pull knot close to zipper. Clip threads.

⑪ **Turn** garment to right side. Remove tape. Carefully remove machine basting in seamline.

⑫ **Press**, using a press cloth to protect fabric from shine. Trim zipper tape even with the top edge of the garment.

How to Insert a Fly-front Zipper

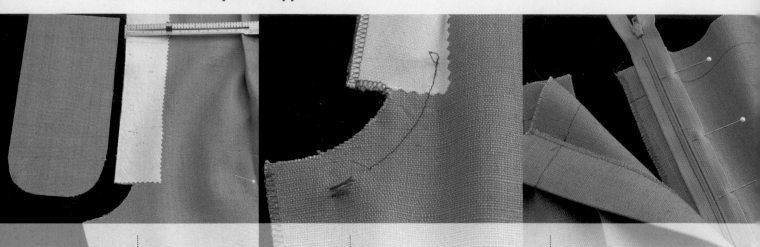

1) For a flat method of construction, apply the zipper before stitching the pants seams. Cut interfacing 1¾" (4.5 cm) wide by the length of the fly facing, using pinking shears; fuse to wrong side of overlap facing. Cut fly shield from pants fabric 4" (10 cm) wide by length of fly facing; curve lower edge, if desired.

2) **Finish** raw edges of fly facings. Press fold on overlap facing at center front. Stitch front crotch seam, using short stitches, beginning about 1½" (3.8 cm) from crotch point and ending at bottom of zipper opening; backstitch three or four stitches.

3) **Use** a zipper 1" to 2" (2.5 to 5 cm) longer than the finished zipper opening. Place closed zipper face down on underlap facing, with edge of zipper tape at center front and zipper stop ⅛" (3 mm) above bottom of zipper opening. Pin outer edge of zipper tape to facing. Using zipper foot, stitch zipper tape to facing only.

4) **Fold** underlap facing to wrong side; machine-baste next to foldline.

5) **Match** center front markings at upper edge, and pin. From wrong side, pin remaining edge of zipper tape to overlap facing only. With facing held away from pants, stitch zipper tape to facing.

6) **Mark** stitching line on right side of pants about 1½" (3.2 cm) from center fold. Hand-baste next to stitching line, if desired. Stitch, backstitching three or four stitches at center fold. Remove basting. Open zipper.

⑦ **Press** fly shield in half length-wise; finish raw edges. Place fly shield under zipper on underlap side, with upper edges matching and folded edge about 1" (2.5 cm) beyond zipper teeth. Stitch close to fold through all layers. Remove basting.

⑧ **Staystitch**, with zipper open, across both ends of zipper at upper edge; trim off excess zipper ends. Clip crotch seam allowances below the fly facing to within ¼" (6 mm) of stitching.

⑨ **Close** zipper. From wrong side, tack lower edge of fly shield to over-lap facing. From right side, stitch a bar tack at lower end of zipper opening, if desired.

How to Insert a Covered Separating Zipper

① **Use** basting tape, pins, or glue to hold closed zipper, face up, under faced opening edges. Position pull tab ⅛" (3 mm) below neck seamline. Edges of the opening should meet at center of zipper, covering the teeth.

② **Open** zipper. Turn ends of zipper tape under at top of garment. Pin in place.

③ **Topstitch** ⅜" (1 cm) from each opening edge, sewing through fabric and zipper tape. Stitch from bottom to top on each side, adjusting zipper foot to correct side.

How to Insert an Exposed Separating Zipper

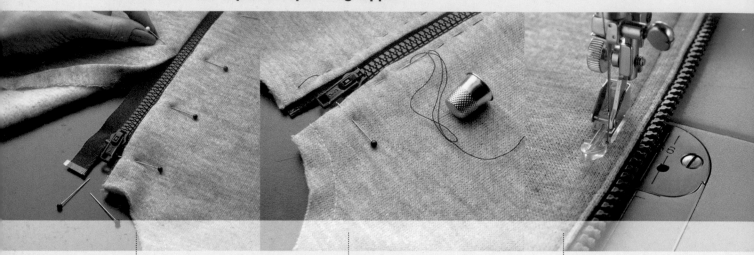

1) **Pin** faced opening edges to closed zipper so that edges are close to but not covering zipper teeth, with pull tab ⅛" (3 mm) below neck seamline.

2) **Baste** zipper in place with tape ends extending above neck seamline. Turn ends of zipper tape under at top of garment if facing is already attached. Open zipper.

3) **Topstitch** close to opening edges on right side of garment, using zipper foot and stitching from bottom to top on each side. To hold zipper tape flat, add another line of stitching ¼" (6 mm) from first stitching line on each side.

How to Insert an Invisible Zipper

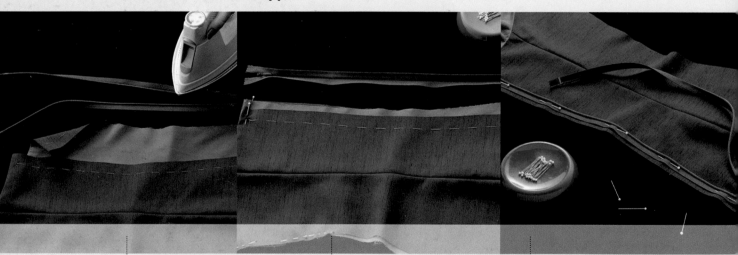

1) **Invisible** zippers can be most easily inserted by stitching them into the garment before stitching any part of the seam. Hand-baste a line the length of the zipper on garment pieces, a scant ¾" (2 cm) from the raw edge. Open zipper. Steam press zipper tape from wrong side, to unroll coils.

2) **Position** closed zipper on the right side of the garment section, with zipper tab ⅜" (1 cm) from neckline seam; pin-mark garment pieces at upper and lower edges of zipper, making sure the pattern markings are aligned.

3) **Open** zipper; position on right garment section, right sides together, with left side of the zipper coil aligned to basted line and ends of zipper aligned to pin marks; zipper tape is in seam allowance. Pin or hand-baste zipper tape in place.

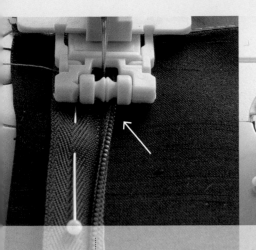

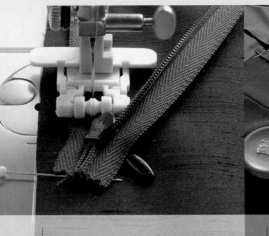

4 **Attach** invisible zipper foot to machine; position zipper coil under groove on right side of foot (arrow). Slide zipper foot on adapter to adjust needle position so stitching will be very close to the coil; on heavier fabric, set needle position slightly farther from coil.

5 **Stitch**, starting at upper edge of zipper coil, until zipper foot touches the pull tab at bottom, taking care not to stretch fabric. Secure thread at ends.

6 **Pin** or hand-baste remaining side of zipper to left garment section, as in step 3, making sure to align ends of zipper to pin marks.

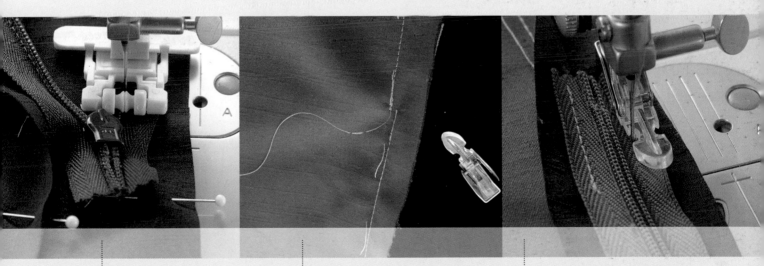

7 **Position** coil under zipper foot; slide zipper foot on adapter to the opposite side, and adjust the needle position. Stitch until zipper foot touches the pull tab; secure thread.

8 **Close** the zipper and stitch the remainder of garment seam; use a regular zipper foot to get as close as possible to the zipper seam.

9 **Secure** lower end of tape to seam allowances, using a regular zipper foot.

Tailoring

Tailoring differs from dressmaking in a number of ways. The term tailored applies to fashions styled like menswear, such as a suit jacket. It also describes certain methods of construction and pattern design. The undercollar and collar on a tailored jacket, for example, are cut from two different pattern pieces to shape the collar. In dressmaking, both collar layers are usually cut from the same pattern piece. Details such as a welt pocket, notched collar, and full lining are typical in patterns for tailored fashions.

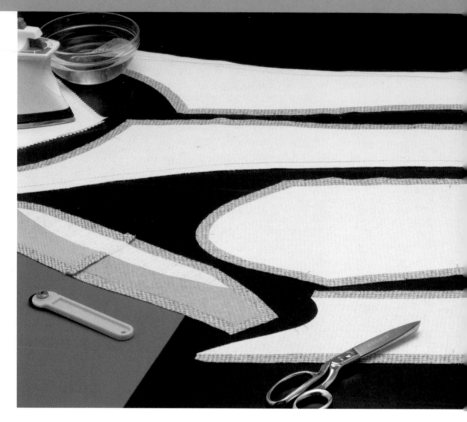

Tailoring also calls for extensive use of interfacings for building in shape. Entire garment sections, not just the details, are backed with interfacing when tailored. Two layers of interfacing may be used for shaping the roll line on jacket lapels. Because different kinds of interfacings have distinctive effects, a single tailored jacket may require several types of interfacing.

Fusible interfacings have eliminated most of the time-consuming handwork that was once the trademark of tailoring. With fusibles you can tailor expertly with just a little practice. However, it's important to choose the right fashion fabric and interfacing for the tailoring task at hand.

Using Fusible Interfacings

Four types of fusible interfacings may be used for tailoring; often all four are used in one garment. Fusible tricot, a knitted interfacing, adds body and support to the fabric without causing stiffness. Use it to stabilize garment sections such as sleeves, hems, front facings, and the upper collar. Fusible hair canvas, a woven interfacing, is firm and resilient. Use it for the jacket front and undercollar when the fabric needs strong support. Weft insertion fusible is a knitted interfacing with extra yarns inserted crosswise. In a medium weight, it is a softer alternative to hair canvas and is used to stabilize fashion details, such as

Textured fabrics, such as tweeds and linen weaves, tailor well; their surfaces give the fusible adhesive something to grip for a strong bond. On the other hand, some fabrics with tight weaves and smooth surfaces, such as fine polyester gabardines, resist smooth fusing and should be used with sew-in interfacing.

Preshrink tailoring fabrics to prepare them for the extra steam used when fusing interfacings and to prevent shrinkage of the garment. Thorough steam-pressing preshrinks fabric effectively without sacrificing the fresh, new look. Steam-press fabric at home, or have a dry cleaner do it for you. A faster and easier preshrinking method is tossing the fabric into a clothes dryer with a few damp towels. Tumble for seven to ten minutes at a medium-high heat. Remove immediately; lay flat to dry. Steam-press if necessary.

Sequence for Tailoring a Jacket

The first step in tailoring a jacket is to fuse interfacing onto the major sections. Make pockets next. Then sew the jacket together and make a notched or shawl collar. Finish the sleeves, including the sleeve hems, and set them in. Shape the shoulders with shoulder pads and sleeve heads. Hem the jacket, and sew the lining as the final step.

vents on jacket hems and the roll lines of lapels and undercollars. In a lighter weight, it is an alternative to fusible tricot. Crisp, nonwoven fusible interfacing is used to keep small details, such as pocket flaps, firm and smooth.

Test fusible interfacings by making a sample when tailoring. Because entire sections of the garment will be interfaced, the sample should be large enough to drape over your hand, at least 6" (15 cm) square (larger if you can spare the fabric). The ideal method for testing fusible interfacings is to fuse 6" (15 cm) squares of different types of interfacing on a long panel, leaving plain fabric in between. The contrast in

feeling between interfaced and non-interfaced areas clearly shows the effect of each interfacing.

Choosing Tailoring Fabrics

When tailoring with fusible interfacings, you'll be more satisfied if you begin with a durable fabric of good quality. Natural fiber fabrics, such as wool, cotton, silk, and linen, respond well to fusing. Many fabrics made from synthetic fibers and blends, such as polyester and rayon, fuse nicely, too. However, some synthetics and metallic fibers are too heat sensitive for fusible interfacings.

INTERFACING THE JACKET SECTIONS

In one session, fuse interfacing to the jacket front, facing, back, collar, undercollar, and sleeves. Grouping the work is an efficient way to prepare major jacket sections for the steps that follow. After fusing, let the sections cool and dry on a flat surface. Wait overnight before handling medium- to heavy-weight woolens and textured tweeds. Wait one or two hours for fabrics of lighter weight.

Fusible interfacing is cut on the seamline rather than the cutting line in all places except at the armhole. Stitch interfacing in the seam at the armhole to support the sleeve. For lightweight fabrics, use the cutting line at the hem instead of the hem foldline.

How to Interface a Jacket Front and Facing

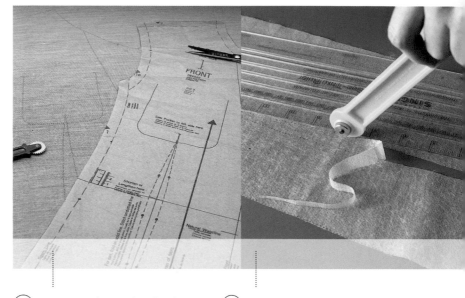

1 **Trace** seamlines of jacket front and side front pattern pieces on fusible weft insertion or hair canvas. Transfer all pattern markings to interfacing, including lapel roll line and dart stitching lines; it is unnecessary to mark fashion fabric.

2 **Cut** out any darts on dart stitching lines to eliminate bulk. Dart in fashion fabric will be stitched along cut edge of interfacing.

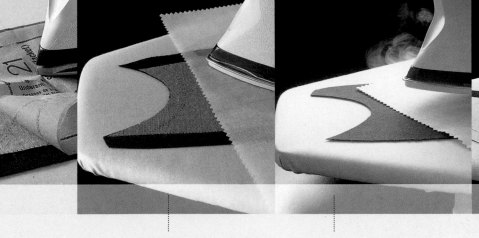

③ **Place** interfacing, adhesive side down, on wrong side of jacket sections. Place pattern on top to position darts and edges of interfacing at seamlines. Using dry iron, tack interfacing in place to prepare for permanent fusing. Set pattern piece aside.

④ **Place** press cloth on interfacing. Begin at center of section, then fuse each end. To avoid disturbing fused sections, fuse remaining areas by alternating from one side to the other. Never slide iron, which could cause layers to shift.

⑤ **Turn** jacket section over to right side. Using dry press cloth to protect right side of fabric, press thoroughly with steam iron. Lay flat to allow fused sections to cool and dry completely.

⑥ **Fuse** tricot knit interfacing or lightweight nonwoven interfacing to front facings after trimming seam allowances at front of facings. Interfacing extends to outer edge of facing.

Shaping Lapels

Layer. Add second layer of interfacing to lapel area only. Use weft insertion fusible interfacing, and cut it to fit from roll line to seamline of lapel; roll line should be placed on straight grain of interfacing to stabilize bias grain of jacket at roll line.

Hinge. When using fusible hair canvas, use a hinged roll line for a sharper edge on bulky or heavyweight fabrics. To make a hinge, cut interfacing on lapel roll line before fusing interfacing to jacket front.

Tape. Use narrow twill tape ¼" to ½" (6 mm to 1.3 cm) shorter than lapel roll line to contour roll line; shorten tape ½" (1.3 cm) for full bust. Place one edge of tape next to roll line; zigzag both tape edges to jacket, easing interfacing to fit tape.

Fold fused lapel on roll line, and press a crease. Do not press crease at lower 2" (5 cm) of lapel roll line; gently steam this area instead. Lay lapel over tailor's ham for pressing. Leave lapel on ham until lapel is completely cool and dry.

How to Interface a Jacket Back with Fusible Interfacing

(1) **Cut** interfacing for jacket back from same interfacing used for jacket front, or use lighter weight interfacing. Cut and mark as for jacket front interfacing, page 186, steps 1 and 2.

(2) **Fuse** interfacing to jacket back, using same technique as for interfacing jacket front, page 187, steps 3 to 5. Fuse interfacing to both jacket back sections before stitching center back seam.

How to Interface a Jacket Back and Hem

(1) **Cut** partial jacket back interfacing from lightweight woven fabric when garment does not need a fused interfacing for the entire back. Stitch darts separately in interfacing and garment. Press interfacing darts toward armhole and garment darts toward center back.

(2) **Staystitch** interfacing to jacket back, ½" (1.3 cm) from raw edges. Include narrow twill tape stay in staystitching at shoulders to prevent bias shoulder seam from stretching.

Hem without vent. Cut fusible knit or nonwoven interfacing crosswise to fit shape of hem from hem fold to raw edge; cut fusible weft insertion on the bias. Fuse as for jacket front interfacing, page 187, steps 3 to 6.

Hem with vent. Cut interfacing to stabilize vent underlap and overlap. Place straight grain of interfacing on lap foldlines.

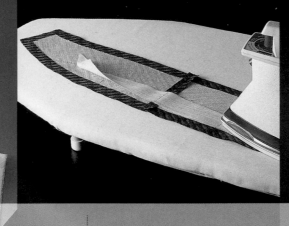

How to Interface and Shape a Jacket Undercollar

1 **Cut** undercollar from fusible weft insertion or hair canvas on bias grain. To cut collar stand interfacing, trace undercollar pattern from roll line to neckline seam; place center back seam on straight grain fold.

2 **Transfer** all pattern markings to both layers of interfacing. Fuse interfacing to undercollar; stitch center back seam. Fuse stand after stitching seam.

3 **Fold** undercollar on roll line, and press a sharp crease. Pin as pressed around tailor's ham, and steam. Leave in place on ham until completely cool and dry.

How to Interface Sleeves

1 **Use** lightweight fusible interfacing for comfort and appearance. Cut interfacing on seamlines of sleeve pattern. At sleeve hem, use cutting line instead of seamline. Transfer all pattern markings to sleeve interfacing.

2 **Fuse** interfacing to sleeve sections before sewing seams.

Alternative method: Back the jacket sleeves with batiste. Transfer pattern markings to batiste. Staystitch batiste to sleeve, ½" (1.3 cm) from raw edges. Machine-baste along hem and vent foldlines.

TAILORING A NOTCHED COLLAR

A notched collar takes its name from the angle of the jacket collar where it joins the jacket lapels. The seams that meet there form a notch, or V-shaped cutout, on each side of the neckline. The seam is the gorge line. A crisp, flat, even notch is a hallmark of fine tailoring. The key to this detail is an artful combination of stitching and pressing, plus careful trimming of enclosed seam allowances to reduce bulk.

Several pattern pieces are needed to make a notched collar. The undercollar, interfaced and shaped, is the first section to be sewn to the jacket. Next, sew the upper collar to the facing; a portion of this facing becomes the outside of the lapels when the collar is finished. After sewing the final seam, which attaches the collar/facing section to the jacket, press and edgestitch or topstitch, using techniques on page 193 to shape and stitch the notches.

How to Sew a Notched Collar

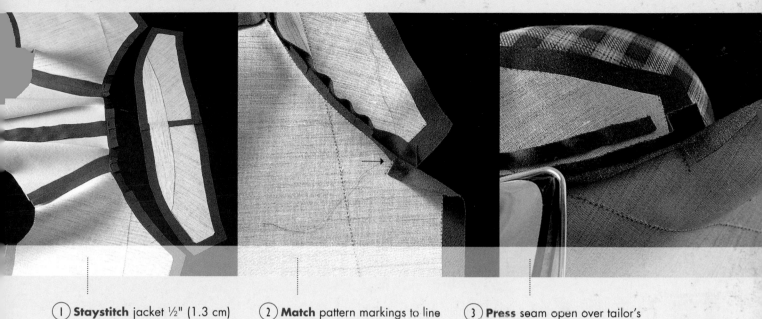

(1) Staystitch jacket ½" (1.3 cm) from neckline raw edge. Clip to staystitching. This releases curved neckline seam allowance so it lies flat for easier sewing.

(2) Match pattern markings to line up undercollar and jacket neckline edge. Stitch undercollar to jacket neckline up to pattern markings on lapels (arrow); clip to marking.

(3) Press seam open over tailor's ham. Trim seam allowances to ¼" (6 mm) to reduce bulk.

(4) Staystitch facing ½" (1.3 cm) from neckline edge. Clip to staystitching. Stitch collar to facing neckline up to pattern markings on lapels; clip to marking.

(5) Press seam open over tailor's ham. Trim seam allowances to ⅜" (1 cm), slightly wider than undercollar to reduce bulk.

(6) Pin collar/facing section to undercollar/jacket section, pinning through seams at collar notches (arrow) to be sure the seams line up precisely.

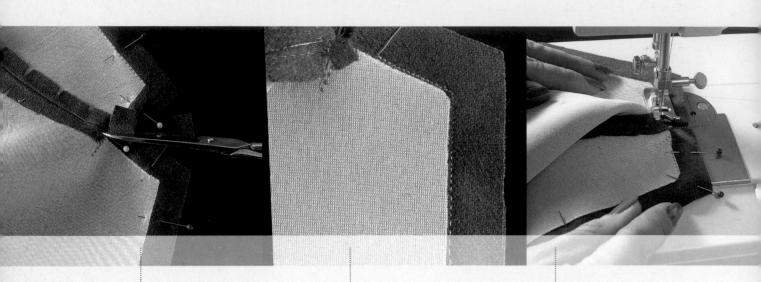

(7) **Trim** excess fabric of collar seam allowance to stitching line on upper and undercollar.

(8) **Stitch** seam, starting at bottom of one jacket edge. Shorten stitches 1" (2.5 cm) from lapel. Take one or two short stitches diagonally across lapel point. (Lapel removed from machine to show stitching.)

(9) **Stitch** from lapel point to collar point, holding seam straight to ensure that notches match on both sides of jacket collar. Finish stitching seam, using same technique on other side.

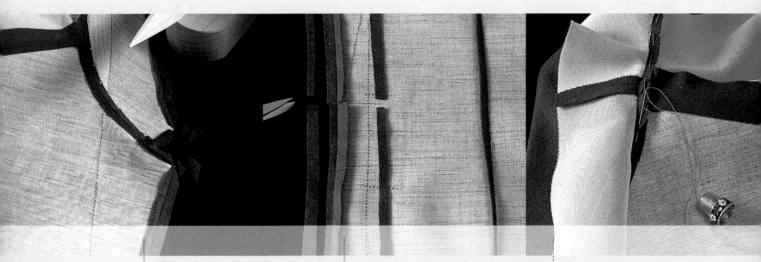

(10) **Press** seam open, using point presser at lapel and collar points. Diagonally trim corners close to stitching. Grade seam allowance on undercollar/lapel to ¼" (6 mm), and on collar/facing to ⅜" (1 cm). Continue grading to lapel roll line.

(11) **Clip** seam at ends of lapel roll line. Below clips, grade jacket front seam allowance to ⅜" (1 cm) and facing to ¼" (6 mm). Press seam open; turn right side out.

(12) **Tack** upper and undercollar seams together with loose running stitch. If seams do not line up exactly because of bulk of fabric, tack the seams where they meet.

Tips for Pressing a Tailored Collar

1) **Press** collar and lapels from underside. Roll seam toward underside of collar and lapels, stopping about 1" (2.5 cm) from end of lapel roll line. Press, using tailor's clapper to force steam out of fabric; this creates crisp edge.

2) **Press** lower 1" (2.5 cm) of lapel roll line so seam is at edge. Work from underside of lapels.

3) **Press** jacket front below lapel roll line from inside. Press so seam rolls toward jacket facing.

How to Topstitch a Tailored Collar

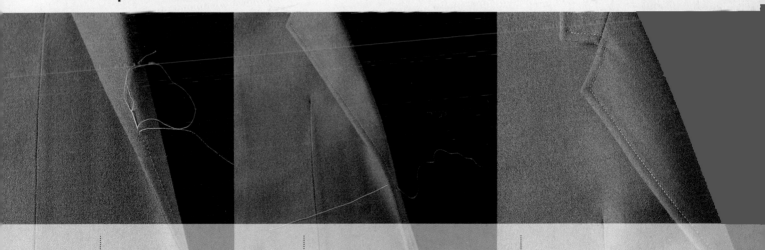

1) **Topstitch** on right side of jacket, beginning at one lower edge. When using topstitching thread in the needle, stop at bottom of lapel roll line. Clip threads. Pull threads through to facing side; bury ends between facing and garment.

2) **Continue** topstitching from right side of lapel. Start at exact point where stitching ended, or overlap two stitches. At collar notch, pivot and stitch up to notch edge. (The garment is off the machine only to show detail. Do not remove from machine.)

3) **Shorten** stitch length, pivot, and stitch in the ditch to topstitching line of collar. Pivot, and stitch around collar to other notch. Repeat at second notch. Break topstitching at end of lapel roll line as described in step 1.

SHAPING THE SHOULDERS

Jackets need inside support for firm, smooth shape at the shoulders. In tailoring, the two important shaping aids are shoulder pads and sleeve heads.

Shoulder pads can be custom-made to fit the jacket armhole, using the jacket pattern pieces. To fit your figure, adjust the size and thickness of the shoulder pad. If one shoulder is higher than the other one, the pad can be made thicker to compensate for the difference. If your shoulders are sloping, use a thicker pad than the pattern suggests. For square shoulders, use a thinner shoulder pad.

On tailored garments such as jackets and coats, the front of the shoulder pad is wider than the back to fill in the hollow area below the shoulder and to create a smooth line. The back is narrower than the front to fit around the shoulder blades. For a full bust, make the shoulder pad slightly shorter in front. Whenever you try on the jacket or coat for fitting, slip the shoulder pads in place. The shape and size of the shoulder pads can make a big difference in the way the shoulder and sleeve fit.

To build the pads to the desired thickness, cut graduated layers of a thin filler, such as polyester fleece or cotton/polyester quilt batting. These fillers add lift without being too soft.

For the upper layer of a shoulder pad, use fusible hair canvas. The goat's hair fibers in the canvas grip the jacket fabric, helping to secure the pad to the garment. Also, the strong, resilient canvas makes the shoulder pads firm and wrinkle free.

Sleeve heads are strips of filler that support the sleeve caps on a tailored jacket to boost the caps and smooth out any wrinkles where the sleeve was eased to fit the armhole. Sleeve heads also improve the way the jacket sleeves drape. The same filler used for shoulder pads (fleece or quilt batting) can be used to make sleeve heads. Necktie interfacing cut on the true bias grain can also be used.

How to Make a Custom Shoulder Pad

(1) **Lap** jacket front and back patterns at shoulder seam. Trace armhole between front and back notches. End shoulder pad pattern ½" (1.3 cm) from neck seam edge, about 5" (12.5 cm) from armhole. Mark shoulder seam on pad pattern. Label armhole front and armhole back.

(2) **Cut** pattern from fusible hair canvas. Transfer shoulder seam markings. Mark front and back of armhole on canvas. Also cut four layers of filler, gradually reducing layers by about ¾" (2 cm) in size, to make ½" (1.3 cm) thick pad. Adjust sizes and numbers of layers to make pad desired thickness.

(3) **Stitch** around armhole edge and across shoulder marking with running stitches to hold filler layers together. Add more rows of stitches about 1" (2.5 cm) apart, fanning rows out from armhole edge.

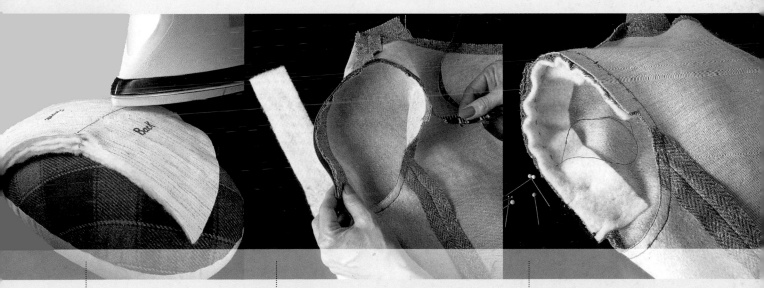

(4) **Fuse** hair canvas to widest layer of fleece, placing pad over tailor's ham to press pad to shape of shoulder. Tack pad to jacket by hand, placing canvas layer next to jacket.

How to Make a Sleeve Head

(1) **Cut** strip of filler 1⅞" (4.7 cm) deep and the length of jacket sleeve cap. Sleeve cap is eased area of set-in sleeve, between pattern markings. Match one long edge of sleeve head to raw edge of armhole seam allowance.

(2) **Stitch** sleeve head to seamline around sleeve cap, using running stitches. When sleeve is turned right side out, sleeve head folds into two layers. Top layer extends beyond bottom layer to prevent ridge on outside of jacket.

TAILORED HEMS

Tailored hems on jackets and jacket sleeves are best put in with a catchstitch. These are small horizontal stitches made in a zigzag pattern. With a blind catchstitch, the stitches do not show from the inside or the outside because they are worked between the hem edge and the jacket or sleeve. The hem is not held tightly against the garment; it should be sewn loosely with some play at the raw edge. A tailored hem should not show a ridge on the outside of the jacket after pressing, even if a bulky fabric is used.

Determine hem lengths on jackets and sleeves before cutting out the pattern pieces. Although the depth can vary, the standard hem on a jacket is 2" (5 cm) deep. The standard sleeve hem is 1½" (3.8 cm) deep. Hem a jacket after completing the collar or before sewing in the lining. For easier handling, sew sleeve hems before setting the sleeves into the jacket.

Trimming. Trim seam allowances within the hem to half their width, from raw edge of hem to hemline only. This reduces bulk and prevents bumps where seams cross hemline.

Edge finishing. Lining covers the hem edge when a jacket is completed, so finish the edge only if the fabric ravels or stretches. Use a nonbulky zigzagged, overlocked, or stitched-and-pinked finish. If you have fused the interfacing, the edge needs no further finishing.

Pressing. Press the hem before sewing. If the hem is very curved, use a line of easestitching along the raw edge to help ease in fabric fullness.

How to Sew a Tailored Hem

① **Turn** hem up and press at hem foldline. Open out pressed hem and trim seam allowances to half width from raw edge of hem to foldline. Baste hem in place close to fold.

② **Press**, letting steam penetrate fabric to ease extra fullness in smoothly. To avoid a ridge on right side, do not press over upper edge of hem.

Catchstitch for lined garments. Work loosely over hem edge from left to right. Make stitch in hem, catching one or two threads; then make a stitch just outside hem edge, catching one garment thread. Alternate stitches in zigzag pattern.

Blind catchstitch for unlined garments. Finish raw edge with appropriate edge finish. Baste hem in place close to finished edge. Fold hem edge down and loosely catchstitch between hem and garment. Stitching is not visible.

How to Hem a Jacket Vent

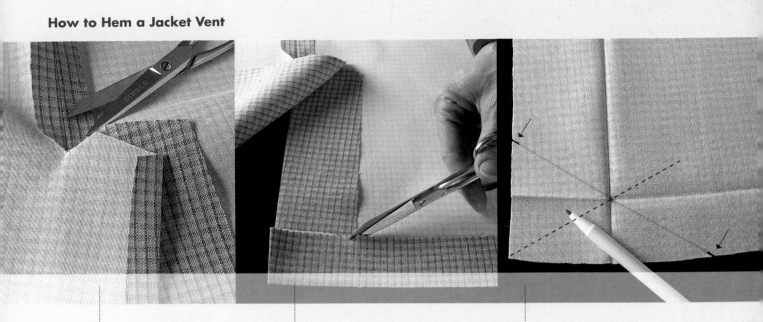

① **Arrange** vent in finished position. Clip seam so underlap lies flat. From inside of jacket, vent underlap is on top with seam allowance pressed back; overlap on bottom has self-facing folded back.

② **Press** hem into position on overlap. Press fold at hem and at vent self-facing to prepare for mitering. Clip vent facing and hem allowance where two edges meet.

③ **Open** out corner. Mark stitching line from clips (arrows) through corner point where pressed lines meet. Fold through corner (dotted line), with right sides together, matching clip marks.

④ **Stitch** on marked line. Trim seam to ¼" (6 mm). Press seam open; turn to right side.

⑤ **Fold** hem to outside on vent underlap, right sides together. Stitch seam from hem fold to top of hem. Trim to ¼" (6 mm) and press open; turn right side out. Catchstitch hem and vent in place.

⑥ **Arrange** vent in finished position. Stitch across top of vent from inside through all layers. Grade seam.

LINING

Lining a garment serves several purposes: it hides seam allowances, protects them from fraying, and helps the garment retain its shape. For jackets and coats, the smooth surface of the lining makes it easier to put on the garment over a shirt or sweater. For skirts and pants, lining often makes the garment more comfortable against the skin.

Lining a Jacket

A lining is cut and sewn along the same style lines as a jacket, but has extra details to add comfort. A pleat in the center back of the lining allows for wearing ease across shoulders and upper back. A pleat also is formed between the lining and hems. This is a jump hem, and it allows you to move comfortably without straining the stitches.

Some jacket patterns provide separate pattern pieces for the lining, and others furnish cutting lines for the lining on the jacket pattern itself. If the same pattern is used for the sleeve and the sleeve lining, cut the sleeve lining ½" (1.3 cm) higher at the underarms. This allows the lining to rest above the jacket underarm seams and prevents binding at the armholes. When a separate sleeve lining pattern is provided, this may have been done for you.

Cut the jacket and sleeve lining ½" (1.3 cm) longer than the finished length after hemming. After the lining is applied to jacket and sleeve hems, the finished edges will fall just below the halfway point on the jacket and sleeve hems. If you adjust the jacket or sleeves, make the same adjustments on the lining patterns.

How to Line a Jacket

1) **Stitch** lining sections together, including sleeves. Reinforce armhole seam with two rows of stitching. Fold and machine-baste center back pleat at top and bottom of lining. Staystitch ½" (1.3 cm) from neckline, sleeve, and lower edges of lining; clip to staystitching at neckline.

2) **Turn** jacket facing out. With right sides together, stitch lining to facing. On each side in front, leave seam unstitched for twice the depth of hem. (Leave 4" [10 cm] unstitched if jacket hem is 2" [5 cm] deep.) Clip seam allowance at curves. Press seam as stitched.

3) **Match** seam allowances of lining and jacket at shoulder (a) and underarm (b) seams; tack in place. Turn lining right side out. Smooth sleeves into position on inside of jacket. Lightly press facing/lining seam allowances toward lining, using a press cloth.

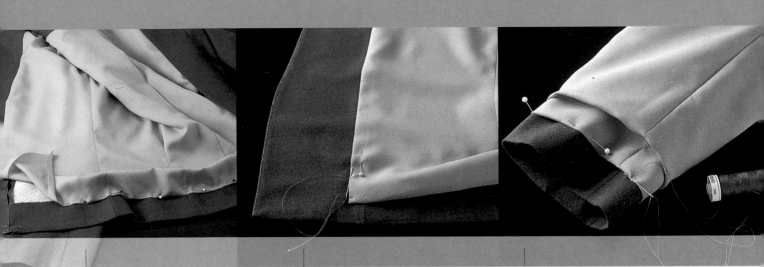

(4) **Trim** raw edges of front facing to neaten them, if necessary. Whipstitch raw edges to hem. Turn lining under on staystitching line at lower edge. Pin so raw edge of lining is even with top edge of jacket hem.

(5) **Slipstitch** lining fold to jacket hem, sewing through jacket hem allowance only. At front edges, fold lining hem down to form pleat, and slipstitch to facing on each side.

(6) **Sew** lining to each sleeve hem, following steps 4 and 5. Sew jump hem around entire sleeve, even if sleeve hem has vent; sleeve vents are decorative and not meant to open and close. Press sleeve lining hem over seam roll.

How to Line a Jacket with a Hem Vent

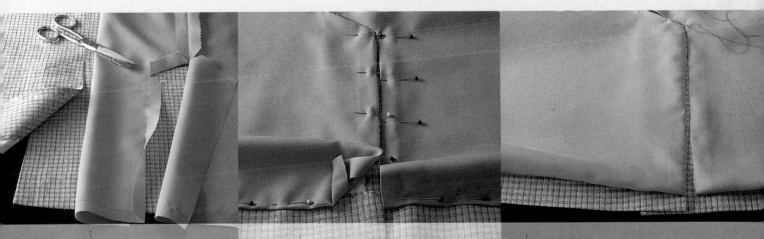

(1) **Stitch** center back seam to marking at top of vent; clip into seam so left side of vent lies flat. Staystitch right side of vent on seamline across top and on foldline. Clip into corner to fold under raw edge on stay stitching. Attach lining to jacket facing, following steps 1 to 3, opposite.

(2) **Match** center back seams of lining and jacket at vent opening. Fold under ⅝" (1.5 cm) seam allowance across top of left vent lining and down side. Pin lining to side edges of vent on jacket; leave top edge unpinned. Match raw edge of lining to jacket hem edge, forming pleat at bottom of vent.

(3) **Sew** lining to hems, following steps 4 and 5, above. Slipstitch vent lining along vent side edges. Stitch across top of vent lining. To prevent lining from pulling at top of vent, slipstitches should not go through to jacket fabric.

LINING A SKIRT OR PANTS

Few patterns provide linings for skirts and pants, but adding a lining makes garments hang better and is easy to accomplish. The method given here is for a slip lining, which is free-hanging and attached at the waistline; the skirt or pants and the lining are hemmed separately. An advantage of a slip lining is that the garment is easy to press because you can lift the whole lining out.

Unlike jacket and coat linings, skirt and pants linings are worn against your skin. In warm or humid climates, fabrics made from rayon, cotton, or cotton blends may feel more comfortable than those made from polyester and similar synthetic fibers.

Tips for Lining Skirts and Pants

Cut the lining from the major front and back pattern pieces. Omit small pattern pieces such as the waistband, facings, and pockets. For a gathered skirt in a lightweight fabric, the skirt and lining may be treated as one layer of fabric. For a heavier weight gathered skirt, cut the lining from a pattern for a simple A-line skirt, or make small pleats or released tucks instead of gathers in the lining. Or pleat out the fullness from the tissue pattern before cutting the lining, allowing some ease for movement. Any of these methods eliminates bulk at the waistline.

Omit any seam extensions for in-seam pockets when you cut out a lining. Straighten the cutting lines on the front and back pattern pieces to change the pocket openings to plain seams. If the garment has slanted pockets, lap the front pattern pieces to cut the lining without pockets.

Shorten the pattern pieces so the lining will be 1" (2.5 cm) shorter than the skirt or pants after hemming. If you plan to make a 1" (2.5 cm) hem in the lining, cut the lower edge of the lining at the hemline of the skirt or pants.

Transfer pattern markings at the zipper opening and the waist to the lining sections after cutting. These markings will help you position the lining inside the skirt or pants.

Assemble the skirt or pants, including the zipper and pockets, before attaching the lining. All stitching on the garment should be completed except for the waistband and the hem. Press seams open. Unless the fabric ravels easily, it is not necessary to finish the seams.

How to Line a Skirt

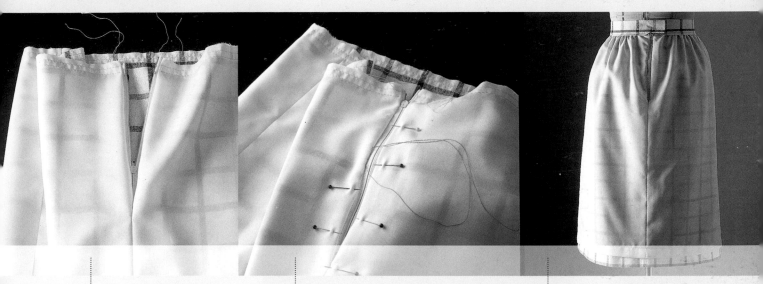

1. **Stitch** lining seams, leaving seam open at zipper; press open. Slip lining over skirt, wrong sides together, matching seams. Machine-baste together on waist seamline, folding lining under at zipper edge.

2. **Fold** lining edges under to expose zipper coil and allow easy opening and closing of zipper. Pin and slipstitch lining to zipper tape.

3. **Apply** waistband. Hem lining so it is 1" (2.5 cm) shorter than skirt. Sew lining hem by hand or machine, as desired.

Darts, Ease, or Pleats in Linings

Darts. Pin tucks in the skirt or pants lining, matching the dart markings. Darts in skirt or pants are pressed toward center front and back. Press tucks in lining in opposite direction to reduce bulk.

Eased or slightly gathered area.

Slip lining over skirt, wrong sides together. Machine-baste at waistline seam. Gather lining and skirt as if they were one layer of fabric, pulling up ease to fit waistband.

Pleat-front skirts or pants.

Machine-baste pleats separately in lining and garment. Press lining pleats flat in opposite direction of skirt pleats. Slip lining over skirt, wrong sides together. Machine-baste at waistline.

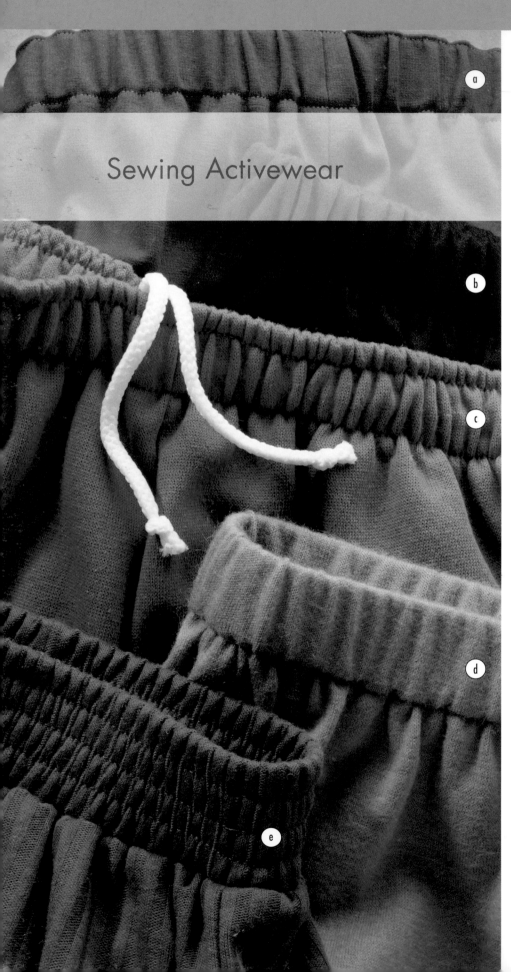

Sewing Activewear

ELASTICIZED WAISTBANDS

Elasticized waistbands are comfortable to wear and easy to sew. They complement the stretch of knit fabrics. Some elasticized waistbands are "cut on," which means the waistbands are cut as an extension of the garment at the waistline edge, while others are a separate waistband piece. Choose an application technique according to the fabric, the garment style, and the type of elastic you are using.

Two techniques for cut-on waistbands are included: one with a casing and one with topstitching. Both are appropriate for garments made from lightweight to medium-weight fabrics. Cut-on waistbands with casings (a) give a casual look. Firm braided or woven elastics are well suited for this technique. Because the elastic is not caught in the waistline seam, it can easily be adjusted for a better fit, if necessary. Cut-on waistbands with topstitching (b) give a variety of looks, depending on the type of topstitching. Use an elastic with good stretch and recovery qualities so the elastic will stretch to the circumference of the garment opening, yet retain its fit. Drawstring elastic (c) may be used for this method.

Two additional techniques are included for waistbands that use a separate waistband piece: smooth waistbands and shirred waistbands. When sewing garments from lightweight or medium-weight knits, you may cut the waistband from self-fabric. When sewing bulky fabrics, such as sweatshirt fleece, choose matching ribbing for the waistband or, for a more decorative effect, a contrasting fabric.

Smooth separate waistbands (d) give the smooth appearance of a traditional waistband when the garment is worn. This waistband style is suitable for a slim-fitting garment made from lightweight or medium weight knit fabric with moderate stretch. Use a firm 1" or 1¼" (2.5 or 3.2 cm) elastic.

Shirred separate waistbands (e) complement fuller garment styles, such as full skirts, and are especially attractive when used with wider elastics. Shirred waistbands may be topstitched or not, depending on the look you prefer. Firm elastic is recommended for this type of waistband.

In general, cut elastics 2" to 3" (5 to 7.5 cm) less than your waist measurement. Cut soft, lightweight elastics, such as knit elastics, 3" to 5" (7.5 to 12.5 cm) less than your waist measurement. Cut very firm elastics, such as nonroll waistband elastic, equal to, or 1" (2.5 cm) less than, your waist measurement. Mark the elastic, and pin it around your waistline before cutting it. Check to see that the elastic fits comfortably around your waist and pulls over your hips easily.

Multiple rows of topstitching can cause elastic to lose some of its recovery. If you are using a method that calls for topstitching, you may want to cut the elastic up to 1" (2.5 cm) shorter than the guidelines, to ensure a snug fit.

Tips for Sewing Elasticized Waistbands

Preshrink elastics for casing applications before measuring. Elastics that will be stitched on do not require preshrinking.

Use longer stitches, about eight to nine stitches per inch (2.5 cm), when stitching through the elastic; the stitches will appear shorter when elastic is relaxed. A stitch length that is too short weakens and stretches out the elastic.

Steam the finished waistband after construction, holding the iron above the fabric, to help the elastic return to its original length.

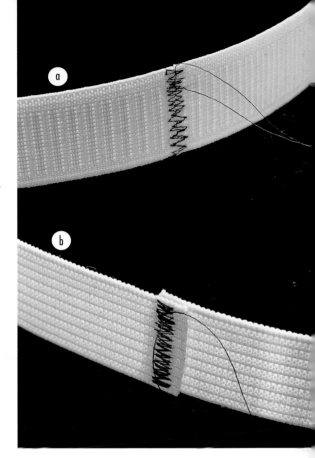

Two Ways to Join the Ends of the Elastic

(a) **Butted method.** Butt ends of elastic. Stitch back and forth, using 3-step zigzag stitch or wide zigzag stitch, catching both ends of elastic in stitching. This method is recommended for firm elastics.

(b) **Overlapped method.** Overlap ends of elastic ½" (1.3 cm). Stitch back and forth through both layers, using wide zigzag stitch or 3-step zigzag stitch. Use for soft elastics, such as knitted elastic.

How to Sew a Cut-on Waistband with a Casing

(1) **Extend** garment pattern pieces above waistline twice the width of the elastic plus ⅝" (1.5 cm). Cut out garment sections, and stitch together.

(2) **Overlock** raw edge at waist, if desired. Fold edge of fabric to wrong side, an amount equal to width of elastic plus ½" (1.3 cm). Edgestitch close to fold.

(3) **Join** ends of elastic (page 203). Position elastic within folded casing area. Stitch next to elastic, using straight stitch and zipper foot; do not catch elastic in stitching. Shift fabric around elastic as necessary while stitching.

(4) **Stretch** waistband to distribute fabric evenly. From right side of garment, stitch in the ditch through all waistband layers, at center front, center back, and side seams, to secure elastic.

Alternate method.

Follow steps 1 and 2, above. Mark elastic to desired length; do not cut. Position elastic within folded casing area. Stitch next to elastic, using straight stitch and zipper foot, leaving 2" (5 cm) unstitched; do not catch elastic in stitching.

Pull elastic through to marking; secure, using safety pin. Try on garment to check fit; adjust elastic, if necessary. Cut and join ends of elastic (page 203). Complete waistband stitching. Stitch in the ditch as in step 4.

How to Sew a Cut-on Waistband with Topstitching

(1) **Extend** garment pattern pieces above waistline twice the width of the elastic. Cut out garment sections, and stitch together. Join ends of elastic (page 203).

(2) **Divide** elastic and garment edge into fourths; pin-mark. Pin elastic to wrong side of garment, with edges even, matching pin marks; overlock or zigzag, stretching elastic to fit between pins. If using overlock machine, guide work carefully or disengage knives to avoid cutting elastic.

(3) **Fold** elastic to wrong side of garment so fabric encases elastic. From right side of garment, stitch in the ditch through all waistband layers, at center front, center back, and side seams, to secure elastic.

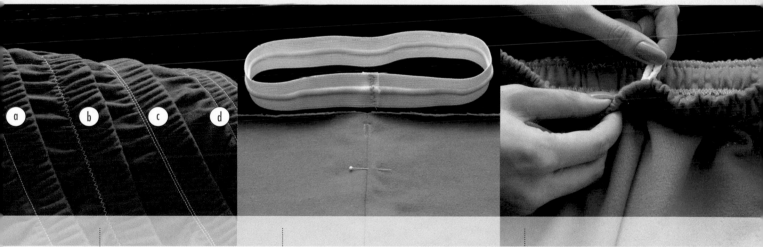

(4) **Topstitch** through all layers, stretching elastic as you sew. Straight-stitch or narrow zigzag close to lower edge of casing, using long stitches (a); zigzag close to lower edge, using medium-to-wide stitches (b); double-needle topstitch close to lower edge (c); or stitch multiple, even rows of straight stitching or double-needle stitching (d).

Drawstring-elastic method.

Extend pattern pieces as in step 1, above. Join ends of drawstring elastic, using overlapped method (page 203). Stitch garment sections together, leaving ½" (1.3 cm) opening in center front seam in drawstring area; topstitch around opening to secure.

Follow step 2, above. Zigzag at lower edge of elastic. Fold elastic to wrong side of garment so fabric encases elastic. Straight-stitch ¼" (6 mm) from upper and lower edges of elastic, through all layers, stretching elastic to fit. Pull drawstring through center front opening. Cut drawstring, and knot ends.

How to Sew a Smooth Separate Waistband

(1) **Mark** cutting line on garment section pattern pieces ⅝" (1.5 cm) above waistline. Cut waistband on crosswise grain, twice the width of elastic plus 1¼" (3.2 cm); length of waistband is equal to your waist measurement plus 3¼" (8 cm). Pin ends of waistband together with ⅝" (1.5 cm) seam allowances; check fit over hips.

(2) **Join** ends of waistband; press seam open. Divide waistband and garment edge into fourths; pin-mark. Pin waistband to right side of garment, with raw edges even, matching pin marks. Stitch ⅝" (1.5 cm) seam, using straight stitch or narrow zigzag stitch; if using straight stitch, stretch fabric as you sew.

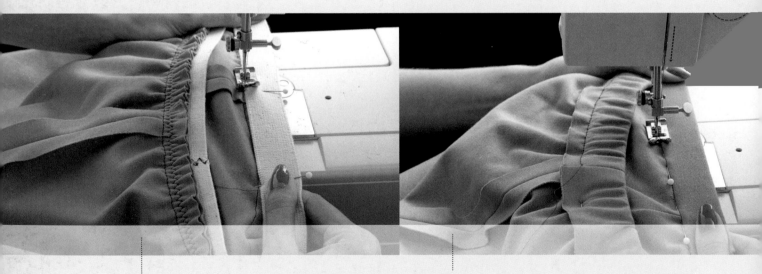

(3) **Join** ends of elastic (page 203). Divide elastic and garment edge into fourths; pin-mark. Place elastic on seam allowance of waistband; pin in place, with lower edge of elastic just above seamline. With elastic on top, stitch through both seam allowances, using wide zigzag or multiple zigzag stitch; stretch elastic to fit between pins. Trim seam allowances.

(4) **Fold** waistband tightly over elastic to wrong side of garment; pin. Stitch in the ditch along seamline from right side of garment, stretching elastic; catch waistband in stitching on wrong side of garment, but do not catch elastic. Trim waistband seam allowance to ¼" (6 mm) from stitching.

How to Sew a Shirred Separate Waistband

(1) **Mark** cutting line on garment section pattern pieces ⅝" (1.5 cm) above waistline. Cut waistband on cross-wise grain, twice the width of elastic plus 1¼" (3.2 cm); length of waistband is equal to your hip measurement plus 1¼" (3.2 cm). Join ends of elastic (page 203).

(2) **Join** ends of waistband in ⅝" (1.5 cm) seam; press seam open. Divide the waistband and garment edges into fourths; pin-mark. Fold the waistband in half lengthwise, wrong sides together, encasing elastic. Baste ½" (1.3 cm) from raw edges, avoiding pins; shift fabric around elastic as necessary.

(3) **Pin** waistband to right side of garment, matching pin marks; if garment is very full, gather waistline edge before attaching waistband. Stitch just inside basting stitches, stretching waistband to fit garment between pins. Trim seam allowances to ¼" (6 mm). Overlock raw edges, if desired.

(4) **Stretch** waistband to distribute fabric evenly. From right side of garment, stitch perpendicular to the waistline through all waistband layers, at the center back and side seams, to secure the elastic. If desired, topstitch through all layers as on page 205, step 4.

RIBBED EDGES

The most common use for ribbing is to finish the edges of knit sportswear garments. Ribbing, which has great crosswise stretch and recovery, enables garment openings to stretch easily when you are getting dressed and return to a neat, comfortable fit during wear. Ribbing is available as yardage and as prefinished ribbed bands.

The width of ribbing yardage ranges from 28" to 60" (71 to 152.5 cm), or 14" to 30" (35.5 to 76 cm) tubular, and is available in several weights. To use ribbing yardage, cut a crosswise strip of the fabric, fold it in half lengthwise, and apply it so the fold becomes the finished edge.

Prefinished ribbed bands have one finished edge and are applied as a single layer. They are available in various widths and lengths, and in different weights and styles.

Ribbing can be used as an edge finish for several styles of necklines, including turtleneck, mock turtleneck, crewneck, and scoop-neck. It is also used on sleeves, lower edges of T-shirts and sweatshirts, and waistlines of pants and skirts. The cut width and cut length of the ribbing varies, depending on where it will be used and the style you want.

If you use ribbing yardage, the cut width of the ribbing is equal to twice the desired finished width plus ½" (1.3 cm) for seam allowances. If you use prefinished ribbed bands, the cut width is equal to the desired finished width plus one ¼" (6 mm) seam allowance.

Many patterns designed for knits indicate what length to cut the ribbing, or they provide a pattern piece to be used as a guide for the ribbing pieces. The cut length for ribbing can also be determined by measuring the garment opening at the seamline, as shown opposite.

For straight, close-fitting edges, the cut length can be determined by pin-fitting the ribbing on the body. On straight edges that do not require a close fit, such as the lower edge of a skirt, cut the ribbing slightly shorter than the garment edge.

To sew ribbed edges, you may use either the flat or the in-the-round method of construction. Flat construction is the fastest method; however, the seams may be noticeable at the edges of the ribbing. For a better-quality finish, the in-the-round method is usually preferred. With this method, the ribbing seams are enclosed for a neater appearance.

If matching ribbing is not available, self-fabric, cut on the crosswise grain, can be substituted for ribbing yardage. Use a knit fabric that stretches at least 50 percent crosswise; for example, 10" (25.5 cm) of knit must stretch to at least 15" (38 cm).

How to Determine the Cut Length

(1) **Measure** seamline of garment opening by standing tape measure on edge. For necklines, cut ribbing as described at right. For other garment openings, ribbing is usually cut two-thirds of the measurement plus ½" (1.3 cm). If self-fabric is substituted for ribbing, cut it three-fourths of the measurement plus ½" (1.3 cm).

(2) **Pin-fit** ribbing or self-fabric around body for straight, close-fitting edges, such as at hiplines, wrists, and ankles. Fold ribbing crosswise for double thickness, and pin ribbing so it lies flat, without gaping; do not distort the ribs. Add ½" (1.3 cm) for seam allowances.

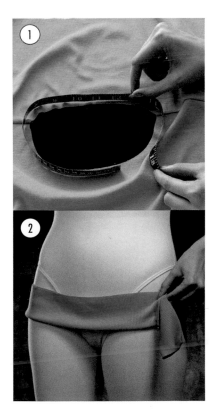

Types of Ribbed Necklines

Crewneck garments (a) usually have ribbing with a finished width of 1" to 1¼" (2.5 to 3.2 cm); the neckline seam falls ¾" (2 cm) below the natural neckline. Cut the ribbing two-thirds of the neckline measurement plus ½" (1.3 cm).

Turtleneck garments (b) have ribbing with a finished width of 4" to 6" (10 to 15 cm). The neckline seam falls at the natural neckline. Cut the ribbing the length of the neckline measurement plus ½" (1.3 cm).

Mock turtleneck garments (c) have ribbing with a finished width of 2" to 2⅜" (5 to 6 cm). The neckline seam falls ½" (1.3 cm) below the natural neckline. Cut the ribbing three-fourths of the neckline measurement plus ½" (1.3 cm).

Scoop-neck garments (d) have rounded necklines, with the edge of the ribbing falling lower than the natural neckline in the front and, sometimes, in the back. Cut the ribbing two-thirds of the neckline measurement plus ½" (1.3 cm). The finished width of the ribbing varies from ¾" to 1" (2 to 2.5 cm).

Self-fabric may be used instead of ribbing. For turtlenecks, cut the self-fabric the length of the neckline measurement plus ½" (1.3 cm); for crew necks, mock turtlenecks, and scoop necks, cut it three-fourths of the neckline plus ½" (1.3 cm).

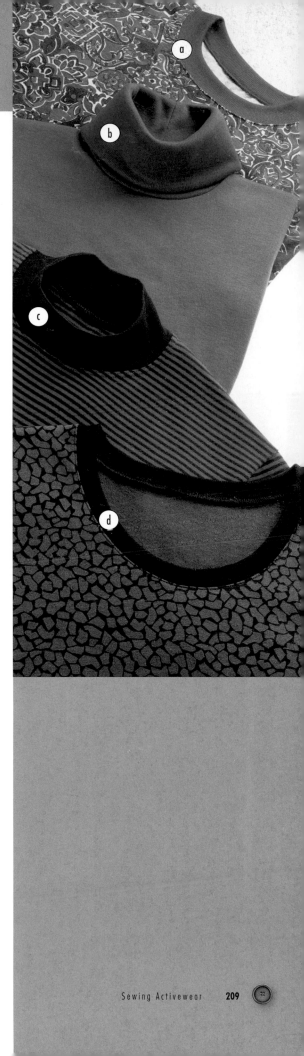

How to Sew Ribbed Edges (flat method)

1 **Cut** garment pieces, allowing ¼" (6 mm) seam allowances at garment openings. Leave one seam unstitched. If using ribbing yardage, fold ribbing in half lengthwise, wrong sides together. Divide ribbing and garment opening into fourths; pin-mark.

2 **Pin** ribbing to right side of garment, matching pin marks. With ribbing on top, stitch ¼" (6 mm) seam, using narrow zigzag or overlock stitch; stretch ribbing to fit garment opening as you sew. Lightly press seam toward garment.

3 **Stitch** remaining garment seam, matching ribbing seam and ends carefully. If desired, topstitch close to seamline as in step 3, below.

How to Sew Ribbed Edges (in-the-round method)

1 **Join** ends of ribbing in ¼" (6 mm) seam. If using ribbing yardage, fold ribbing in half lengthwise, wrong sides together. Divide ribbing and garment opening into fourths; pin-mark.

2 **Pin** ribbing to right side of garment, matching pin marks. With ribbing on top, stitch ¼" (6 mm) seam, using narrow zigzag or overlock stitch; stretch ribbing to fit garment opening as you sew. Lightly press seam toward garment.

3 **Topstitch** close to seamline, if desired, stitching through garment and seam allowances, using single or double needle. If single needle is used, stretch fabric slightly as you sew.

How to Apply Lapped Ribbing to a V-Neckline

(1) **Cut** ribbing slightly longer than the cut edge of neckline. With short stitches, staystitch on the seamline 2" (5 cm) on either side of the V. Clip carefully to the V. Fold ribbing in half lengthwise.

(2) **Pin** ribbing to right-hand side of neckline in ¼" (6 mm) seam; leave 1" (2.5 cm) for lapping. With garment on top, begin stitching at center front. Stretch ribbing slightly as you sew.

(3) **Stop** stitching at shoulder seam. Measure back neckline between shoulder seams. Mark ribbing with pin at point equal to two-thirds the measured length. Match pin mark to shoulder seam.

(4) **Stitch** ribbing to garment across back neckline and down left-hand side of neckline, stretching ribbing slightly. Stop stitching before reaching point of V, leaving an opening equal to width of ribbing. Remove garment from machine.

(5) **Turn** ribbing seam to inside and then lay garment out flat. Tuck the extensions inside the seam opening with right-hand side overlapping left. Pin ribbing at center front in lapped position.

(6) **Fold** front of garment out of the way. From wrong side, stitch opening closed; pivot at point of V, and stitch free end of ribbing to right-hand seam allowance. Trim extensions close to stitches.

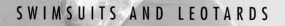

SWIMSUITS AND LEOTARDS

area. Purchased bra cups may be sewn into the bandeau if firmer support is desired.

Two-way stretch fabric stretches to fit the contours of many different figure types. Select the pattern according to the bust measurement to avoid extensive fitting adjustments at the bustline. If you require different pattern sizes for the hips and the bust, choose a multisize pattern, following the cutting lines for the appropriate sizes and blending the lines in the waistline area.

Adjusting the Pattern

For one-piece swimsuits and leotards, measure your torso length as shown, below, and compare it to the torso lengths given in the chart at right; do not measure the pattern pieces for this comparison, because they will measure less than the actual body measurement. If your torso measurement falls within the range given for your bust size, no pattern adjustment is needed.

If your torso measurement is different from the length given in the chart, first adjust the pattern front an amount equal to one-fourth the difference, then adjust the pattern back the same amount. The total pattern adjustment is only one-half the difference between your torso measurement and the chart; the

Patterns for swimsuits and leotards are usually closely fitted for comfort and easy motion. A wide range of pattern styles is available. Styles with princess seams are slenderizing. So are patterns with a center panel of a contrasting color; to minimize hips, use a dark color for the side panels. High-cut leg openings on swimsuits and leotards give the appearance of longer legs and a slimmer torso. For a full-busted figure, choose a

pattern with a bustline shaped by darts or seams. To fill out a slender figure, use a pattern with shirring, draping, or ruffles. Or choose a simple pattern style and a splashy printed fabric to enhance a slender figure.

By sewing your own swimsuits and leotards, you can make garments that meet your needs. Add a full-front lining to a swimsuit, if desired; this is especially important for light-colored and lightweight fabrics. Or you may line just the crotch area or add a bandeau lining in the bust two-way stretch fabric will be stretched when it is worn, automatically giving you the rest of the length needed. If each pattern piece has two adjustment lines, divide the total amount of adjustment needed equally among all four lines.

Linings can limit the stretch of the swimsuit fabric, so if you are going to line the front of a swimsuit, add an extra ½" (1.3 cm) of length to the front and back pattern pieces.

Comparison of Bust Size and Torso Length

Bust size	Torso length
30" (76 cm)	52" to 54" (132 to 137 cm)
32" (81.5 cm)	53" to 55" (134.5 to 139.5 cm)
34" (86.5 cm)	54" to 56" (137 to 142 cm)
36" (91.5 cm)	55" to 57" (139.5 to 145 cm)
38" (96.5 cm)	56" to 58" (142 to 147 cm)
40" (102 cm)	57" to 59" (145 to 150 cm)
42" (107 cm)	58" to 60" (147 to 152.5 cm)
44" (112 cm)	59" to 61" (150 to 155 cm)

How to Adjust the Torso Length on the Pattern

(1) **Measure** from indentation at breast bone in front; bring tape measure between your legs to prominent bone at back of neck. Keep the tape measure snug to duplicate fit of finished garment. It is helpful to have someone help you take this measurement.

(2) **Determine** the difference between your torso measurement and the torso length given in the chart, above, that corresponds to your bust size. The pattern needs to be adjusted an amount equal to one-half the difference; distribute this amount equally among the pattern adjustment lines.

(3) **Adjust** the pattern, adding or subtracting length to the pattern by spreading or overlapping front and back pattern pieces on the adjustment lines. In the example shown here, front and back pieces are lengthened ¼" (6 mm) on each adjustment line for a total adjustment of 1" (2.5 cm).

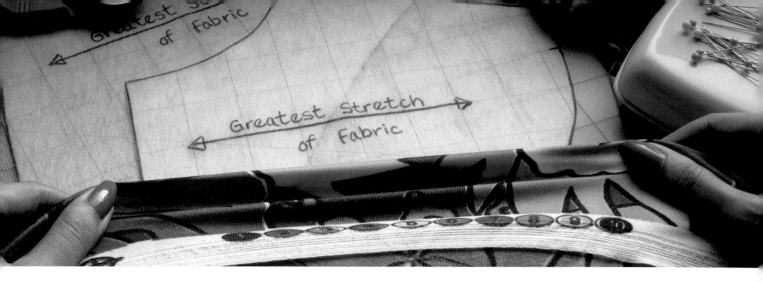

Sewing Swimsuits and Leotards

Before laying out a swimsuit or leotard pattern, determine which direction of the fabric has the greater amount of stretch. Nylon/spandex knits usually stretch more in the lengthwise direction; cotton/spandex, in the crosswise. For a comfortable fit, lay out the pattern on the fabric so the greater amount of stretch will encircle the body.

Swimsuits and leotards are fast and easy to sew. Most styles have only a few seams and edge finishes. Stitch the side seams and crotch seam first; then try on the garment and adjust the fit as needed.

If a one-piece swimsuit or leotard is too long in the torso, shorten it at the shoulder seams; if this raises the neckline, the neck opening can be trimmed as necessary. If the

armholes are too small, causing the garment to bind under the arms, enlarge them by trimming the openings. Leg openings should fit smoothly; if they are too large, take in the side seams at the lower edge, tapering the seams gradually. Stitch the shoulder seams after the fitting, and apply the elastic (pages 216 and 217).

How to Sew a Basic One-piece Swimsuit or Leotard

(1) **Determine** whether the fabric stretches more on lengthwise or crosswise grain. Lay out pattern on fabric so the greater amount of stretch will encircle the body.

(2) **Stitch** center back seam; then stitch crotch seam, applying crotch lining if desired. Stitch side seams. Check garment for fit, opposite.

(3) **Apply** full-front lining, if desired. Stitch shoulder seams. Apply elastic to garment openings (pages 216 and 217).

How to Sew a Basic Two-piece Swimsuit

(1) **Lay** out the pattern as in step 1, opposite. Stitch seams, and machine-baste lining to wrong side of swimsuit top, basting a distance equal to width of elastic from raw edges; trim lining close to the stitching. Center boning, if used, on side seam allowance, positioned so the ends will curve away from body. Stitch over previous stitches along inner edge of boning.

(2) **Apply** elastic to edges of swimsuit top (pages 216 and 217). Make straps; stitch to garment, using narrow zigzag stitch. Pull right end through swimsuit hook, folding ½" (1.3 cm) to wrong side; zigzag across end. Fold left end ½" (1.3 cm) to wrong side; zigzag in place. Garment details, such as center front detail, are sewn following pattern.

(3) **Stitch** center back seam of the swimsuit bottom. Apply full-front lining, if desired. Apply elastic to upper edge and leg openings of swimsuit bottom (pages 216 and 217).

Adjusting for a Good Fit

(1) **Adjust** shoulder seams for snug fit if garment is too long in torso. Adjust neck opening if shoulder adjustment raised the neckline, marking adjustment with chalk, then trimming on marked lines.

(2) **Adjust** armhole openings if the garment binds under the arms, marking the adjustment with chalk, then trimming away excess fabric.

(3) **Adjust** side seams, if necessary, so leg openings fit snugly before the elastic is applied.

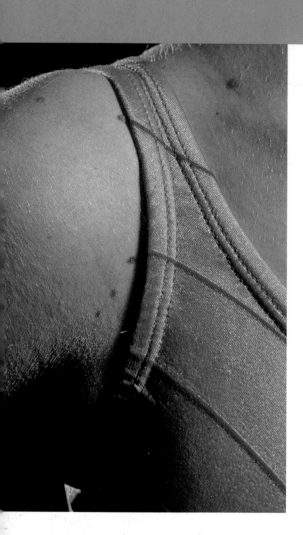

Elasticized Edges

To stabilize edges and to ensure a snug fit on swimsuits and leotards, use elastic at necklines, armholes, waistlines, and leg openings. Elasticized edges also allow you to slip the garment on and off easily. Although elasticized edges do self-adjust to your figure, do not depend on them to solve fitting problems.

If you have not adjusted the neckline, armhole, or leg openings, cut the elastic to the lengths specified by the pattern. If you have changed the size of the openings, follow the guidelines given in the chart below. Most patterns print the cutting information for the elastic on the guide sheet or provide a cutting guide on the pattern tissue. If using a pattern with several views, be sure to cut the elastic for the style you have chosen; for example, a high-cut leg opening requires longer elastic than a standard leg opening.

Cotton braided swimwear elastic or transparent elastic may be used. Both types of elastic, with excellent stretch and recovery, are chlorine-resistant and salt-resistant. Most patterns call for ⅜" (1 cm) elastic for adults' swimwear and ¼" (6 mm) elastic for children's.

Guidelines for Cutting Elastic

Type of Edge	Length to Cut Elastic
Leg opening	Measurement of leg opening minus 2" (5 cm) for adult's garment or minus 1" (2.5 cm) for the child's.
Upper edge of two-piece swimsuit bottom	Measurement of upper edge minus 2" to 3" (5 to 7.5 cm), depending on desired fit. Check to see that elastic fits comfortably over hips.
Armhole	Measurement of armhole.
Neckline	Measurement of neckline. Or for a snug fit on V-necked, low, or scoop necklines, use elastic 1" to 3" (2.5 to 7.5 cm) shorter than neckline.

How to Apply Elastic

Neckline or waistline openings.

① **Join** ends of elastic, using overlapped method (page 203). Divide elastic into fourths; pin-mark, with one pin next to joined ends of elastic. Divide garment opening into fourths; pin-mark. Seams may not be halfway between center front and center back.

② **Pin** elastic to wrong side of fabric, matching edges and pin marks. Place joined ends at center back of neckline or waistline.

③ **Stitch** outer edge of elastic to the garment, using overlock or narrow zigzag stitch; stretch elastic to fit between pins. If using overlock machine, guide work carefully or disengage knives to avoid cutting elastic.

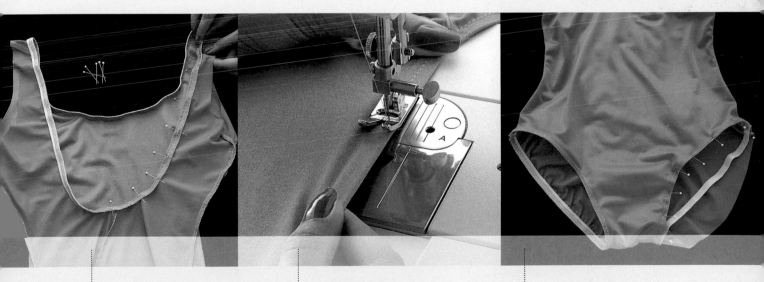

④ **Fold** elastic toward inside of garment, encasing it in garment fabric.

⑤ **Stitch** through all layers, ¼" (6 mm) from folded edge, using long straight stitches or narrow zigzag stitches, stretching as you sew. Or topstitch, using double needle.

Leg openings. Join ends of elastic (page 203). Pin elastic to leg opening, with joint at side seam. Keep elastic relaxed on garment front; remaining elastic will stretch to fit the back of leg opening. Follow steps 3 to 5, stretching elastic as you sew.

HOME DECORATING

Decorator Fabrics

Decorator fabrics have characteristics not found in fashion fabrics. Thread counts, meaning the number of threads per square inch (centimeter), are generally higher in decorator fabrics, making them stronger. Stain-resistant finishes are usually applied to decorator fabrics, since they must go for long periods of time without being cleaned. When cleaning is necessary, most decorator fabrics must be dry cleaned to avoid shrinkage.

The weave pattern, fiber content, and weight of the fabric will have an impact on the finished appearance and durability of home décor items. For window treatments, these fabric characteristics will also determine how they control light and privacy.

Lightweight open weaves include casements, laces, eyelets, and sheers. Often these fabrics are woven in 118" (300 cm) widths, with the width intended to run vertically, allowing you to make floor-length sheer curtains without seams. Novelty sheers have interesting textural features, sometimes arranged in stripes. Most sheers are made of polyester for strength and stability, though they may also contain other decorative fibers. Natural fibers, including cotton and linen, are also used for sheer and lightweight fabrics.

Medium-weight fabrics include a wide range of fiber contents and weave structures. Plain weaves (a) may be solid in color or printed. Their strength is determined by the closeness of the yarns in the weave. Satin weaves (b) are woven so that warp yarns float on the surface over two or three weft yarns, giving the fabric a subtle sheen. They also may be solid in color or printed. Jacquard weaves (c), including damasks, tapestries, and brocades, have woven-in designs. Novelty weaves (d) often solid colors, feature textural interest created by complicated weave patterns. These fabrics are very versatile in any decorating scheme. Decorator pile fabrics (e), such as suede, corduroy, and chenille, have interesting surface textures. They are usually heavier than their fashion-fabric counterparts.

Decorator fabrics for the interior are often made of natural fibers, which include cotton, linen, silk, and wool. Natural fibers are breathable, comfortable, and easy to sew. Unfortunately, these fabrics don't perform well for porches, sunrooms, or outdoors. To keep up with the strong trend toward outdoor decorating, manufacturers are also making water-repellant, fade-resistant, acrylic or polyester decorator fabrics that look and feel like interior fabrics. They are colorfast and are treated to resist stains and mildew.

Performance fabrics intended for use outdoors look and feel like interior decorator fabrics and are available in some of the same prints and colors.

Fabric Preparation

Preshrink any dry-clean-only fabrics by steaming. Move the iron evenly along the grainlines, hovering just above the surface of the fabric. Allow the fabric to dry before moving it. Preshrink washable fabrics by washing and drying in the same way you intend to care for the finished item.

CUTTING DECORATOR FABRICS

After preshrinking, straighten the cut ends of the fabric, using one of the three methods at right. Then mark the other cutting lines, using the straightened edge as a guide. Before cutting full-width pieces of fabric for large home décor projects, such as tablecloths, curtains, or bed covers, pin-mark the placement of each cut along the selvage. Mark out pieces for smaller projects, such as pillows or napkins, with chalk. Double check your measurements and inspect the fabric for flaws. Once you have cut into the fabric, you cannot return it.

To ensure that large décor items will hang or lay straight, the fabric lengths must be cut on-grain. This means that the cuts are made along the exact crosswise grain of the fabric. Patterned decorator fabrics are cut following the pattern repeat rather than the grainline so make sure the fabric you buy is printed on-grain.

a **For tightly woven fabrics** without a matchable pattern, mark straight cuts on the crosswise grain, using a carpenter's square. Align one edge to a selvage and mark along the perpendicular side.

b **For loosely woven fabrics,** such as linen tablecloth fabric, pull out a yarn along the crosswise grain, from selvage to selvage. Cut along the line left by the missing yarn.

c **For tightly woven patterned** decorator fabric, mark both selvages at the exact same point in the pattern repeat. Using a long straightedge, draw a line connecting the two points. If you will be stitching two or more full widths of fabric together, make all the cuts at the same location in the repeat. This usually means that you cut the pieces longer than necessary, stitch them together, and then trim them to the necessary length.

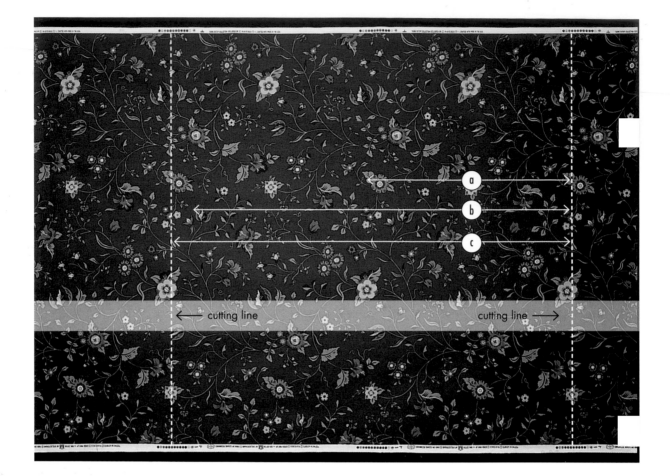

cutting line ←   cutting line →

WORKING WITH PATTERNED FABRICS

Patterned decorator fabrics are designed to match at the seam. Cuts are made across the fabric, from selvage to selvage, following the pattern repeat rather than the fabric grain, so it is very important to purchase fabric that has been printed on grain. Fabrics that are printed slightly off grain can usually be corrected by stretching diagonally, unless they have a polished finish.

The pattern repeat is the lengthwise distance from one distinctive point in the pattern, such as the tip of a particular petal in a floral pattern, to the same point in the next pattern design. Some patterned fabrics have pattern repeat markings (+) printed on the selvage. These markings indicate the beginning of each pattern repeat, and they are especially helpful for fabrics that include several similar designs.

When sewing large items such as curtains or duvet covers, extra yardage is usually needed to match the pattern. Add the amounts needed for any hems, rod pockets, headings, ease, and seam allowances to the finished length, to determine how long the lengths of fabric need to be. Then round this measurement up to the next number divisible by the size of the pattern repeat to determine the cut length. For example, if the pattern repeat (a) is 24" (61 cm), and the needed length (b) is 45" (115 cm), the actual cut length (c) is 48" (122 cm). To have patterns match from one panel to the next, each panel must be cut at exactly the same point of the pattern repeat.

To calculate the amount of fabric needed, multiply the cut length by the number of fabric widths required for the project; add one additional pattern repeat so you can adjust the placement of the pattern on the cut lengths. This is the total fabric length in inches (centimeters); divide this measurement by 36" (100 cm) to determine the number of yards (meters) required.

How to Match a Patterned Fabric

(1) **Place** two fabric widths right sides together, aligning the selvages. Fold back the upper selvage until the pattern matches. Adjust the top layer slightly up or down so that the pattern lines up exactly. Press the foldline.

(2) **Unfold** the pressed selvage, and pin the fabric widths together, inserting the pins in and parallel to the foldline.

(3) **Turn** the fabric over, and check the match from the right side. Make any necessary adjustments.

(4) **Repin** the fabric so the pins are perpendicular to the foldline. Stitch the seam following the foldline; remove the pins as you come to them.

(5) **Check** the match from the right side again. Make any necessary adjustments. Trim away the selvages, cutting the seam allowances to ½" (1.3 cm).

(6) **Trim** the entire fabric panel to the necessary cut length as determined in the project instructions. (Remember your initial cut length for the patterned fabric included extra length to accommodate the pattern repeat.)

SEAMS

All seams in home décor sewing are ½" (1.3 cm) unless otherwise specified. To secure straight seams, backstitch a few stitches at each end. For most projects, avoid using the selvage as a seam allowance edge. Though this tightly woven, nonraveling edge would eliminate the need for extra finishing, it will make the seam pucker and may shrink excessively when steamed or laundered. The exception to this rule is stitching long seams in loosely woven fabrics such as casements or laces.

Long seams tend to pucker in some fabrics. To prevent this, practice taut sewing. As you sew, pull equally on the fabric in front and back of the needle as if the fabric were in an embroidery hoop. Do not stretch. Pull the fabric taut, and let it feed through the machine on its own.

The following seams are the most commonly used seams for home decorator sewing.

Seams for Home Décor Sewing

Plain seam, pressed open, is suitable for almost every fabric and application when you plan to enclose the seam or cover it with lining. If the seam allowances will be exposed or if the item will be laundered often, finish the seam allowances with a zigzag or overlock with a serger.

Plain seam, pressed to one side, is most commonly used for window treatments. The seam allowances are pressed toward the return edge of the curtain (away from the center of the window). Finish the seam allowance edges together, especially if the item will not be lined or if the fabric tends to ravel.

4-Thread or 5-thread safety stitch on a serger trims the seam allowances to a uniform width while stitching a seam and overcasting the seam allowances together. Use this stitch for curtains or any item where the seam allowances are exposed.

Narrow zigzag stitch is used for long seams in loosely woven fabrics or laces. The zigzag allows the seam to relax slightly and prevents puckers. If removing the selvages would cause excessive raveling, leave the selvages on and clip them up to the stitching line every 1" to 6" (2.5 to 15 cm) to allow them to relax.

French seam eliminates raw edges by encasing them. It is especially suitable for lightweight, sheer, and loosely woven fabrics when the item will be laundered or exposed to abrasion. This seam is also used for fashion sewing (page 106), however, for home décor sewing, where the seam allowances are only ½" (1.3 cm), two ¼" (6 mm) seam allowances are sewn.

Pillows

Pillows come in several basic styles: knife-edge, mock box, flange, box, and bolster. From these styles, you can design countless pillows in a wide range of fabrics, using decorative techniques and embellishments to suit every décor, mood, and budget.

The instructions for each style described in this section are for a pillow cover that is stitched closed. If you think you'll never need to remove the stuffing to clean the pillow cover, this is a suitable finish. For pillow covers that are removable, see the section on closures (pages 240 to 245).

Pillow covers can be made to fit ready-made square, rectangular, and round pillow forms. If you want the pillow to be plump and firm, plan the finished size to be at least 1" (2.5 cm) smaller than the pillow form size. If you prefer that your pillow be softer and less plump, plan the finished size to be the same as the form. For pillows in nonstandard sizes and shapes, you can make forms to fit and fill them with the loose stuffing of your choice. For pillows without removable inserts, stuff the filling directly into the pillow cover.

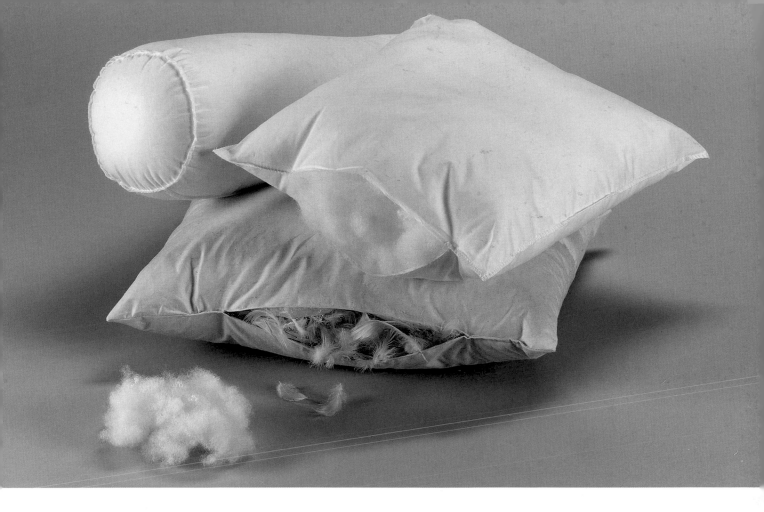

Forms and Fillings

Pillows get their shape from natural or synthetic fillings. Depending on the shape, size, and purpose of a pillow, you can fill it with loose filling or with a pillow form. Forms are great for pillows that will be laundered or dry cleaned because they are easily inserted and removed through a zippered or lapped closure. If you want to be able to remove the filling for cleaning a pillow that is a nonstandard size or shape, make a muslin-covered form in the same shape as the pillow and fill it with the desired material. Loose filling can be stuffed directly into the pillow cover if you intend to stitch it closed.

Forms are available in knife-edge squares from 10" to 30" (25.5 to 76 cm), rectangles, rounds, and bolsters. The most expensive forms are filled with down or a mix of down and feathers. Down-filled pillows can be shaped and slouched to conform to the corner of a sofa. They mold comfortably to your body when you lean on them, but they are brought back to billowy plumpness with a little fluffing. Polyester fiberfill forms imitate some features of down, but they are more resilient or springy than down. Fiberfill forms are lower in cost, washable, and nonallergenic. Different brands of fiberfill forms vary in quality and price—some are more plump, guaranteed not to separate or clump, and have fabric covers as opposed to thin nonwoven synthetic covers.

Manufactured forms aren't necessarily ready for use, especially if they seem high through the center with filling that doesn't reach the corners. You can open a seam and adjust the filling, if necessary, filling out the corners and creating a more even thickness. If you want more plumpness, add some loose fiberfill before sewing the form closed. To use a knife-edge form for a box or mock box pillow, move filling out of the corners and follow steps 3 and 4 for the Mock Box Pillow, page 231, stitching from the outside of the form.

KNIFE-EDGE PILLOWS

The term "knife-edge" means that the front and back of the pillow are the same size and shape and are joined by a single seam around the perimeter. If desired, that seam can also incorporate a decorative element, such as welting, fringe, or a ruffle. Knife-edge pillows can be square, rectangular, or almost any shape you wish to create, though some shapes are better suited to this style than others. Round knife-edge pillows, for instance, will pucker unattractively around the edge.

Square and rectangular knife-edge pillows tend to develop "dog ears" when they are stuffed, because they are thicker in the center than around the edges. This effect can be prevented with the simple shaping technique described in steps 2 to 4, opposite.

How to Make a Knife-edge Pillow

(1) **Determine** the desired finished size of your pillow and add 1" (2.5 cm) in both directions for seam allowances. Cut the pillow front and back along the fabric grainlines.

(2) **Fold** the front into fourths. Mark a point halfway between the corner and the fold on each open side. At the corner, mark a point ½" (1.3 cm) from each edge.

(3) **Trim** a gradually tapering sliver of fabric from the marked point on the fabric edge to the marked corner point. Repeat on the adjoining side to shape the corner.

(4) **Unfold** the front and use it as a pattern for trimming the back.

(5) **Pin** the pillow front to the back, right sides together. Stitch ½" (1.3 cm) seam, pivoting at the corners. Leave an opening on one lengthwise-grain side for stuffing the pillow.

If you will be inserting a pillow form, leave an opening about two-thirds the length of the side. For loose stuffing, a smaller opening will do.

(6) **Press** the seams flat. Then turn back the upper seam allowance and press with the tip of the iron in the crease of the seam. In the area of the opening, press both seam allowances back.

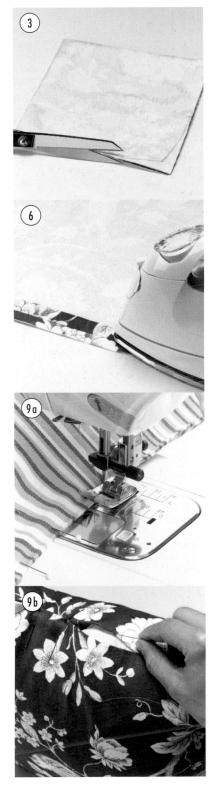

✂ **TIP**

Cut through all four layers at once, if the fabric is fairly lightweight. For heavier fabrics, trim both sides of one corner and then use it as a pattern to trim the remaining three corners.

(7) **Turn** the pillow cover right side out. Square up the corners, using a point turner or similar pointed utensil inserted through the opening. Press lightly.

(8) **Compress** and insert the pillow form, making sure the form sits squarely inside the cover; add fiberfill in the corners, if necessary. Or stuff the pillow with the desired stuffing.

(9a) **Pin** the opening closed, aligning the pressed folds. Edgestitch by machine.

(9b) **Pin** the opening closed, aligning the pressed folds. Slipstitch the opening closed by hand.

MOCK BOX PILLOWS

The mock box pillow, a variation of the knife-edge style, is cube-shaped with soft, undefined edges. Unlike the knife-edge pillow that tapers in depth toward the outer edges, the mock box pillow is chunkier with a consistent depth from center to sides. The depth is created by stitching a vertical seam in each corner of the pillow cover, which shortens the length and width. The length of that seam determines the pillow depth. The larger the pillow, the deeper it can be. For instance, a large floor pillow looks well proportioned with a depth of 6" (15 cm), whereas a smaller sofa pillow looks better at a depth of 2½" to 3" (6.5 to 7.5 cm). The perimeter seam circles the pillow halfway between the front and back. If desired, this seam can incorporate welting.

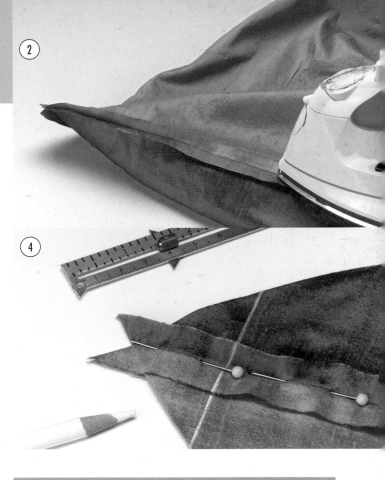

How to Make a Mock Box Pillow

(1) **Cut** out the pillow front and back, aligning the sides to the fabric grainlines. Refer to the chart below for cut size guidelines.

(2) **Pin** the pillow front to the back, right sides together. Stitch ½" (1.3 cm) seam, pivoting at the corners. Leave an opening on one lengthwise-grain side for the stuffing. Press the seam allowances open.

(3) **Pull** the front and back away from each other at one corner, and refold the fabric so that a new corner is formed with the seams in the center. Pin through the seams from front to back to ensure they are aligned.

(4) **Measure** along the seam and mark a point a distance from the corner that equals half the desired pillow depth. Draw a line through the point, perpendicular to the seam, from fold to fold. The length of the line equals the total desired pillow depth. Stitch on the marked line. Do not trim off the corner triangle.

(5) **Repeat** steps 3 and 4 at each corner. Repeat for the corners of the pillow form, if desired. Turn the pillow cover right side out. Insert the form and close the opening as in steps 7 to 9 on page 229.

> ## ✂ TIP
>
> It is helpful to insert a sleeve roll or firm cardboard tube into the pillow cover for pressing the seam allowances open.

The chart at right shows the cut sizes needed for the finished sizes of mock box pillows that will fit standard pillow forms. Cut sizes include ½" (1.3 cm) seam allowances

Finished Size	Depth	Cut Size	Form Size
10" × 10" (25.5 × 25.5 cm)	2" (5 cm)	13" × 13" (33 × 33 cm)	12" × 12" (30.5 × 30.5 cm)
11½" × 11½" (29 × 29 cm)	2½" (6.5 cm)	15" × 15" (38 × 38 cm)	14" × 14" (35.5 × 35.5 cm)
13" × 13" (33 × 33 cm)	3" (7.5 cm)	17" × 17" (43 × 43 cm)	16" × 16" (40.5 × 40.5 cm)
14½" × 14½" (37 × 37 cm)	3½" (9 cm)	19" × 19" (48.5 × 48.5 cm)	18" × 18" (46 × 46 cm)
16" × 16" (40.5 × 40.5 cm)	4" (10 cm)	21" × 21" (53.5 × 53.5 cm)	20" × 20" (51 × 51 cm)
19" × 19" (48.5 × 48.5 cm)	5" (13 cm)	25" × 25" (63.5 × 63.5 cm)	24" × 24" (61 × 61 cm)
24" × 24" (61 × 61 cm)	6" (15 cm)	31" × 31" (78.5 × 78.5 cm)	30" × 30" (76 × 76 cm)

FLANGE PILLOWS

A flange is flat fabric that extends beyond the stuffed portion of a pillow. There are several ways to make a flange. A single flange is formed from two layers of fabric seamed together around the edge. For a double flange pillow, each flange is self-lined. Raw-edge flange pillows are made from two layers of reversible fabrics that do not ravel, such as fleece, felt, faux suede, real suede, or leather. Individual self-lined flange strips can be sewn into

the seams of a knife-edge pillow to make a pillow with contrasting flanges that are interrupted at the corners. The flange width can vary to suit your pillow's size and design. A good width for sofa pillows is 1½" to 2½" (3.8 to 6.5 cm); larger pillows can have wider flanges. Unless the fabric is quite stiff, however, wide flanges tend to flop forward, so that is something to consider if you want to display the pillow standing upright. The easiest way to make a flange

pillow is to stitch the opening closed by machine. However, if you want to be able to remove the pillow form, plan for a plain or decorative overlap closure, a centered zipper closure on the back, or an invisible zipper closure between double flanges.

How to Make a Single Flange Pillow

1) **Determine** the finished size of the stuffed area of the pillow plus twice the width of the flange. Add 1" (2.5 cm) to the width and length for ½" (1.3 cm) seam allowances all around. Cut out the pillow front and back, aligning sides to the fabric grainlines.

2) **Follow** steps 5 to 7 for the knife-edge pillow (page 229). Mark the depth of the flange from the seamed outer edge. Pin the layers together along the marked line to keep them from shifting. Stitch on the marked line, leaving an opening of the same size parallel to the outer opening.

3) **Insert** the pillow form or stuffing into the inner area; do not stuff the flange.

4) **Topstitch** the inner area closed, using a zipper foot. Slipstitch the flange closed, or edgestitch around the entire flange.

How to Make a Raw-edge Flange Pillow

1) **Determine** the finished size of the stuffed area of the pillow plus twice the width of the flange. Cut out the pillow front and back, aligning sides to the fabric grainlines, if necessary.

2) **Mark** the depth of the flange on the pillow front. Pin the front to the back, wrong sides together, along the marked line to keep them from shifting. Stitch on the marked line, leaving an opening along one side for inserting the pillow form.

3) **Insert** the pillow form or stuffing into the inner area. Topstitch the inner area closed, using a zipper foot.

How to Make a Pillow with Contrasting Flanges

1) **Follow** steps 1 to 4 for a knife-edge pillow (page 229). Cut four flange strips the same lengths as the pillow sides and 1" (2.5 cm) wider than twice the desired width of the flange. Fold each strip in half lengthwise, and stitch ½" (1.3 cm) seams across the ends. Turn right side out and press.

2) **Pin** the flange strips to the outer edges of the pillow front, ½" (1.3 cm) from the corners, aligning the raw edges. Baste a scant ½" (1.3 cm) from the edges.

3) **Follow** steps 5 to 9 for the knife-edge pillow (page 229) to complete. Take care that the finished ends of the flanges do not get caught in the stitching.

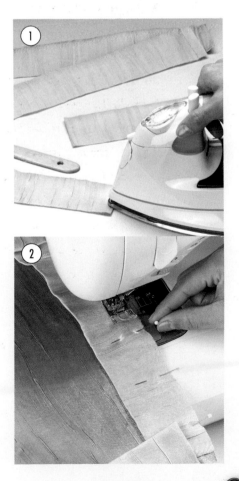

BOX PILLOWS

Box pillows are cube-shaped, with fronts and backs of the same shape and size joined together with a strip of fabric known as a boxing strip. Using this technique, you can make a pillow in any shape, including circles, rectangles, hexagons, triangles, hearts, and stars. Standard pillow forms can be used for square box pillows, but to fill the pillow depth more consistently, make the pillow cover with a width and length 2" (5 cm) smaller than the pillow form size. For nonstandard shapes and sizes, make your own pillow form or insert loose stuffing directly into the cover.

How to Make a Rectangular Box Pillow

(1) **Determine** the finished width, length, and depth of the pillow. Add 1" (2.5 cm) to the width and length for ½" (1.3 cm) seam allowances all around. Cut out the pillow front and back, aligning sides to the fabric grainlines. Cut the boxing strip, with the length equal to the finished distance around the pillow plus 1" (2.5 cm) for seam allowances and the width equal to the finished pillow depth plus 1" (2.5 cm) for seam allowances. If the boxing strip will need to be pieced, allow 1" (2.5 cm) for each piecing seam.

(2) **Piece** the boxing strip together, if necessary, using ½" (1.3 cm) seam allowances. Stitch the short ends of the strip, right sides together, to form a continuous loop. Mark both long edges of the boxing strip with the lengths of each side of the pillow, using a ⅜" (1 cm) clip into the seam allowances. Do not use a joining seam as one of the marks.

(3) **Pin** the boxing strip to the pillow front, right sides together, raw edges even, matching the clip marks on the boxing strip to the pillow corners.

(4) **Stitch** ½" (1.3 cm) seam. At each corner, stop with the needle down in the fabric, and pivot the fabric. The clip marks will spread, allowing the fabric to turn the corner.

(5) **Pin** the other side of the boxing strip to the pillow back, right sides together, matching the clip marks to the corners. Stitch the seam as in step 4, leaving an opening for stuffing the pillow.

(6) **Press** the seams flat. Then, on each seam, turn back the upper seam allowance and press with the tip of the iron in the crease of the seam. In the area of the opening, press both seam allowances back.

(7) **Turn** the pillow cover right side out. Square up the corners, using a point turner or similar pointed utensil inserted through the opening. Press lightly.

(8) **Compress** and insert the pillow form, making sure the form sits squarely inside the cover; add fiberfill in the corners, if necessary. Or stuff the pillow with the desired stuffing. Slipstitch the opening closed.

③

How to Make a Round Box Pillow

① **Make** a pattern for the pillow front and back, using a string-and-pencil compass. Add ½" (1.3 cm) seam allowance all around. Cut out the pattern; use it to cut out the pillow front and back. Multiply the finished diameter by 3.14, and round the measurement up to the nearest fraction of an inch (millimeter) to determine the finished length of the boxing strip; add 1" (2.5 cm) for seam allowances. Cut the boxing strip the desired finished width plus 1" (2.5 cm) for seam allowances.

② **Stitch** the boxing strip into a continuous loop, as in step 2 for the rectangular box pillow. Stitch a scant ½" (1.3 cm) from each edge of the boxing strip. Then clip the seam allowance every ½" (1.3 cm) up to, but not through, the stitching line.

③ **Pin-mark** the pillow front, pillow back, and boxing strip into fourths. Pin the boxing strip to the pillow front, right sides together, raw edges even, matching the pin marks. With the boxing strip facing up, stitch ½" (1.3 cm) seam.

④ **Stitch** the other side of the boxing strip to the pillow back, leaving an opening for turning and stuffing. Finish the pillow as in steps 6 to 8 for the rectangular box pillow, disregarding the reference to corners.

How to Make a Box Pillow with Inside Corners

① **Make** a pattern for the pillow front and back, adding ½" (1.3 cm) for seam allowances all around. Measure the entire outer seamline and add 1" (2.5 cm) to determine the cut length of the boxing strip. Cut the boxing strip to the desired width plus 1" (2.5 cm); piece together as necessary.

② **Mark** the seamlines at any inner corners of the pillow front and back. Using short straight stitches, stay stitch on the seamline, about 1" (2.5 cm) each side of the inner corners, pivoting at the corners. Clip up to, but not through, the stitching lines at the corners.

③ **Prepare** the boxing strip as in step 2 for the round box pillow, left, in areas where the boxing strip will follow an outer curve. Pin the boxing strip to the pillow front, right sides together. Stitch with the boxing strip facing up in areas of straight lines or outer curves. Stop stitching within 2" (5 cm) of any inner corners, and resume stitching 2" (5 cm) beyond the corner.

④ **Complete** the stitching at the inner corners with the boxing strip on the underside. Stitch just to the inside of the staystitching lines.

⑤ **Attach** the other side of the boxing strip to the pillow back, leaving an opening for turning and stuffing. Finish the pillow.

②

④

BOLSTER PILLOWS

Bolsters are cylindrical pillows that offer support for the neck or lower back. With their interesting shape, they are a great addition to the "pillow scene" and versatile enough to be used on beds, sofas, chairs, and window seats. In its simplest form, a bolster is merely a rectangle sewn into a cylinder and drawn closed at each end with a drawstring in a casing. An alternative is to make the cylinder extra long and tie the ends with decorative cording so the pillow resembles a wrapped candy. In a tailored version, the bolster ends are capped with circles of fabric. The cylinder itself can be pieced together from two or more fabrics and the seams can be embellished with welting or other decorator trims.

Bolster forms are available in several sizes, or you can make your own, following step 1, page 238, for a simple bolster.

How to Make a Simple Bolster

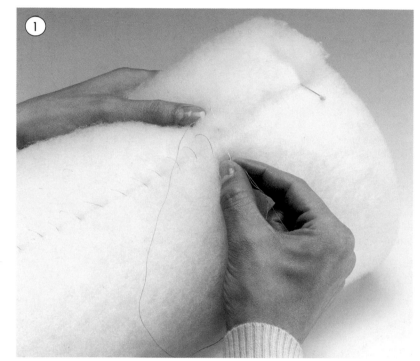

(1) **Cut** a rectangle of batting about 1 yd. (1 m) long, with the width equal to the desired finished length of the bolster. Roll the batting with the desired firmness (the looser you roll it, the softer the bolster will be) until it is the desired diameter; cut off any excess. Whipstitch the cut end to the roll.

(2) **Cut** a rectangle of fabric with the width equal to the circumference of the bolster form plus 1" (2.5 cm) and the length equal to the length of the bolster form plus the diameter plus 1½" (3.8 cm) for casings.

(3) **Press** under ¼" (6 mm), then ½" (1.3 cm) on each short end of the fabric to form the casings. Unfold the ends. Fold the fabric in half lengthwise, right sides together. Stitch ½" (1.3 cm) seam on the lengthwise edge, beginning and ending with backstitches ¾" (2 cm) from the ends; press the seam open.

(4) **Refold** the casings. Edgestitch along the inner folds; reinforce the stitches at the openings. Turn the bolster cover right side out.

(5) **Thread** narrow cording into the casings. Insert the bolster form. Draw up the cording and tie securely. Tuck the cord ends inside the opening, if desired.

✂ TIP

If the bolster form is not completely covered at the ends, place pieces of matching fabric over the ends before tying the cords. The tightness of the drawstring will keep them in place.

How to Make a Candy Wrapper Bolster

(1) **Make** a bolster form as in step 1 for a simple bolster, if necessary. Cut a rectangle of fabric with the width equal to the circumference of the bolster form plus 1" (2.5 cm) and the length equal to the length of the bolster form plus three times the diameter.

(2) **Press** under ¼" (6 mm) on each short end; unfold. Fold the fabric in half lengthwise, right sides together. Stitch a ½" (1.3 cm) seam on the lengthwise edge, beginning and ending with backstitches ¾" (2 cm) from the ends; press the seam open.

(3) **Refold** ¼" (6 mm) at the open ends. Fold the ends under half the diameter of the bolster. Edgestitch along the inner folds; reinforce the stitches at the openings. Stitch again ½" (1.3 cm) from the fold, forming a casing.

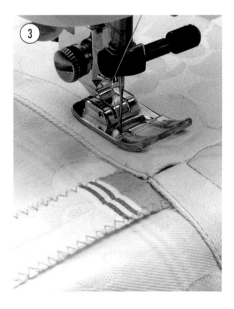

(4) **Thread** narrow cording into the casings. Turn the bolster cover right side out. Insert the bolster form. Draw up the cording and tie securely. Tuck the cord ends inside the opening. Tie decorative cording around the gathers at each end, if desired.

How to Make a Tailored Bolster

(1) **Make** a bolster form as in step 1 for a simple bolster, if necessary. Cut a rectangle of fabric with the width equal to the circumference of the bolster form plus 1" (2.5 cm) and the length equal to the length of the bolster form plus 1" (2.5 cm). Cut two circles of fabric for the ends with the diameter equal to the diameter of the bolster form plus 1" (2.5 cm).

(2) **Fold** the rectangle in half lengthwise, right sides together. Stitch a ½" (1.3 cm) seam on the lengthwise edge, leaving an opening for turning and inserting the bolster form; press the seam open.

(3) **Stitch** a scant ½" (1.3 cm) from the outer edge of each end of the cylinder. Clip into the fabric every ½" (1.3 cm) up to, but not through, the stitching line.

(4) **Pin** a circle to one end, right sides together, aligning the raw edges. The cylinder ends will fan out at the clips. Stitch a ½" (1.3 cm) seam, keeping the outer edges even. You should be stitching just inside the first stitching line. Repeat at the opposite end.

(5) **Turn** the bolster cover right side out. Insert the bolster form. Slipstitch the opening closed.

CLOSURE OPTIONS

Pillows that are used for comfort, tossed about, and handled a lot need closures that will allow you to easily remove the stuffing so the covers can be laundered or dry cleaned occasionally. The options include conventional zippers, invisible zippers, and lapped closures.

The pillow style influences the closure choice as well as the closure location. Invisible zippers, for instance, work well in the seams of plain knife-edge pillows or mock box pillows, especially when the pillows are decorative on both sides. If a knife-edge pillow has welting or ruffles, though, it can be more difficult to insert a zipper in the seam. A conventional zipper or lapped closure in the pillow back would be easier in such cases. If a box pillow needs a zippered closure, it is usually applied into a section of the boxing strip so that the pillow is reversible. Flange pillows that require removable covers can

have zippered, lapped, hook and loop tape, or buttoned closures in the back or decorative buttoned closures in the front.

Sometimes the closure itself is the main decorative feature of the pillow. Items borrowed from the fashion world—like fancy buttons, toggles, frogs, buckles, and fabric or ribbon ties—give these home décor pieces a couture touch.

Zippers

Conventional polyester zippers (not the separating kind) can be inserted in a seam between pieces of the pillow back. The seam can be centered in the pillow back or placed close to one edge so that it is less visible; the seam allowances hide the zipper teeth. Invisible zippers, which must be installed with the use of a special presser foot, are usually placed in the seam between the pillow front and back, where they almost disappear.

Make the zipper closure long enough so that removing and inserting the pillow form will not strain the zipper ends. As a general rule, use a zipper that is at least three-fourths the pillow width. Zippers can be shortened, if necessary, following the directions on page 175.

How to Insert a Conventional Zipper

(1) **Cut** the pillow back 1" (2.5 cm) wider than the front to allow for ½" (1.3 cm) seam allowances at the closure. Fold the pillow back in half, right sides together, if you want the closure to be centered in the pillow back. Fold one edge in 1¾" (4.5 cm), if you want the closure near one edge. Press.

(2) **Mark** the fold at the location of the zipper stops. Stitch ½" (1.3 cm) from the fold, from the pillow edge to the first mark; backstitch. Machine-baste to the second mark. Shorten the stitch length again and backstitch; then stitch to the opposite edge. Cut on the fold; press the seam allowances open.

(3) **Center** the closed zipper facedown over the seam, with the stops at the marks. Glue-baste or pin to the seam allowances only. Finish the seam allowances, catching the zipper tape in the stitches.

(4) **Spread** the pillow back flat, right side up. Mark the top and bottom of the zipper coil with pins. Center a strip of ½" (1.3 cm) transparent tape over the seam from pin to pin. Topstitch a narrow rectangle along the edges of the tape, using a zipper foot. Stitch slowly as you cross the zipper teeth just beyond the stops. Remove the tape. Pull threads to the underside and knot. Remove the basting stitches.

(5) **Finish** the pillow, following the general directions for the pillow style. Rather than leave an opening for turning, simply open the zipper before stitching the final seam.

How to Make a Zipper Closure in a Boxing Strip

1. **Purchase** a zipper that is about 2" (5 cm) shorter than one side of a square box pillow or one-third the circumference of a round pillow. Cut a boxing strip for the zipper section 2" (5 cm) wider than the desired finished width of the boxing strip and equal in length to the zipper tape. Cut a boxing strip for the remaining pillow circumference 1" (2.5 cm) wider than the desired finished width and about 6" (15 cm) longer than the remaining circumference.

2. **Press** the boxing/zipper strip in half lengthwise, right sides together. Machine-baste ½" (1.3 cm) from the fold. Cut on the fold; press the seam allowances open.

3. **Center** the closed zipper facedown over the seam. Glue-baste or pin to the seam allowances only. Finish the seam allowances, catching the zipper tape in the stitches.

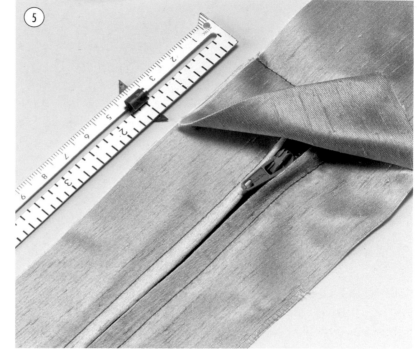

4. **Turn** the zipper strip faceup. Center a strip of ½" (1.3 cm) transparent tape over the entire seam. Topstitch along the edges of the tape from end to end, using a zipper foot (no need to cross the zipper). Remove the tape. Remove the basting stitches.

5. **Press** under 2" (5 cm) on one short end of the boxing strip. Lap the fold over the upper end of the zipper strip to cover the tab. Stitch through all the layers 1½" (3.8 cm) from the fold.

6. **Trim** the boxing/zipper strip to the finished pillow circumference plus 1" (2.5 cm) for seam allowances. Pin the cut end to the bottom of the zipper strip, right sides together. Stitch ½" (1.3 cm) seam, stitching slowly over the zipper teeth. Press the seam allowances away from the zipper. Finish the pillow, following the general directions on page 235. Rather than leave an opening for turning, simply open the zipper before stitching the final seam.

How to Insert an Invisible Zipper

(1) **Open** the zipper; press open the zipper tape from the wrong side to unroll the coils. Center the zipper along one long edge of the pillow back. Mark the right side of the pillow back at the ends of the zipper coil; transfer the marks to the pillow front. Mark the ½" (1.3 cm) seamline on the fabric, using removable fabric marker or chalk.

(2) **Position** the open zipper on the pillow back, right sides together, with the zipper coil aligned to the seamline and ends of coil aligned to the marks. Glue-baste or pin in place. Finish the seam allowance, catching the zipper tape in the stitches.

(3) **Attach** the invisible zipper foot to the machine; position the top of the zipper coil under the appropriate groove of the foot. Slide the zipper foot on the adapter to adjust the needle position so stitching will be very close to the coil; on heavier fabrics set the needle position slightly away from the coil. Stitch, starting at the top of the zipper, until the zipper foot touches the pull tab at the bottom.

(4) **Secure** the other side of the zipper to the pillow front, as in step 2. Position the coils under the zipper foot; slide the zipper foot on the adapter to the opposite side, and adjust the needle position. The bulk of the fabric will be on the opposite side of the needle. Stitch until the zipper foot touches the tab.

(5) **Close** the zipper; pin the pillow front and back right sides together above and below the zipper. Adjust the zipper foot to get as close as possible to the zipper. Stitch the rest of the seam.

(6) **Open** the zipper. Attach the general purpose presser foot, and finish the pillow, following the general directions for the pillow style. Rather than leave an opening for turning, simply open the zipper before stitching the final seam.

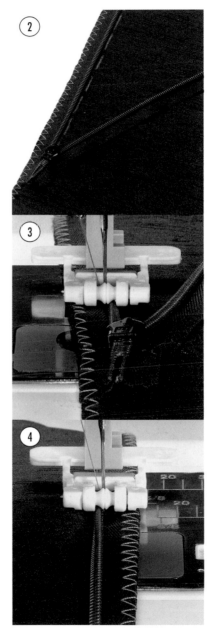

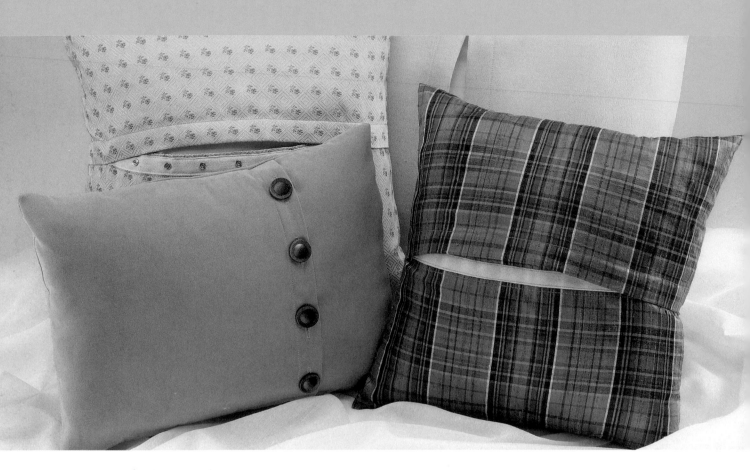

Lapped Closures

A lapped closure is simply two hemmed edges that overlap, similar to that on a button-down shirt. The edges can be held together with fasteners, such as hook and loop tape, snap tape, or buttons. If the edges are overlapped slightly deeper, fasteners are not necessary. Closures that are strictly functional can be placed in the center of the pillow back or near one side. On the other hand, decorative closures showing off fancy buttons or toggles can be positioned on the pillow front.

How to Sew a Plain Lapped Closure

(1) **Cut** two pieces for the pillow back with the length equal to the finished pillow length plus 1" (2.5 cm) and the width equal to half the finished pillow width plus 3½" (9 cm). Press a 1" (2.5 cm) double-fold hem in one long edge of each back piece. Stitch along the inner fold of each piece.

(2) **Overlap** the hemmed edges 2" (5 cm), right sides up. The inner folds will align. Baste across the hem ends. Follow the general pillow directions to complete the pillow. Rather than leave an opening for turning, turn the pillow right side out through the overlapped hems.

How to Sew a Hook and Loop Tape Lapped Closure

(1) **Cut** two pieces for the pillow back with the length equal to the finished pillow length plus 1" (2.5 cm) and the width equal to half the finished pillow width plus 3" (7.5 cm). Press a 1" (2.5 cm) double-fold hem in one long edge of each back piece. Stitch along the inner fold of one piece.

(2) **Cut** strips of ¾" (2 cm) hook and loop tape 3" (7.5 cm) shorter than the hemmed side. Center the loop side of the tape on the right side of the stitched hem. Stitch around the outer edges of the tape.

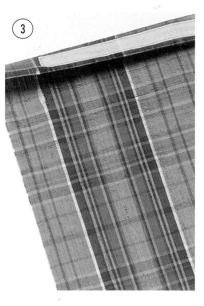

(3) **Unfold** the hem edge of the other pillow back piece. Center the hook side of the tape on the right side of the fabric, between the two pressed folds; stitch around the outer edges of the tape. Refold the hem, and stitch.

(4) **Overlap** the hems and seal the tape. Baste across the hem ends. Follow the general pillow directions to complete the pillow. Rather than leave an opening for turning, unseal the tapes to turn the pillow right side out.

How to Sew a Buttoned Closure

(1) **Follow** step 1 for the hook and loop closure, but stitch both hems in place. Stitch the desired number of evenly spaced buttonholes parallel to and down the center of the

hem of one pillow back piece (or front piece, if closure is decorative). Overlap the hems and mark the button placement through the center of each buttonhole onto the underlapped hem. Sew on the buttons.

(2) **Overlap** and button the hems. Baste across the hem ends. Finish the pillow, following the general directions for the pillow style. Rather than leave an opening for turning, unbutton the hems to turn the pillow right side out.

How to Sew a Snap Tape Lapped Closure

(1) **Follow** the directions for the hook and loop tape closure, left, but extend the snap tape sides into the seam allowances at the ends of the opening. Be sure the snaps align before stitching.

DECORATIVE EDGES

The seams around a pillow are the perfect place for decorative accents. While defining the pillow's lines, accents such as fabric-covered welting and twisted cord welting also lend stability and give the pillow a tailored, classic look. Ruffles soften the pillow lines and create a casual, romantic appearance. Fringes, in every style imaginable, boost plain pillows into the designer category.

Welting

Cording, available in several sizes, can be covered with fabric to make welting. Choose a cording diameter that will complement the pillow's size and shape and work well with the pillow fabric. Narrower welting is more tailored and well suited to small pillows made with lightweight fabrics. Thicker welting is more casual and more prominent in the overall design of the pillow. In order to round corners and fit curves smoothly, fabric strips for making welting are cut on the bias.

Twisted cord welting is an ornate alternative to fabric-covered welting, and is available in a wide range of styles, colors, and sizes. A welt tape, or lip, is attached to a decorative cord for sewing into a seam. From the right side of the welting, the inner edge of the lip is not visible. For easier stitching and a neat appearance on the pillow front, the welting is applied to the pillow back first, right side up. The ends of the welting can be twisted together to join them inconspicuously.

Decorative trims, including twisted welting, tend to unravel easily. Before cutting these trims in the fabric store, the clerk should wrap the trim with tape and cut through the center of the taped area. Likewise, when you begin a project, wrap the trim with tape before cutting to a workable length. Before making final cuts, saturate the trim with liquid fray preventer or fabric glue and allow it to dry completely, then cut through the center of the sealed area.

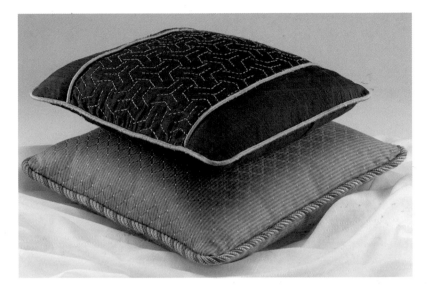

How to Make Fabric-covered Welting

(1) **Fold** the fabric diagonally, aligning the cut end to the selvage. Cut bias strips parallel to the fold 1" (2.5 cm) wider than the cording circumference. Piece strips together to a length a few inches (centimeters) longer than the distance to be welted.

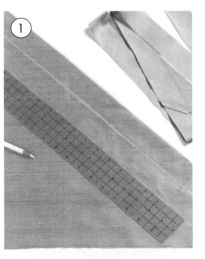

(2) **Fold** the fabric strip around the cording, right side out, aligning the raw edges. Using a cording foot or zipper foot, machine-baste close to the cording. Keep the cording straight and smooth as you sew.

(3) **Stitch** the welting to the right side of the pillow, aligning the raw edges and starting 2" (5 cm) from the end of the welting. Clip and ease the welting at corners; ease the welting around curves.

(4) **Stop** stitching 2" (5 cm) from the point where the ends will meet. Cut off one end of the welting so it overlaps the other by 1" (2.5 cm).

(5) **Remove** the stitching from one end of the welting, and trim the ends of the cording so they just meet.

(6) **Fold** under ½" (1.3 cm) of fabric on the overlapping end of the welting. Lap it around the other end; finish stitching the welting to the pillow edge.

(7) **Finish** the pillow, following the general directions. On seams that carry welting, use a cording foot or zipper. With the wrong side of the welted piece facing up, stitch inside the previous stitching line, crowding the stitches against the welting.

TIP

When you attach twisted welting to a square or rectangular pillow, be sure to taper the pillow corners as in steps 2 and 3 on page 231.

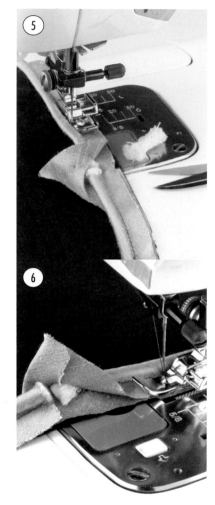

How to Attach Twisted Cord Welting

(1) **Pin** the twisted welting to the pillow back, right sides up, with the beginning and end along one side (not at a corner). Mark each corner with a pin. Remove the trim.

(2) **Hand-tack** the lip to the cord ¼" (6 mm) from each side of each pin. Cut away ½" (1.3 cm) of lip at each corner mark. This will make it easier to attach the welting as it rounds the corners.

(3) **Stitch** the twisted welting to the pillow back, right sides up, using a zipper foot; align the edge of the welt lip to the raw edge of the fabric. Round the cord at the corners and stitch only on the fabric. Leave 1½" (3.8 cm) unstitched between ends; leave 3" (7.5 cm) tails.

(4) **Loosen** the cord from the lip in the area of the join. Trim the lip ends so they overlap 1" (2.5 cm). Separate the cord plies; wrap the end of each ply with tape. Arrange the plies so those on the right turn up and those on the left turn down.

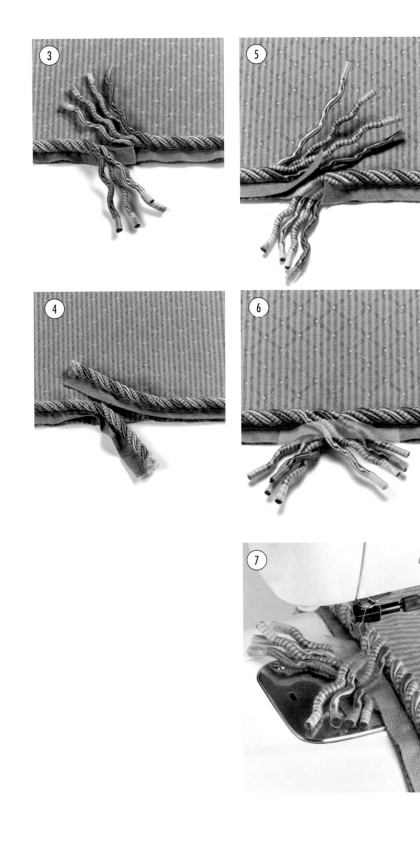

5 **Insert** the plies on the right under the crossed lip ends, twisting and pulling them down until the welting is returned to its original shape. Secure in place using tape.

6 **Twist** and pull the plies on the left over the right plies until the twisted ends look like continuous twisted welting from both sides. Tape in place.

7 **Position** the zipper foot on the left of the needle, if possible. Place the pillow back to the right of the needle; this will allow you to stitch in the direction of the cord twists. Machine-baste through all layers to secure the welting. If you are unable to adjust your machine to stitch in this position, remove the presser foot and stitch manually over the thick cords. Be sure the presser foot lever is down so the thread tension is engaged.

8 **Finish** the pillow, following the general directions for the style. On seams that carry twisted welting, use a zipper foot. With the wrong side of the welted piece facing up, stitch inside the previous stitching line, crowding the stitches against the welting.

Ruffles

Because they will be visible from both sides, self-lined ruffles are best for pillows. Taper square pillow corners, as in steps 2 and 3 on page 229, before attaching ruffles. Then round the corners rather than pivot sharply. The finished pillow will appear square and the ruffles will lie more smoothly around the corners.

How to Make Ruffles

① **Cut** strips of fabric for the ruffles on the lengthwise or crosswise grain of the fabric twice the desired finished width plus 1" (2.5 cm). Piece enough strips together to reach a length two to three times the pillow circumference; piece the strips together in diagonal seams to reduce bulk.

② **Stitch** the ends of the ruffle strip together in a diagonal seam, forming a circle. Fold the strip in half lengthwise, right sides together. Press the fold, if desired, or leave it unpressed for softer ruffles. Prepare the raw edges for gathering by zigzagging over a cord, such as crochet cotton or dental floss, within the ½" (1.3 cm) seam allowance.

③ **Fold** the ruffle into fourths. Make a ⅜" (1 cm) clip into the seam allowances at each fold. Arrange the ruffle on the right side of the pillow front, with the zigzagged cord on top and raw edges even. For a square pillow, match the clips to the corners of the pillow front; for a rectangular pillow, match the clips to the centers of the sides; for a round pillow, match the clips to quarter-marks along the outer edge. Pin at the marks.

④ **Pull** up the gathering cord until the ruffle fits the areas between the marks. Distribute the fullness evenly, allowing extra fullness at the corners so the ruffle can fan out. Pin the ruffle in place. Secure the gathering cord by wrapping the ends around pins.

⑤ **Machine-baste** the ruffle to the pillow front, stitching just inside the gathering row.

⑥ **Finish** the pillow, following the general directions for the style. On seams that have ruffles, with the wrong side of the ruffled piece facing up, stitch just inside the previous stitching line.

Fringe

Types of Fringe

Brush fringe (a) is a dense row of yarns, all cut to the same length. When you see it in the store, the cut edge is usually secured with a chain stitch, which should be left intact until you have finished the pillow. The stitches are then easily removed and the brush fringe can be fluffed out by steaming and gently rubbing.

Cut fringe has a decorative heading and is similar to brush fringe, but is usually not as dense. The cut yarns of this fringe are often multicolored in a blend of fibers.

Loop fringe (b) is made with either a decorative or plain heading and is available in a variety of fibers. Just as the name implies, the fringe is composed of a series of overlapping looped yarns, cords, or ribbons. The loops may be all the same length or arranged in a pattern of varying lengths.

Tassel fringe (c) is a continuous row of miniature tassels attached to a decorative heading. The tassels are often separated by loops and may be multicolored and multifibered.

Ball fringe (d) is a continuous row of pompoms hanging from a plain heading. Though recognized as a casual craft fringe, some styles of ball fringe are more ornate and suitable for embellishing pillows.

Bullion fringe (e) is a continuous row of twisted cords attached to a plain or decorative heading. Styles range from very heavy, long fringe to lightweight, short fringe with single-color or multicolor cords.

Beaded fringes (f) are very chic. They are available in many styles; some resemble cut, loop, or ball fiber fringes but are made with hundreds of beads in all sorts of shapes, sizes, and colors. Bead fringes with decorative headings or ribbons can be sewn to the outer surface of a pillow; those with a plain heading are caught in outer seams where the beads can dangle and swish.

Feather fringe (g) is a trendy embellishment for pillows that are meant to be more decorative than useful. The feathers are usually secured to a plain tape that can be concealed inside a seam or covered with another trim.

How to Attach Fringes

Fringe without decorative heading

(1) **Taper** the corners on square-corner pillows. Machine-baste the fringe to the right side of the pillow front, placing the heading within the ½" (1.3 cm) seam allowance and the fringe facing inward. At the ends, cut the fringe between the loops and hand-stitch the cut ends to prevent raveling; butt the ends together. Finish the pillow following the general directions for the style.

Fringe with decorative heading

(2) **Before** stuffing the pillow, pin the fringe around the front outer edge of the finished pillow cover, aligning the inner edge of the heading to the outer edge of the pillow. Miter the heading at corners. If the heading is thick or textured, use paper-backed, two-sided fabric adhesive. Secure a thin, flat heading using fabric glue or paper-backed fusible adhesive strips.

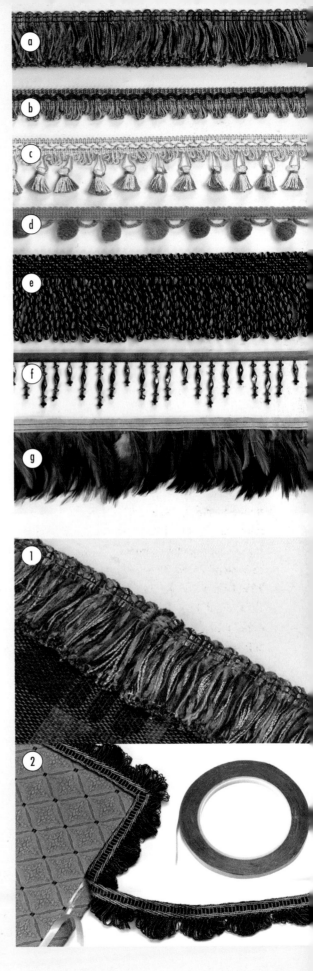

Slipcovers

Slipcovers can give your furniture a fresh start when you want to change the color scheme of a room, update faded or worn upholstery, or simply alter the mood with the changing of the seasons. Whether you are making simple dining chair covers or a fitted cover for a futon mattress, there are some basic techniques you'll use over and over. Follow these guidelines for successful results.

Laying Out and Cutting the Fabric

Whenever possible, lay out all the pattern pieces on the fabric before you start to cut. This allows you to rearrange the pieces as necessary to make the best use of the fabric.

When a patterned fabric with an all-over design is used for slipcovers, little matching is required. When seaming widths of fabric together, the pattern should be matched. If a patterned fabric with a one-way design is used, be careful to lay the pieces in the correct direction of the fabric.

Center large motifs in a print fabric on the top and bottom of the cushion. It is usually impossible to match a fabric pattern across all the seams in a slipcover. Match the pattern in the areas that are most visible, such as the seam between the seat and chair back and the seam between the seat front and the skirt front.

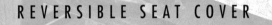

REVERSIBLE SEAT COVER

Simple seat covers give your dining room or kitchen chairs a fresh look. These covers are made with two coordinating decorator fabrics, so they can be flipped over for an instant décor change. Darts sewn at the front corners shape the covers to fit the chair seats smoothly. The back corners are held in place with a button tab that wraps around the back of the leg.

These covers wrap over all four edges of the seat, so they are suitable for armless chairs with straight sides and fronts that are open between the back posts. Because the amount of fabric needed depends on your chair size and the fabric design size, make the pattern first so you'll know how much fabric to buy.

When making covers for two or more chairs, you'll want to center the same motif on each seat cover. If you choose fabric with large motifs, such as the toile shown here, take the pattern with you when you shop for fabric.

YOU WILL NEED

- muslin for making patterns
- two coordinating decorator fabrics, such as a print and a stripe; amount depends on chair size and fabric design size
- four buttons for each cover, ⅞" to 1" (2 to 2.5 cm) in diameter
- ½ yd. (0.5 m) grosgrain ribbon, ⅞" (2 cm) wide, in a color to match the fabrics

Seat Covers

① **Measure** the chair seat side to side and front to back. Add 10" (25.5 cm) in each direction. Cut muslin to this size to make a pattern. Press the muslin pattern in half in both directions. Unfold. Center the pattern on the chair seat, allowing it to fall down over the front and sides. At the back, turn the pattern up along the posts. If necessary, tape the pattern in place.

② **Mark** a dot at one front corner. Pinch the fabric together from the dot down, bringing the front to meet the side. Pin out excess fabric, inserting the pins parallel to the chair leg, forming a dart. Mark lines on both sides of the dart from the dot down to the bottom. Repeat on the other front corner.

③ **Mark** dots at the back of the seat, at the inside front corners of the back posts. (If your posts are round, mark each dot at a point in line with the front and side of the post.) Trace the outline of the chair seat on the pattern.

④ **Remove** the pattern from the chair; remove the pins. Draw lines 4½" (11.5 cm) outside the traced seat lines. At the back corners, draw lines from the dots to the outer lines, forming squares.

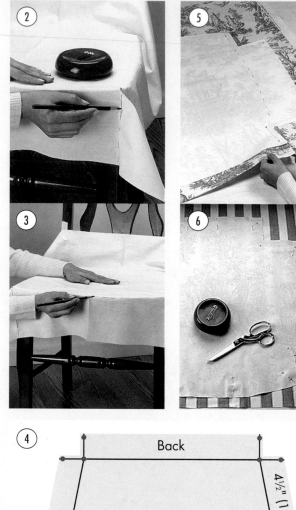

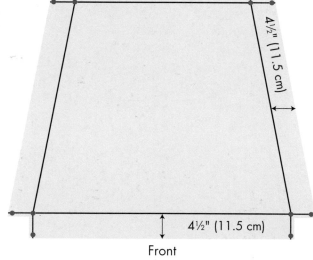

Back

4½" (11.5 cm)

4½" (11.5 cm)

Front

(These will be the stitching lines.) Mark pivot points (shown in blue) on the stitching lines ½" (1.3 cm) from the outer edge. Draw cutting lines ½" (1.3 cm) outside the stitching lines at the legs and the front darts. Fold the pattern in half to make sure it is symmetrical, and make any necessary corrections. Cut out the pattern on the outer lines.

⑤ **Place** the pattern on the top fabric, aligning the front-to-back crease with the lengthwise grain and the side-to-side crease with the crosswise grain. Position the pattern so that the intersection of the creases is at the exact center of the design motif, if using a large print. Cut out the seat cover top. Transfer the pivot points and dart dots to the wrong side of the fabric.

⑥ **Cut out** the remaining seat cover tops, using the first piece as a guide. This will make it easier to center the design motifs. Place each of the tops on the bottom fabric, right sides together. Pin near the outer edges. Cut them out; remove the pins.

⑦ **Fold** the dart on one front corner, right sides together, aligning the raw edges; pin. Stitch the dart.

8) Repeat step 7 for the remaining front corners on the top and bottom pieces. Press the seam allowances of the darts open.

9) Place the top and bottom seat covers right sides together, aligning the raw edges; pin. Align the seams of the front darts. Stitch the layers together ½" (1.3 cm) from the edge all around, pivoting at the corners. Leave a 6" (15 cm) opening along one straight edge for turning.

10) Trim the seam allowances diagonally at the outer corners. Clip to, but not through, the stitches at the inner corners.

11) Turn back the top seam allowances and press, applying light pressure with the tip of the iron down the crease of the seam. In the area of the opening, turn back and press the seam allowances ½" (1.3 cm) where they meet.

12) Turn the cover right side out through the opening. Insert a point turner or similar tool into the opening and gently push the pivot points out to form perfect corners. Push the seam out so that it is centered all around the outer edge; press. Align the folded edges of the opening and pin them closed.

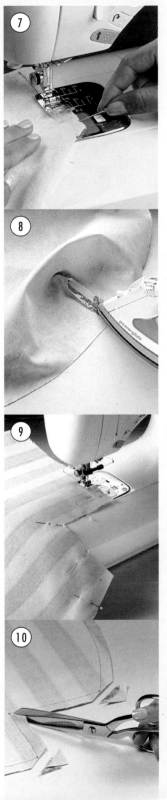

13) Edgestitch around the seat cover, stitching the opening closed; pivot at the corners.

14) Mark placement lines for the four buttonholes parallel to and 1" (2.5 cm) above the lower side and back edges. Mark lines that equal the diameter plus the thickness of the buttons, with one end 1" (2.5 cm) from the vertical edges. Attach a buttonhole presser foot or buttonhole attachment. Stitch the buttonholes over the marked lines. Cut the buttonholes open, using a buttonhole cutter or small, sharp scissors.

15) Place the cover on the chair seat. At the back of one chair leg, measure the distance between buttonholes. Cut ribbon 4" (10 cm) longer than this measurement. Turn under 1" (2.5 cm) twice on each end of the ribbon; press. Stitch across the inner folds, forming double-fold hems. Stitch a button to the center of each hem. Repeat for the other leg. Button the chair seat cover in place.

CUSHIONS

You can make slipcovers for cushions on benches or window seats, as well as for those on sofas or chairs. Most cushions fall into one of the three styles shown at left: knife-edge (top), waterfall (middle), and boxed (bottom). Any of these styles can be fitted flush to the front of the chair or T-shaped, wrapping around the front of the chair arms.

To make it easier to insert the cushion, install a zipper across the back of the slipcover, extending about 4" (10 cm) onto each side. For cushions that are exposed on three sides, install a zipper across the back of the slipcover only. Use upholstery zippers, which are available in longer lengths than dressmaker zippers. For boxed and waterfall cushions, the tab of the zipper will be concealed in a pocket at the end of the zipper opening. This is an upholsterer's technique that gives a professional finish.

Boxed and knife-edge cushions can be sewn with or without welting at the seams. See page 248 for instructions on making and attaching welting. Knife-edge cushions on chairs or sofas usually have a welted seam around the center on sides where the cushion is exposed. If there are hidden sides, such as for a knife-edge seat cushion on a wing chair, the hidden sides are often constructed with a boxing strip. Waterfall cushions, more common in contemporary furniture, are sewn with one continuous piece of fabric wrapping over the front, from top to bottom. This style has a boxing strip around the sides and back and is usually made without welting.

Slipcovers for cushions can often be put on right over the existing upholstery. Sometimes, however, it is better to remove the old cover and insert the cushion into the new slipcover. This is a better option if the slipcover fabric is lighter weight than the upholstery or if there is existing welting that will show through or cause wear on the new slipcover.

For the best fit, pin-fit muslin to the existing cushion to make a pattern for the new cushion cover.

Cutting Directions

Knife-edge Cushion

• If the cushion is rectangular, fairly flat, and soft, like a pillow, cut a cushion cover top to the same dimensions as the original cushion plus 1" (2.5 cm) for seam allowances. Cut the cushion cover bottom 1" (2.5 cm) longer than the top to allow for ½" (1.3 cm) seam allowances at the zipper closure.

• To cover a rectangular cushion that has a thick, firm, foam insert, cut a top and bottom with the width and length equal to the cushion width and length plus the foam depth plus 1" (2.5 cm) for seam allowances.

• If continuous zipper tape is used, cut the zipper tape with the length equal to at least three-fourths of the cushion width, or purchase a conventional zipper with this approximate length.

• Cut fabric strips for the welting long enough to fit the welted section of the cushion.

Waterfall Cushion

• Pin-fit a muslin pattern for the continuous top/bottom piece. Cut a cushion top and bottom piece, using the pattern. Mark the end of the piece that will become the cushion top (with a directional print or napped fabric, the fabric will run in the correct direction only on the top).

• Cut the side boxing strips. Measure the original boxing strip between the seams and add 1" (2.5 cm) for seam allowances. Cut each boxing strip with the length equal to the side measurement of the cushion plus 1" (2.5 cm). Excess length will be cut off during construction.

• If continuous zipper tape is used, cut the zipper tape with the length equal to the back cushion measurement plus 8" (20.5 cm), or purchase an upholstery zipper with this approximate length. Cut two fabric strips for the zipper closure, with the length equal to the length of the zipper tape and the width equal to half the cut width of the boxing strip plus ¾" (2 cm).

Boxed Cushion

• Cut the top and bottom pieces 1" (2.5 cm) larger than the cushion size to allow for seam allowances. For boxed T-cushions, pin-fit a muslin pattern to ensure accurate cutting.

• Measure the original boxing strip between seams and add 1" (2.5 cm) for seam allowances. Cut the boxing strip with the length equal to the total measurement of the front and sides of the cushion. Excess length will be cut off during construction. If piecing is necessary, allow 1" (2.5 cm) for each seam, planning the placement of the seams out of view along the sides of the cushion.

• If continuous zipper tape is used, cut the zipper tape 8" (20.5 cm) longer than the back cushion measurement, or purchase an upholstery zipper with this approximate length. Cut two fabric strips for the zipper closure with the length equal to the length of the zipper tape and the width equal to half the cut width of the boxing strip plus ¾" (2 cm).

• If the cushion will be welted, cut fabric strips for the welting (page 248) with the length equal to twice the circumference of the cushion plus additional length for seaming strips, joining ends, and inconspicuously positioning seams.

Sewing a Knife-edge Cushion Cover

1. **Fold** in the lower edge of the cushion back 1¾" (4.5 cm), right sides together; press. Place the zipper alongside the fold and mark the fold at the location of the zipper stops. Stitch ½" (1.3 cm) from the fold, from the side to the first mark; backstitch. Machine-baste to the second mark; backstitch, then finish the seam to the opposite edge.

2. **Cut** on the fold. Press the seam allowances open.

3. **Center** the closed zipper face-down over the seam, with the stops at the marks. Glue-baste or pin the zipper tape to the seam allowances only. Finish the seam allowances, catching the zipper tape in the stitches.

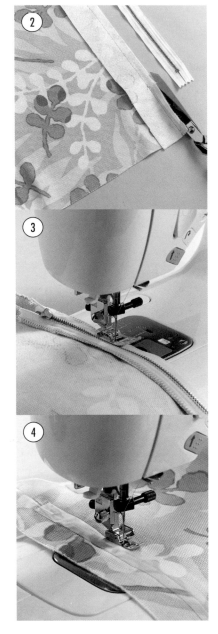

4. **Spread** the cushion cover back flat, right side up. Mark the top and bottom of the zipper coil with pins. Center a strip of ½" (1.3 cm) transparent tape over the seam from pin to pin. Topstitch a narrow rectangle along the edges of the tape, using a zipper foot. Stitch slowly as you cross the zipper just beyond the stops. Remove the tape. Pull threads to the underside and knot. Remove the basting stitches.

5. **Make** welting as on page 248. Sew the welting around the outer edge of the cushion cover top, following the continuous circle method.

6. **Open** the zipper partially. Pin the cover top and bottom right sides together. With the wrong side of the top facing up, stitch just inside the first welting stitches, crowding the cording.

7. **Turn** the cover right side out through the zipper opening.

Sewing a Waterfall Cushion Cover

① **Follow** steps 2 and 3 for the box cushion on page 260. Fold the zipper strip straight across at the corner; mark the opposite edge with a ⅜" (1 cm) clip into the seam allowance. Repeat at the other corner. Pin the zipper strip to the back edge of the cushion bottom, matching the clip marks to the corners. Stitch, beginning and ending about 1½" (3.8 cm) beyond the corners.

② **Mark** the center of the front short end of each side of the boxing strip; round the front corners of the side boxing strips slightly. Mark the outer edges of the top/bottom cushion at the center front. Staystitch a scant ½" (1.3 cm) from the outer edges of the top/bottom piece a distance on either side of the marks equal to the cushion height.

③ **Clip** the seam allowances to the staystitching every ½" (1.3 cm). Pin the side boxing strip to the top/bottom, right sides together, aligning the center marks. Check to see that corresponding points on the top/bottom match up directly across from each other on the boxing strip. Sew ½" (1.3 cm) seam, beginning and ending 6" (15 cm) from the back corners. Repeat on the opposite side.

④ **Follow** steps 7 to 10 on page 261. Open the zipper partially. Finish sewing the boxing strip to the top/bottom on both sides. Turn the cushion cover right side out through the zipper opening.

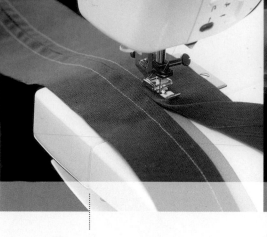

Sewing a Rectangular Boxed Cushion Cover

(1) **Make** welting as on page 248. Sew the welting around the outer edge of the cushion top and cushion bottom, following the continuous circle method.

(2) **Press** under ¾" (2 cm) seam allowance on one long edge of the zipper strip. Position the folded edge of the strip along the center of the zipper teeth, right side up. Using a zipper foot, topstitch ⅜" (1 cm) from the fold. Repeat for the opposite side, making sure folds meet at the center of the zipper. If using continuous zipper tape, attach the zipper pull to the tape.

(3) **Center** the zipper strip over the back edge of the cushion top, right sides together. Stitch the zipper strip to the cushion top, beginning and ending on the sides about 1½" (3.8 cm) beyond the corners. Clip into the zipper strip seam allowance at each corner to allow the fabric to spread, and pivot.

(4) **Align** the center of the boxing strip to the front center of the cushion top, matching the print, if necessary; pin-mark the pieces separately. Smooth the boxing strip to the right front corner; mark with a ⅜" (1 cm) clip into the seam allowance. Smooth the boxing strip along the right side of the cushion top; pin the boxing strip to the cushion top about 6" (15 cm) from the back corner.

(5) **Stitch** the boxing strip to the cushion top, beginning at the side pin and sewing ½" (1.3 cm) seam. For a welted cover, use a welting foot or zipper foot. Match the clip mark to the front corner; pivot the stitching at the corner.

(6) **Continue** stitching the boxing strip to the cushion top, matching the center marks. Clip once into the boxing strip seam allowance at the left front corner; pivot. Stop stitching about 6" (15 cm) from the back left corner.

7 **Cut** the boxing strip 4" (10 cm) beyond the point where it overlaps the zipper pull end of the zipper strip. Pin the end of the boxing strip to the end of the zipper strip, right sides together, matching all cut edges.

8 **Stitch** together 2" (5 cm) from the end; pivot at the zipper tape. Stitch along the outer edge of the zipper tape to within ½" (1.3 cm) of the end; pivot. Place a small scrap of fabric over the zipper teeth. Stitch slowly across the teeth to the opposite side of the zipper tape; pivot. Stitch along the opposite side of the zipper tape until 2" (5 cm) from the end; pivot, and stitch to the edge.

9 **Fingerpress** the seam allowance toward the boxing strip. Finish sewing the zipper strip and boxing strip to the cushion top. A small pocket forms to hide the zipper pull when the cover is closed.

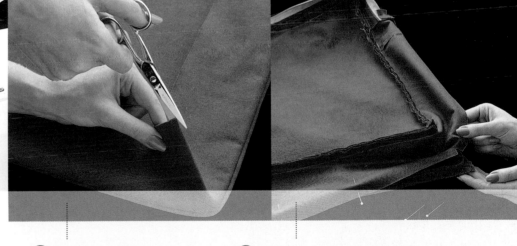

10 **Cut** the opposite end of the boxing strip 1" (2.5 cm) beyond the point where it overlaps the end of the zipper strip. Pin the ends together. Stitch ½" (1.3 cm) from the ends, placing a scrap of fabric over the zipper teeth and stitching slowly. Turn the seam allowance toward the boxing strip. Finish sewing the zipper strip and boxing strip to the cushion top.

11 **Fold** the boxing strip straight across at the corner; mark the opposite side of the boxing strip with a ⅜" (1 cm) clip into the seam allowance. Repeat for all the corners.

12 **Open** the zipper partially. Pin the boxing strip to the cushion bottom, matching the clip marks to the corners. Stitch. Turn the cover right side out through the zipper opening.

Sewing a Boxed T-cushion Cover

(1) **Cut** muslin about 4" (10 cm) larger than the top of the cushion; mark the grain line at the center of the fabric. Place the muslin over the cushion; pin along the seamline, smoothing out the fabric. Mark the seamline along the pin marks.

(2) **Remove** the muslin. True the seamlines, using a straightedge. Fold the muslin in half to check that the piece is symmetrical; make any necessary adjustments. Add ½" (1.3 cm) seam allowances to the pattern. Cut the pieces as in the cutting directions (page 257).

(3) **Press** under a ½" (1.3 cm) seam allowance on one long edge of each zipper strip. Position the folded edges of the strips along the center of the zipper teeth, right sides up. Using a zipper foot, topstitch ⅜" (1 cm) from folds.

(4) **Press** under 2" (5 cm) on one short end of the boxing strip. Lap the boxing strip over the zipper strip to cover the zipper tab. Stitch through all layers 1½" (3.8 cm) from the folded edge of the boxing strip.

(5) **Make** and apply welting as on page 248. Stitch welting to the right side of top and bottom pieces.

(6) **Place** the boxing strip on the slipcover top, right sides together; center the zipper on the back edge. Start stitching 2" (5 cm) from the zipper end, crowding the cording. Clip the corners as you come to them; stop stitching 4" (10 cm) from the starting point.

(7) **Clip** to mark the seam allowances at the ends of the boxing strip. Stitch the boxing strip ends together. Trim off excess fabric; finger press the seam open. Finish stitching the boxing strip to the slipcover top.

(8) **Fold** the boxing strip, and clip the seam allowance to mark the lower corners; be sure all corners are aligned with the corners on the slipcover top. Open the zipper.

(9) **Place** the boxing strip and slipcover bottom right sides together. Match the clips of the boxing strip to the corners of the slipcover bottom; stitch. Turn the cover right side out.

(10) **Fold** the cushion to insert it into the cover. Stretch the cover from front to back. Close the zipper. Smooth the cover from center to edges. Stretch the welting taut from corner to corner to square the cushion.

Alternative zipper placement. Install the zipper across the back of the slipcover, without extending it around the sides, if the slipcover will be exposed on three sides.

FUTON COVER

A futon is affordable and multi-functional. It can easily be converted from a chair or sofa to a bed by changing the position of the futon frame from an upright to a reclining position. The futon mattress often comes with a fabric cover that is not only decorative, but also protects the mattress from becoming stained or worn. You can sew your own futon mattress cover that coordinates with the decorating scheme of the room.

Make the cover so the lengthwise grain runs from the seat to the back, rather than from arm to arm. Run the seams from the seat to the back. For ease in inserting or removing the mattress, the cover is constructed with a zippered closure that extends along three sides. Custom-sized zippers are available from upholstery shops and many fabric stores. Or you can use continuous zipper strip, cut it to the right length, and add the zipper tab.

Working with large pieces of fabric can be awkward. Set up a table next to your sewing cabinet or table, on your left side. By holding excess fabric at the same height as the sewing machine, it will be easier to feed the fabric to the machine and control the extra weight.

Cutting Directions

• Cut the front and back pieces for the futon cover, with the length and width of the pieces 1" (2.5 cm) longer and wider than the finished width of the futon cover. To piece decorator fabric, run a full width of fabric up the center and add equal, partial widths at the sides of both the front and back.

• Cut one piece for the boxing strip that is 1" (2.5 cm) longer than the length of the futon cover and 1" (2.5 cm) wider than the thickness of the mattress. Cut one zipper tab, 4" (10 cm) long, with the cut width of the tab equal to the cut width of the boxing strip.

• For the zippered boxing on one long side of the cover, cut two zipper strips, with the length of the strips 1" (2.5 cm) longer than the finished length of the mattress; the cut width of the zipper strips is 1¼" (3.2 cm) wider than one-half the finished width of the boxing strip. For the zippered boxing on the short sides of the cover, cut four zipper strips, each 1" (2.5 cm) longer than the finished width of the mattress and 1¼" (3.2 cm) wider than one-half the finished width of the boxing strip.

- decorator fabric

- zipper, with the length of the zipper tape equal to combined length of the two ends and one side of the mattress plus 1" (2.5 cm)

Sewing the Futon Cover

① **Stitch** one short zipper strip to each end of one long zipper strip in ½" (1.3 cm) seams, right sides together; start stitching at the raw edge and stop ½" (1.3 cm) from the opposite raw edge. Finish seams, using overlock or zigzag stitch; press open. Repeat, using remaining short and long zipper strips.

② **Place** the zipper strips right sides together, matching the raw edges and seams. Machine-baste ¾" (2 cm) from the long edge where stitching of the end seams extends to the raw edge. Finish seams; press open.

③ **Fold** the strip in half, right sides together, with one seam allowance extending. Place the closed zipper facedown over seam allowances, with the teeth centered on the seamline and the ends of the zipper tape even with the ends of the strip. Machine-baste the zipper tape to the extended seam allowance.

④ **Unfold** the strip. On right side, center a strip of ¾" (2 cm) transparent tape over seamline. Stitch on both sides of the tape, securing the zipper. Remove the tape and basting stitches.

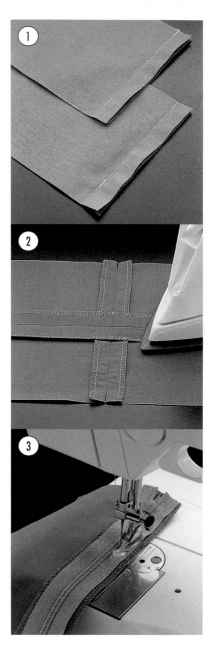

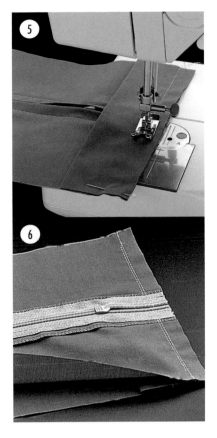

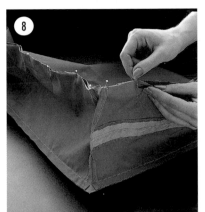

5) **Press** the zipper tab in half, with wrong sides together. Open the zipper about 2" (5 cm). At the top end of the zipper, place the tab over the zipper strip, right sides up; stitch across the end, a scant ½" (1.3 cm) from the raw edges, stitching carefully over the zipper teeth.

6) **Stitch** ends of the boxing strip to ends of the zipper strip, right sides together, stitching ½" (1.3 cm) seams; start and stop ½" (1.3 cm) from the raw edges. Finish seams; press open.

7) **Pin** the boxing strip to the futon cover front, right sides together, matching seams to corners. With the boxing strip faceup, stitch ½" (1.3 cm) seam, pivoting at corners.

8) **Pin** the opposite side of boxing strip to the futon cover back, right sides together, matching seams to corners; stitch. Finish remaining seams.

9) **Open** the zipper; turn the futon cover right side out. Insert the futon mattress; close the zipper, hiding the zipper pull under the tab.

PARSONS CHAIR

Parsons chairs are popular dining room chairs, with upholstered backs that adjoin upholstered seats. The lines are very tailored and straight, and there is often a floor-length skirt. These one-piece slipcovers conceal the entire chair and have skirts with inverted box pleats at the corners.

These directions are suitable for chairs with straight backs. The upper edge of the chair back must be no wider than the lower back, or you won't be able to slip the cover on. When measuring the front and back of the chair back, measure as if there are centered side seams, even if the seams on the upholstered chair are not centered.

The skirt for this style is self-lined, eliminating any noticeable hemline and giving the skirt extra body.

Pin-fitting the Pattern

(1) **Measure** the length and width of the front of the chair back. Add 4" (10 cm) to the length and the width. Cut muslin to size. Mark a center line on the lengthwise grain. Mark a line 1" (2.5 cm) from the raw edge at the upper edge on the muslin.

(2) **Repeat** step 1 for the back of the chair back. Label the pattern pieces.

(3) **Pin** the front and back pattern pieces of the chair back, wrong sides together, at the upper marked line matching the center lines. Center the patterns on the chair back and pin the patterns at the sides of the chair, allowing ample ease. Mark the side seams on both the front and back pieces.

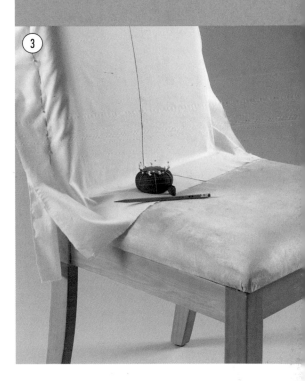

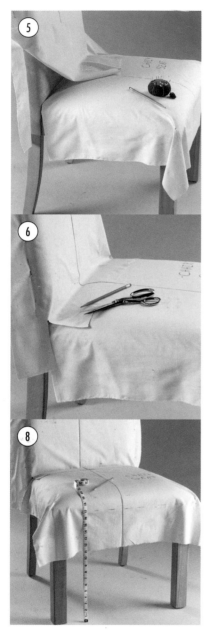

4 **Measure** the length of the chair seat from the back to where the cushion meets the frame at the front. Measure the width from where the cushion meets the frame at the sides. Cut muslin 6" (15 cm) larger than measurement. Mark a center line on the lengthwise grain. Label the pattern piece.

5 **Press** under 1" (2.5 cm) along the back of the chair seat pattern perpendicular to the center line. This will become the stitching line. Center the pattern on the chair seat with the pressed fold even with the chair back and smooth the fabric in place. Pin out excess fabric at the front corners, forming darts. Mark the dart seam lines with a pencil.

6 **Mark** dots on the front of the chair back pattern and on the fold of the chair seat pattern where the patterns meet at the outer edges of the seat back. Cut straight up from the bottom to the dots on the front chair back piece, allowing the fabric to spread so the side can be smoothed downward and the center bottom between dots can be smoothed forward under the seat pattern.

7 **Pin** the seat pattern to the front chair back pattern at the sides. Mark the seam on the front chair back piece between dots, even with the fold of the seat pattern. Continue marking the seam line down the sides of the front chair back even with the fold of the seat pattern.

8 **Measure** the distance from the floor to where the seat cushion meets the frame at the chair front. Record the measurement. Mark a seam line on the patterns all around the chair at this height from the floor.

9 **Remove** the patterns from the chair and redraw seam lines as necessary. Reposition the patterns on the chair; adjust as necessary. Add ½" (1.3 cm) seam allowances to all pattern pieces. Cut out the patterns.

Sewing the Slipcover

1. **Using** the muslin patterns, cut one of each piece from the decorator fabric, matching the fabric design across seams, if necessary. Transfer all markings.

2. **Staystitch** the lower corners of the front piece, pivoting at the dots. Clip up to, but not through, the stitched corner.

3. **Stitch** darts on the front corners of the chair seat. Trim the excess fabric ¼" (6 mm) from the stitching, and press the seam allowances open.

4. **Pin** the chair seat to the front, matching the dots and lower edges. Stitch ½" (1.3 cm) seam. Finish the seam allowances and press them open.

5. **Pin** the front/seat to the back at the sides and top. Stitch. Using a ½" (1.3 cm) seam, stitch the chair front and back together across the top and down the sides. Finish the seam allowances and press them open.

6. **If welting** is desired, cut bias strips 1⅝" (4 cm) wide. The length of the welting is equal to the circumference of the lower edge of the slipcover. Make and apply welting as on page 248.

7. **Measure** the lower edge of the slipcover between the front darts. Add 14" (35.5 cm) for seam and pleat allowances to determine the width of the front skirt piece. Repeat for the sides, measuring from the dart to the side seam. Repeat for the back, measuring between side seams. To determine the length of the skirt pieces, double the measurement you recorded in step 8 of making the pattern, and add 1" (2.5 cm). At this length, the skirt will brush the floor. Adjust the measurement if you want it shorter. Cut the four skirt pieces.

8. **Stitch** the skirt pieces together into a circle, using ½" (1.3 cm) seams. Press the seam allowances open. Fold the skirt in half crosswise, wrong sides together. Baste the upper edges together within the ½" (1.3 cm) seam allowance.

9. **Mark** with pins 6½" (16.3 cm) on each side of one of the skirt seams. Fold the skirt at the pin marks and bring the folds to the seam to form an inverted box pleat. Pin the pleat in place. Repeat at the three remaining seams.

10. **Check** the fit of the skirt; adjust the sizes of the pleats if necessary. Baste across the tops of the pleats within the ½" (1.3 cm) seam allowance. Baste the skirt to the chair seat and back, right sides together. Place the slipcover on the chair and check the length of the skirt. Adjust if necessary. Stitch ½" (1.3 cm) seam. Finish the seam allowances together, and press them away from the skirt.

Window Treatments

TERMS TO KNOW

These words and phrases are often used to describe window treatments and construction techniques.

Bias. Any diagonal line intersecting the lengthwise and crosswise grains of fabric. While woven fabric is very stable on the lengthwise and crosswise grains, it has considerable stretch on the bias.

Buckram. Stiffened fabric that gives support to the headings of pleated draperies. Buckram, available in the decorating department of fabric stores, comes on a roll in a standard width of 4" (10 cm). It is also available, though sometimes harder to find, in 5" and 6" (13 and 15 cm) widths for making draperies with deeper headings. You can purchase the length you need. Because cut edges of buckram will not fray, it is also useful for making templates for marking the pleats and spaces.

Clearance. The distance between the back of the rod or treatment and the wall or undertreatment, measured at the front and sides. There must be enough clearance so the layers of the window treatment do not interfere with each other.

Crosswise grain. On woven fabrics, the crosswise grain is perpendicular to the selvages. Fabric has slight "give" in the crosswise grain.

Cut length. The total length at which fabric pieces should be cut for the treatment. It includes allowances for any hems, headings, rod pockets, and ease.

Cut width. The total width the fabric should be cut. If more than one width of fabric is needed, the cut width refers to the entire panel after seams are sewn, including allowances for any side hems.

Finish. To improve the durability of a seam, the raw edges are secured with stitches that prevent them from fraying. This can be done with zig-zag stitches that wrap over the edge or with serging.

Finished length. The total length of a treatment after it is sewn.

Finished width. The total width of the treatment after it is sewn, including the depth of the returns.

Flounce. An extra-long heading sewn at the top of a rod-pocket curtain that falls forward over the rod pocket.

Fullness. The finished width of a treatment compared to the length of the rod or mounting board. For example, two times fullness means that the width of the fabric is two times the length of the rod.

Heading. The portion at the top of a rod-pocket treatment that forms a ruffle when the treatment is on the rod. The depth of the heading is the distance from the finished upper edge to the top stitching line for the rod pocket.

Interlining. A layer of fabric encased between the top fabric and the lining to prevent light from shining through or to add body to the treatment.

Lengthwise grain. On woven fabrics, the lengthwise grain runs parallel to the selvages. Fabrics are generally stronger along the lengthwise grain.

Lining. A fabric backing sewn to the face fabric to provide extra body, protection from sunlight, and support for side hems.

Miter. A square corner is made by joining two pieces with a seam at a 45-degree angle.

Mock up. Sometimes it is necessary to make a test curtain to find accurate measurements. Do this by cutting up inexpensive muslin or an old sheet and hanging it from the rod in the same manner you intend to hang the finished treatment.

On-grain. When the lengthwise and crosswise yarns in woven fabric are perfectly perpendicular to each other. If the fabric is not on-grain as it is printed, it will be impossible

to match up the pattern or to have a treatment that hangs evenly with straight-cut lower edges.

Overlap. On traversing draperies, the panels lap over each other at the center. The standard overlap distance is 3½" (9 cm).

Pattern repeat. The lengthwise distance from one distinctive point in the fabric pattern, such as the tip of a particular petal in a floral pattern, to the same point in the next pattern design.

Projection. The distance a rod or mounting board stands out from the wall.

Railroading. Normally the lengthwise grain of the fabric runs vertically in a window treatment. Since decorator fabric is usually 54" (137 cm) wide, treatments that are wider than this must have vertical seams joining additional widths of fabric. Railroading means the fabric is turned sideways, so the lengthwise grain runs horizontally. The full width can then be cut in one piece, eliminating the need for any seams.

Return. The portion of the treatment that extends from the end of the rod or mounting board to the wall, blocking the side light and view.

Rod pocket. The fabric tunnel where the curtain rod or pole is inserted. Stitching lines at the top and bottom of the pocket keep the rod in place.

Self-lined. A fabric panel lined to the edge with the same fabric. Rather than cutting two pieces and sewing them together, one double-length piece is cut, folded right sides together, and stitched on the remaining three sides, so one edge will have a fold instead of a seam.

Selvage. The narrow, tightly woven edges of the fabric that do not ravel or fray. These should be cut away on firmly woven fabrics before seaming to prevent puckering of long seams. On loosely woven fabrics, the selvages should not be trimmed off because they are needed for support.

Stacking space. The distance from the sides of the window to the end brackets of the hardware that allows traversing draperies to clear or partially clear the window when the draperies are open. This is sometimes referred to as stackback. Roughly estimated at one-third of the total treatment width, this distance must be figured into the finished width of the treatment so you know what size rod to buy.

Undertreatment. A window treatment—curtains, draperies, blinds, or a shade—installed under the top treatment, either inside or outside the window frame. The undertreatment is mounted on its own hardware, independent of the top treatment.

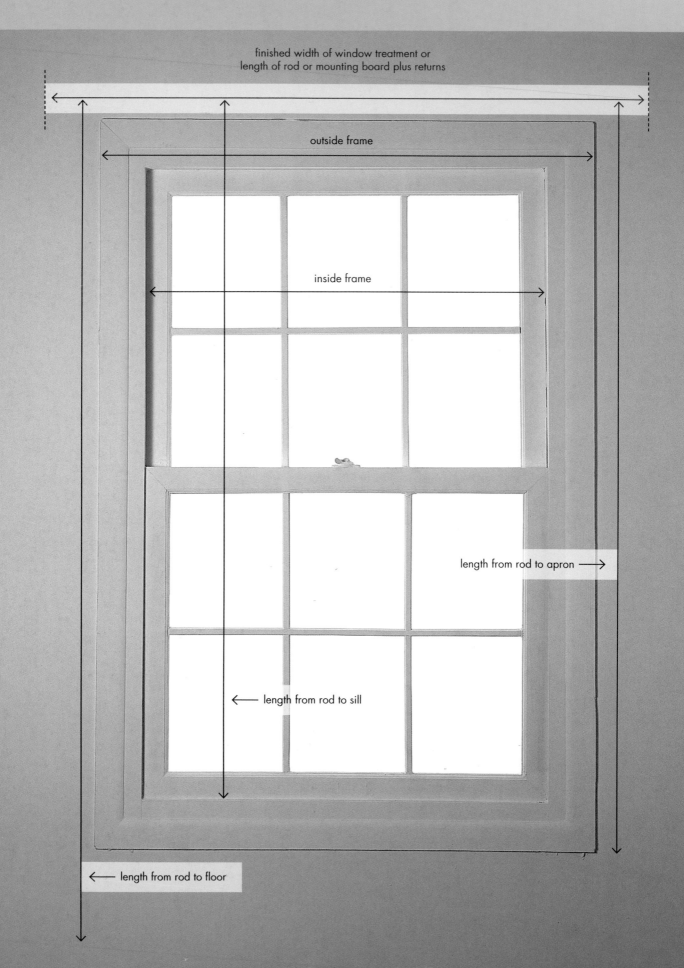

finished width of window treatment or
length of rod or mounting board plus returns

outside frame

inside frame

length from rod to apron →

← length from rod to sill

← length from rod to floor

MEASURING THE WINDOW

Sketch the window treatment to scale on graph paper, to help you determine the most pleasing proportion for the treatment as well as the correct placement of any hardware. After installing the hardware, take all necessary measurements, using a steel tape measure for accuracy, and record the measurements on the sketch.

For each project, you will need to determine the finished length and width of the treatment. The finished length is measured from the top of the mounting board or rod, or from where you want the upper edge of a curtain, to where you want the lower edge of the window treatment. The finished width is determined by measuring the length of the rod or mounting board. For treatments with returns, the finished width includes twice the projection of the rod or mounting board.

Specific instructions for determining the cut lengths and widths of the fabric are given for each project in this book. In general, the cut width is determined by multiplying the finished width by the amount of fullness desired. Fullness describes the finished width of the curtain or valance in proportion to the length of the rod or mounting board. For example, two times fullness means that the width of the curtain measures two times the length of the rod.

Yardage requirements can be determined by multiplying the cut length by the number of fabric widths needed to obtain the cut width. Special considerations for determining yardage requirements for patterned fabrics are given on page 222.

Tips for Measuring

Plan the proportion of the layers in a window treatment so the length of the top treatment is about one-fifth the length of the overall treatment. The top treatment may be installed higher than the window, to add visual height to the overall treatment. In some cases, it may be desirable to start the top treatment at the ceiling, provided the top of the window frame is not visible at the lower edge of the top treatment.

Plan for the shortest point of a top treatment to fall at least 4" to 6" (10 to 15 cm) below the top of the window glass. This prevents you from seeing the window frame as you look upward at the top treatment.

Allow ½" (1.3 cm) clearance between the lower edge of the curtain and the floor when measuring for floor-length curtains.

Add 2" (5 cm) to the measurement for floor-length curtains for a window treatment that breaks on the floor.

Add 20" (51 cm) to the measurement for floor-length curtains for a window treatment that puddles on the floor.

Measure for all curtains in the room to the same height from the floor, for a uniform look. Use the highest window in the room as the standard for measuring the other windows.

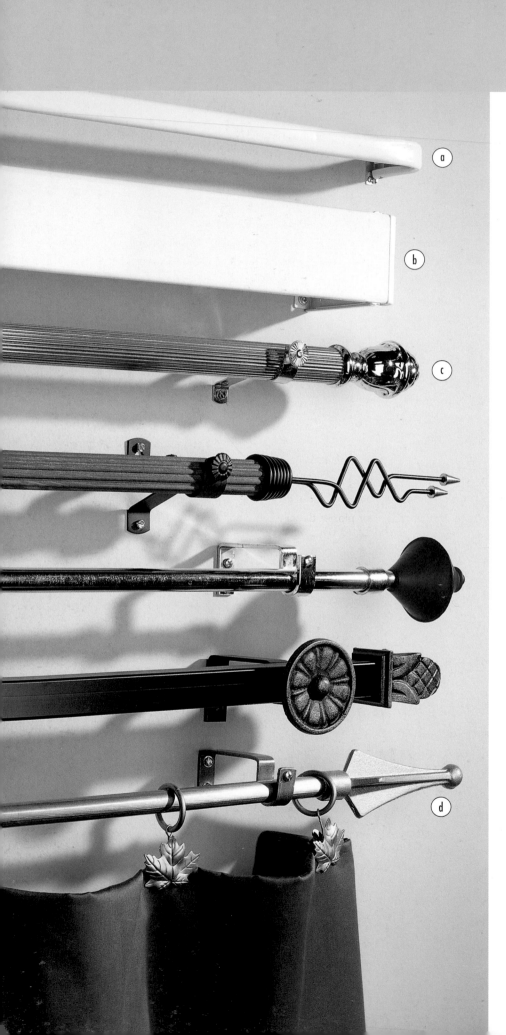

SELECTING AND INSTALLING HARDWARE

Conventional and decorative rods are available in many styles. Window treatments that have a rod pocket may be mounted on narrow curtain rods (a) or wide curtain rods (b), which are available in either 2½" (6.5 cm) or 4½" (11.5 cm) widths. Decorative metal rods and wood poles with ornate finials (c) are suitable for treatment styles that reveal all or part of the rod, such as tab curtains. They may be used with decorative rings (d), which are sewn or clipped to the top of a curtain panel.

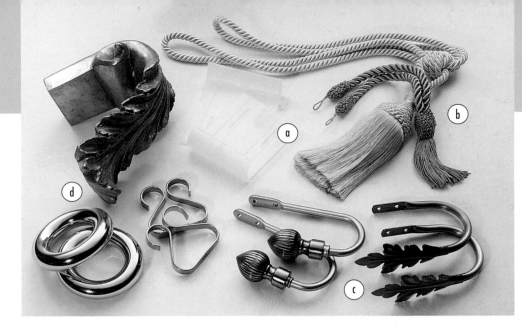

Hardware accessories are both decorative and functional. Concealed tieback holders (a) fit behind the last fold of pleated or rod-pocket draperies to prevent the tieback from crushing the draperies. Cord-and-tassel tiebacks (b) are used with concealed or decorative holders to hold draperies in place. Holdbacks (c), as the name implies, hold back a stationary curtain or drapery without the use of tiebacks. Swag holders (d), in a wide range of styles, support the draped fabric in swag window treatments. Some styles are meant to be concealed, while others are obviously decorative.

Conventional traverse rods, designed for pleated draperies, are available in white, ivory, and wood tones. Drapery hooks are inserted so the pleats conceal the rod when the treatment is closed. Valances or cornices are used over the top of the draperies to completely conceal the rod. Flexible traverse rods are used for pleated draperies on bow windows.

Window treatment hardware is available in a wide range of styles to suit any decorating plan. Consider both decorative and functional needs when selecting hardware. Some curtain rods are designed to be covered completely by the fabric, while others may have decorative finishes and ornate finials that enhance the treatment. Select and install the hardware before measuring for the window treatment, because the cut length of the fabric will vary depending on the hardware placement.

Window treatment hardware is packaged complete with mounting brackets, screws or nails, and installation instructions. Use screws alone if installing through drywall or plaster directly into wall studs. When brackets are positioned between wall studs, support the screws for lightweight treatments with plastic anchors in the correct size for the screws. If the brackets must support a heavy window treatment, use plastic toggle anchors in the correct size for the wallboard depth, or use molly bolts. If nails are supplied with the hardware, use them only for lightweight treatments installed directly to the window frame. Otherwise, substitute screws or molly bolts that fit through the holes in the brackets.

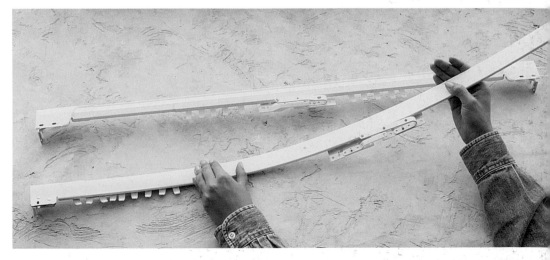

How to Install Brackets Using Plastic Anchors

(1) **Mark** screw locations on wall. Drill holes for plastic anchors, using drill bit slightly smaller than diameter of plastic anchor. Tap anchors into drilled holes, using hammer.

(2) **Insert** screw through hole in bracket and into installed plastic anchor. Tighten screw securely; anchor expands in drywall, preventing it from pulling out of wall.

How to Install Brackets Using Plastic Toggle Anchors

(1) **Mark** screw locations on wall. Drill holes for plastic toggle anchors, using drill bit slightly smaller than diameter of toggle anchor shank.

(2) **Squeeze** wings of toggle anchor flat, and push toggle anchor into hole; tap in with hammer until it is flush with wall.

(3) **Insert** screw through hole in bracket and into installed anchor; tighten screw. Wings spread out and flatten against the back side of drywall.

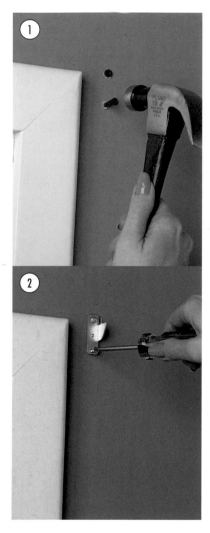

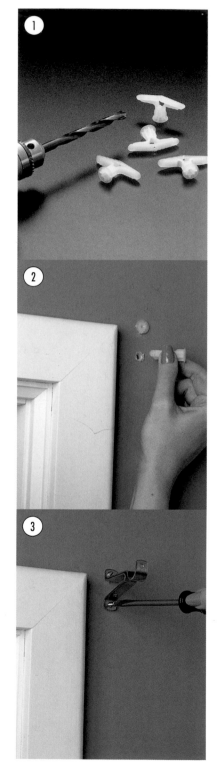

How to Install Brackets Using Molly Bolts

(1) **Mark** screw locations on wall. Drill holes for molly bolts, using drill bit slightly smaller than the diameter of molly bolt.

(2) **Tap** molly bolt into drilled hole, using hammer; tighten screw. Molly bolt expands and flattens against back of drywall.

(3) **Remove** screw from molly bolt; insert the screw through hole in bracket and into installed molly bolt. Screw the bracket securely in place.

How to Install a Traverse Rod

(1) **Mount** the end rod brackets with the U-shaped socket facing upward.

(2) **Hook** the lipped support clip of the center bracket over the center of the rod; position the rod, fitting the ends of the rod into the end brackets. Mark the screw holes for the center bracket.

(3) **Take** the rod down, and mount the center bracket. Lift the rod into position again; snap the center support clip over the rod, hooking it into the groove at the front of the rod. Using a screwdriver, turn the cam on the underside of the bracket, locking the clip in place.

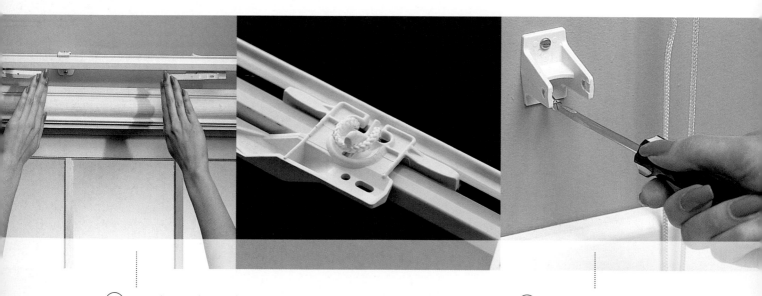

(4) **Push** the overlap and underlap master slides to the opposite ends of the rod. At the left side, reach behind the underlap slide for the cord. Pull

the cord slightly to form a small loop; hook the loop securely over the plastic finger that projects from the back of the master slide.

(5) **Separate** the stem from the pulley base; hold the base against the wall near the floor, directly below a point 2" (5 cm) in from the right end bracket of the rod. Mark screw locations; mount the bracket.

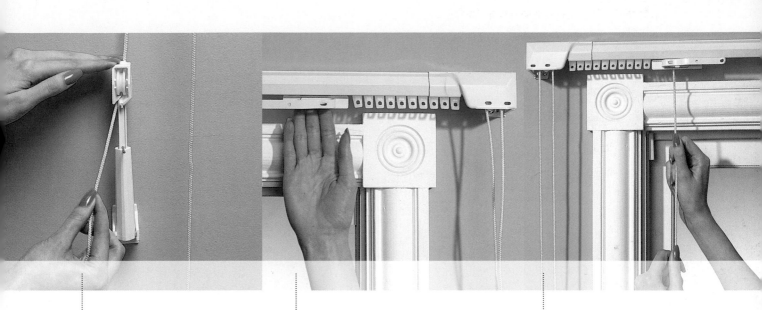

6 **Attach** the stem to the pulley base. Pull up on the cord housing, exposing the hole on the inner stem. Insert a small nail through the hole so the stem remains extended. Attach the cord to the pulley, slipping the loop end of the cord through the slot in the cord housing.

7 **Reach** behind the overlap master slide at the right end of the rod; locate the two knots at the back of the slide.

8 **Pull** the knot nearest the glides until the cord hanging at the side of the rod is taut against the pulley wheel. Tie a new knot in the cord at the back of the slide, with excess cord hanging down. Remove the nail from the inner stem of the pulley. Cut off the excess cord; tighten the knot securely.

COVERING AND INSTALLING MOUNTING BOARDS

Many window treatments, including Roman shades and a variety of valance styles, are mounted on boards, rather than on drapery hardware.

The mounting board is covered with fabric to match the window treatment or with drapery lining, and the window treatment is then stapled to the board. The treatment may be installed as an outside mount, securing it to the window frame or to the wall above the window frame. For an inside mount, the treatment is installed inside the upper window frame, flush with the front of the frame.

Supplies include mounting board, angle irons, pan-head screws, and molly bolts.

The size of the mounting board varies, depending on whether the board-mounted window treatment is an inside or outside mount and whether it is being used alone or with an undertreatment. When using stock, or nominal, lumber, keep in mind that the actual measurement differs from the nominal measurement. A 1 × 2 board measures ¾" × 1½" (2 × 3.8 cm), a 1 × 4 measures ¾" × 3½" (2 × 9 cm), a 1 × 6 measures ¾" × 5½" (2 × 14 cm), and a 1 × 8 measures ¾" × 7¼" (2 × 19 cm).

For an inside-mounted window treatment, the depth of the window frame must be at least 1½" (3.8 cm), to accommodate a 1 × 2 mounting board. Cut the mounting board ½" (1.3 cm) shorter than the inside measurement across the window frame, to ensure that the board will fit inside the frame after it is covered with fabric.

The projection (page 273) necessary for an outside-mounted top treatment depends on the projection of any existing undertreatment. If the undertreatment is stationary, allow at least 2" (5 cm) of clearance between it and the top treatment; if the undertreatment traverses, allow at least 3" (7.5 cm) of clearance. If there is no undertreatment or if the undertreatment is mounted inside the window frame, use a 1 × 4 board for the top treatment. Cut the mounting board at least 2" (5 cm) wider than the outside width of the window frame. Install the board using angle irons that measure more than one-half the projection of the board.

For an outside-mounted Roman shade, use 1 × 2 board, cut 2" (5 cm) longer than the outside width of the window frame. Attach the board flat to the wall for a ¾" (2 cm) projection. This allows the shade to rest close to the window frame for optimum light control and privacy.

Cutting Directions

Cut the fabric to cover the mounting board, with the width of the fabric equal to the distance around the board plus 1" (2.5 cm) and the length of the fabric equal to the length of the board plus 3" (7.5 cm).

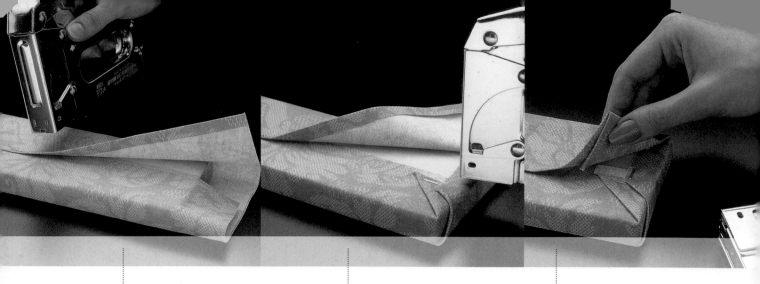

How to Cover the Mounting Board with Fabric

(1) **Center** board on wrong side of fabric. Staple one long edge of fabric to board, placing staples about 8" (20.5 cm) apart; do not staple within 6" (15 cm) of ends. Wrap fabric around board. Fold under ⅜" (1 cm) on long edge; staple to board, placing staples about 6" (15 cm) apart.

(2) **Miter** fabric at corners on side of the board with unfolded fabric edge; fingerpress. Staple miters in place near raw edge.

(3) **Miter** fabric at corners on side of the board with folded fabric edge; fingerpress. Fold under excess fabric at ends; staple near fold.

How to Install an Inside-mounted Board

(1) **Cover** mounting board. Attach window treatment to mounting board. Hold board in place against upper window frame, with wide side of board up; align front edge to frame.

(2) **Predrill** screw holes through the board and up into window frame, using ⅛" drill bit; drill holes within 1" (2.5 cm) of each end of board and in center for wide window treatments. Adjust the placement of holes to avoid screw eyes, if any. Secure board, using 8" x 1½" (20 x 3.8 cm) round-head screws.

How to Install an Outside-mounted Board

1. **Cover** mounting board. Attach window treatment to board. Mark screw holes for angle irons on bottom of board, positioning angle irons within 1" (2.5 cm) of each end of board and at 45" (115 cm) intervals or less.

2. **Predrill** screw holes into the board; size of drill bit depends on screw size required for angle iron. Screw angle irons to board.

3. **Hold** board at desired placement, making sure it is level; mark screw holes on wall or window frame. Remove angle irons from board.

4. **Secure** angle irons to the wall, using 1½" (3.8 cm) flat-head screws, into wall studs; if angle irons are not positioned at wall studs, use molly bolts or toggle anchors instead of flat-head screws.

5. **Reposition** window treatment on angle irons, aligning screw holes; fasten screws.

Roman shade mounted with ¾" (2 cm) projection. Install board flat to wall at desired location above window, predrilling holes through board into wall. Secure with 8 x 2½" (6.5 cm) flat-head screws into wall studs; use molly bolts or toggle anchors if not screwing into wall studs.

HEMS

If you have measured, figured, and cut accurately, your window treatments should fit perfectly once they are hemmed. For curtains and draperies, follow the procedure used in professional workrooms: sew the lower hems first, the side hems next, and the heading last.

Side and lower hems of curtains are always double to provide strength, weight, and stability. The most accurate way to make a double-fold hem is to press the full hem depth under first, and then open and turn the cut edge under up to the foldline. Cut off the selvages evenly before pressing the side hems.

Curtains hang better when hems are weighted or anchored. Sew small weights into the hems at the lower corners and bottoms of seams to keep the curtain from pulling or puckering.

How to Sew a Double-fold Hem

Lower hem. ① Turn under and press the full hem allowance on the lower edge; 8" (20.5 cm) for floor-length curtains or 6" (15 cm) for sill-length curtains. Unfold and turn the cut edge under to meet the foldline; press outer fold.

② **Tack** drapery weight to hem allowance at each seam. Refold on inner foldline, encasing cut edge; pin. Stitch hem.

Side hem. Turn under and press 1½" (3.8 cm) double-fold side hems as in step 1 for lower hem; pin. Tack drapery weights inside hems, about 3" (7.5 cm) from lower edge. Refold and stitch hem.

Three Ways to Finish Hems

Straight-stitch on folded hem edge, using eight to ten stitches per inch (2.5 cm). Use thread to match solid color fabric or blend with multicolor fabric. Stitch slowly through multiple layers.

Machine blindstitch. Adjust machine to blindstitch setting and attach blindstitch foot. Fold hem under, leaving inner fold extending ⅛" (3 mm). Align guide in foot to soft fold. Adjust stitch width to take tiny bite into soft fold.

Fused hem. Fuse paper-backed adhesive strip to hem; remove paper backing, and fuse hem in place. Follow manufacturer's instructions for fusing. Press from both sides.

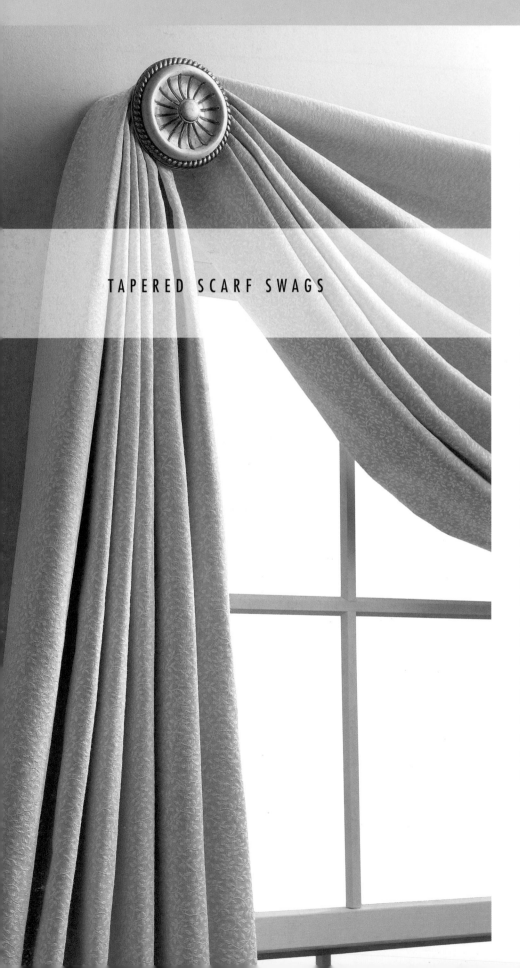

TAPERED SCARF SWAGS

Tapered scarf swags drape into smooth, even folds and are lined for extra body. Used alone to punctuate the top of a window or as a complement to draperies or blinds, the versatile tapered scarf swag is suited for many décor styles. Depending on the fabric and hardware chosen, as well as the length of the tails, a tapered scarf can work in rooms as varied as a breakfast nook and a stately living room.

Design swags that drape into a single swoop or into multiple swoops. The tails can stop just short of, break at, or puddle on the floor (the last is most formal). Shorter tails that come to the bottom of the window frame or to points two-thirds or one-third the window length have ends that angle up and in toward the window. In this method, the shaping of the swag is achieved by cutting wedges of excess fullness from a length of fabric at each point where the swag crosses a swag holder or pole. The swag is then constructed by sewing the angled pieces together and adding a lining.

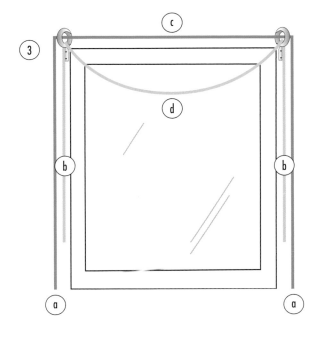

This scarf swag uses the full width of the fabric and can be either self-lined or lined in a contrasting fabric. Nearly any decorator fabric can be used, from semisheer to brocade. Even one-way prints are suitable, because the direction of the fabric can be switched at a tail seam.

Holders for mounting the swags are available in several styles, including medallions and scarf rings; decorative tieback holders and holdbacks can also be used. A tapered swag with a single swoop can also be draped over a decorative pole. Mount the holders at the upper corners of the window frame and in any other desired locations before beginning the project, and measure for the treatment using twill tape.

How to Measure for a Single Swoop

(1) **Mount** the swag holders or decorative pole in the desired locations. Drape a length of twill tape over the holders or pole, extending to the desired length of the sides and stretching straight across the top of the window. This will be the finished length of the top and outer sides of the swag.

(2) **Drape** a second length of twill tape over the holders or pole, extending to the desired shortest points of the tapered sides and dipping to the lowest point desired at the center of the swoop. This will be the finished length of the bottom and inner sides of the swag. Mark both tapes at the holders or outermost points on the pole.

YOU WILL NEED

- decorative swag holders (one holder at each upper corner of the window for a swag with a single swoop, and one holder for each additional swoop) or decorative pole

- tools and hardware for installation

- twill tape

- decorator fabric for swag, length determined in step 1, page 290 for swag with single swoop or step 1, page 291 for swag with multiple swoops

- matching or contrasting fabric for lining, length equal to decorator fabric

- double-sided carpet tape, optional

(3) **Measure** and record the lengths of the tape for each section. Measurement (a) is from the long point to the holder or pole, (b) is from the short point to the holder or pole, (c) is the distance straight across between the holders or along the pole, and (d) is the length of the lower edge of the swoop.

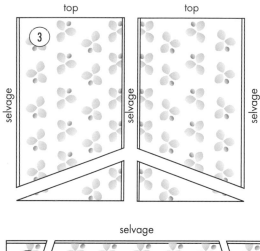

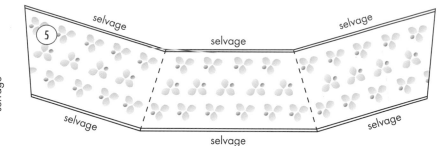

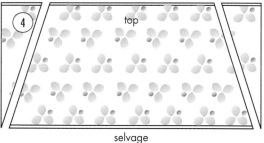

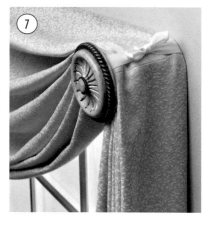

How to Sew a Single Swoop

(1) **Cut** the full width of the fabric, with the length equal to measurement (d) plus two times measurement (a) plus 3" (7.5 cm) for seam allowances. Measure from each end of the fabric a distance equal to (a) plus 1" (2.5 cm). Cut across the fabric perpendicular to the selvages at these points, to separate the end pieces from the center.

(2) **Turn** one end piece completely around, if you are using fabric with an obvious one-way design, so the upward direction on both ends points toward the middle; when hung the design will face in the correct direction on both end pieces. Label the top of each end piece.

(3) **Subtract** measurement (b) from measurement (a). Mark a point on the inner edge of one end piece this distance from the lower cut edge. Draw a line from this point to the lower outside corner; cut away the triangular wedge. Repeat for the other end piece, cutting the angle in the opposite direction.

(4) **Subtract** measurement (c) from measurement (d); divide this measurement in half. Mark a point on the top edge of the center piece this distance from one cut end. Draw a line from this point to the lower corner; cut away the triangular wedge. Repeat for the opposite cut end of the center piece.

(5) **Trim** off the selvages. Cut the lining, using the swag pieces as patterns; label the tops of the lining pieces. Stitch the swag pieces together using ½" (1.3 cm) seams, easing the edges to fit; repeat for the lining pieces. Press the seam allowances open.

(6) **Pin** the lining to the swag, right sides together. Stitch a ½" (1.3 cm) seam all around, leaving an opening along the center top for turning. Trim the corners diagonally. Press the lining seam allowance toward the lining.

(7) **Turn** the swag right side out; press the seamed edges. Slipstitch the opening closed. Fanfold the swag along the seam lines, keeping the number and depth of folds consistent. Tie the folds with twill tape. Hang the swag through scarf rings or over medallion-style scarf holders or tieback holders. Or hang the swag over a pole, with the center swoop in front. Arrange the folds in the swag and sides. Remove the twill tape. If necessary, secure the fabric to the holder or pole inconspicuously, using double-sided carpet tape.

How to Measure for Multiple Swoops

(1) **Mount** the swag holders or pole in the desired locations. Drape a length of twill tape over the holders or pole, extending to the longest points of the tapered sides and stretching straight across the top of the window or pole. This will be the finished length of the top of the swag.

(2) **Drape** a second length of twill tape over the holders or pole, extending to the shortest points of the tapered sides and dipping to the lowest point desired at the center of each swoop. This will be the finished length on the bottom of the swag. Mark both tapes at the holders or at the attachment points on the pole.

(3) **Measure** and record the lengths of the tape for each section. Measurement (a) is from the long point to the holder or pole. Measurement (b) is from the short point to the holder or pole. Measurement (c) is the distance straight across between the holders or along the pole. Measurement (d) is the total length of all the swoops between the end holders or end attachment points to the pole.

How to Sew Multiple Swoops

(1) **Cut** the full width of the fabric, with the length equal to measurement (d) plus two times measurement (a) plus 1" (2.5 cm) for each swoop plus an additional 2" (5 cm). Measure from each end of the fabric a distance equal to measurement (a) plus 1" (2.5 cm). Cut across the fabric perpendicular to the selvages at these points. Follow steps 2 and 3 on page 290.

(2) **Measure** the length of the center piece; divide this measurement by the number of swoops in the swag. Mark the center piece into lengths of this size; cut the fabric perpendicular to the selvages at these points.

(3) **Subtract** measurement (c) from measurement (d). Divide this measurement by the number of swoops in the swag; then divide this number in half. Mark a point on the top edge of one swoop piece this distance from one cut end. Draw a line from this point to the lower corner; cut away the triangular wedge. Repeat for the opposite cut end of the same piece. Cut identical wedges from each remaining swoop piece. Complete the swag as on page 290, steps 5 to 7.

GATHERED PICKUP VALANCE

A gathered pickup valance begins as a flat, lined rectangle with a rod pocket and heading. At evenly spaced intervals, vertical rows of tucks are sewn into the valance, drawing the lower section of the valance up into graceful bells. The fabric between the bells falls into gentle swags. Welting at the lower edge accents and supports the curves of the bells and swags. A contrasting fabric, used to line the valance, peeks from the inside of each bell.

When planning the design of the valance, work with enough full and half widths of fabric to equal about two-and-one-half times fullness. Bells are positioned at each seam and at each midpoint between seams. Though you usually shouldn't position prominent details of a window treatment at seams, this pattern of placement coincides with the placement of large motifs in most decorator fabrics, allowing the main motifs to fall in the center of each swag.

The valance hangs straight down at the returns to a length that is about 6" (15 cm) longer than the center of each swag. The shortest point at the back of each bell is about 2" (5 cm) shorter than the swags.

Medium-weight decorator fabrics work well for this valance. To add body and a slightly padded appearance, interline the valance with flannel. Select contrasting fabric for the lining and for the fabric-covered welting.

Mount the valance on a plain narrow pole with elbows or a utility rod just above and to the outside of the window frame.

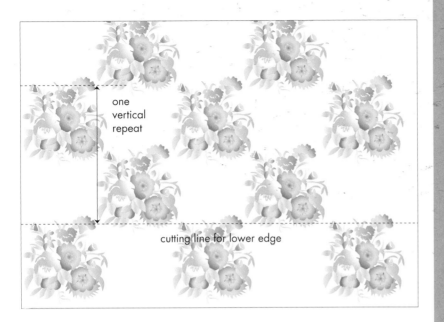

one
vertical
repeat

cutting line for lower edge

Cutting Directions

- The cut length of the valance fabric Is equal to the finished length at the side (from the underside of the rod to the hem) plus twice the rod-pocket depth plus twice the heading height plus 1" (2.5 cm).

- The cut width of the valance is equal to the rod length plus twice the projection of the rod, multiplied by two-and-one-half times fullness. After calculating the full cut width, divide this number by the fabric width and round to the nearest number of full and half widths to piece together.

- Cut the fabric for the contrast lining to the same length and width as the valance fabric.

- If interlining is desired, the cut width of the interlining fabric is equal to the total width of the valance fabric after seaming. The cut length of the interlining fabric Is equal to the finished length of the valance. If possible, railroad (page 273) the interlining to avoid seams.

- Cut bias fabric strips if making fabric-covered welting, following step 1 on page 248.

- In fabrics with large motifs, one complete vertical repeat will have two rows of motifs with staggered placement. One row will have two full motifs, while the second row will have one full motif in the center and two halves of another motif matching at the selvages. Cut the valance pieces with the primary motifs in the lower 12" to 15" (30.5 to 38 cm), so they will be more visible in the finished valance.

How to Make a Gathered Pickup Valance

1. **Seam** the valance fabric widths together. Repeat for the lining. Check to see that the valance and lining are exactly the same size.

2. **Make** fabric-covered welting (page 248), if desired, and stitch it to the lower edge of the valance; begin and end the welting ½" (1.3 cm) from the side edges. Alternatively, attach purchased welting. For a valance without interlining, omit step 3.

3. **Seam** the interlining, if necessary. Pin the interlining to the wrong side of the lining along the sides, with the lower edge of the interlining ½" (1.3 cm) above the lower edge of the lining. Baste within the ½" (1.3 cm) seam allowances on the sides.

4. **Place** the valance and lining right sides together, matching the raw edges; pin along the sides and lower edge. Stitch ½" (1.3 cm) seams on the sides and lower edge, using a zipper foot and stitching with the valance fabric on top. Along the lower edge, stitch inside the previous stitching line, crowding the stitches against the welting.

5. **Trim** the lower corners diagonally. Turn the valance right side out. Press the sides and the lower edges. If the valance is interlined, smooth the interlining in place, checking to see that the upper edge of the interlining stops a distance from the upper edge of the valance equal to the heading depth plus the rod-pocket depth plus ½" (1.3 cm).

6. **Press** under ½" (1.3 cm) on the upper edge, turning under the valance and lining together. Then press under an amount equal to the heading depth plus the rod-pocket depth; pin.

7 **Stitch** close to the first fold; stitch again at the depth of the heading, using tape on the bed of the sewing machine as a stitching guide.

8 **Lay** the valance facedown on a flat surface. Mark for vertical rows of tucks at each seam and at each midpoint between the seams. The distance from the outer row of marks to the side edge equals the distance between rows. Measure up 10" (25.5 cm) from the lower edge for the placement of the first mark in each row. Place the remaining marks evenly spaced between the lower mark and the lower stitching line of the rod pocket, dividing the distance into three equal parts.

9 **Thread** a large-eyed needle with heavy thread. Insert the needle into the valance at the lowest mark in a row. Bring the needle back through to the lining side of the valance at the next mark and insert it back through ¼" (6 mm) above it. Repeat, taking a small stitch at each mark and running the thread on the right side of the valance. Bring the needle through at the lower stitching line of the rod pocket. Insert the needle back through ¼" (6 mm) to the side of the top stitch.

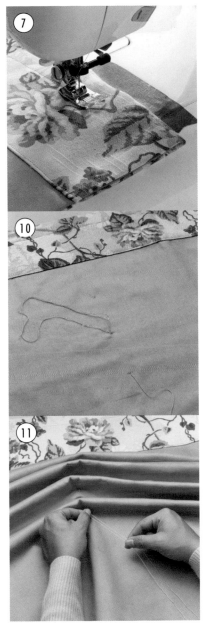

10 **Make** a second row of stitches alongside the first row back to the lowest mark. Cut the thread, leaving tails.

11 **Repeat** steps 9 and 10 for each marked row. Pull up the stitches to make three tucks in each row. Knot the thread securely.

12 **Insert** the rod into the rod pocket. Mount the rod; distribute the gathers evenly. Shape the bells and swags.

FLAT ROMAN SHADES

A flat Roman shade is a tailored, economical window treatment that controls light and provides privacy. Completely flat when lowered, this style is a good choice layered under tied-back curtains, drapery side panels, or swags.

This shade design is minimal and uncomplicated, but it doesn't have to be boring. Lining provides added body, prevents fabric fading, and creates a uniform appearance from the outside. A system of evenly spaced rings through which cords are run on the back of the shade makes it possible to raise and lower the shade. The rings are spaced in even columns and rows so the shade will fold neatly at regular intervals when raised.

Choose a sturdy, firm decorator fabric to give the shade a crisp look. Because the shade is absolutely flat when lowered, it is a great way to show off a large all-over print. These directions are suitable for a shade that is at least 2" (5 cm) narrower than the fabric width. If the window is wider, use one full width of fabric for a center panel and add equal, narrow pieces to the sides.

Mounted on a board, the shade can be installed as an inside mount, secured inside the upper window frame, flush with the front of the frame. For an outside mount, the shade is installed on the wall at least 1" (2.5 cm) above the frame. Use a very narrow projection because the shade does not wrap over the ends of the board. To find the finished length of the shade for an outside mount, measure from the top of the mounting board to the sill or ½" (1.3 cm) below the apron; for an inside mount, measure the inside frame to the sill. The finished width of the shade is equal to the length of the mounting board plus ¼" (6 mm).

Cutting Directions

• Cut a mounting board 2" (5 cm) longer than the outside measurement of the window frame for an outside mount or ½" (1.3 cm) shorter than the inside measurement for an inside mount. Cut a strip of fabric for covering the board ½" (1.3 cm) wider than the board circumference and 2" (5 cm) longer than the board length.

• The cut width of the decorator fabric is equal to the finished width plus 2" (5 cm). The cut length is equal to the finished length plus 7" (18 cm). This includes allowance for length that may be lost in stitching; the exact length is cut after the panel has been sewn. Do not use a selvage as an edge. Cut the lining fabric with the width equal to the finished width and the length equal to the finished length plus 3½" (9 cm).

YOU WILL NEED

- mounting board
- decorator fabric
- 1" (2.5 cm) angle irons with screws for outside mount
- tools for installation
- paper-backed fusible adhesive strip, ¾" (1.9 cm) wide
- drapery lining
- graph paper
- plastic rings, ⅜" or ½" (1 or 1.3 cm)
- flat metal weight bar, ½" (1.3 cm) wide, cut ½" (1.3 cm) shorter than finished width of shade
- staple gun and staples
- screw eyes
- shade cord
- white glue
- drapery pull, optional
- awning cleat

How to Make a Flat Roman Shade

(1) **Cut** the mounting board and cover it with fabric (page 284). If the shade will be mounted outside the window frame, secure angle irons to the bottom of the board, near the ends and at 45" (114 cm) intervals, using pan-head screws. Mount the board (page 285), centered above the window frame. Measure for the finished size of the shade. Remove the screws that hold the mounting board to the angle irons, leaving the angle irons on the wall.

(2) **Press** under 1" (2.5 cm) on the sides of the shade. Cut strips of ¾" (1.9 cm) paper-backed fusible web the length of each side. Turn back the hem and place the strips near the cut edge. Press over the strips to fuse them to the hem allowance, following the manufacturer's directions.

(3) **Place** the lining over the shade fabric, wrong sides together, with the lower edge of the lining 3½" (8.9 cm) above the lower edge of the shade fabric; tuck the lining under the side hems. Remove the protective paper backing from the fusible web, and press to fuse the hems in place.

(4) **Press** under ½" (1.3 cm) at the lower edge; then press under 3" (7.6 cm) to form the hem pocket. The lower edge of the lining should now be even with the bottom fold of the shade. Pin the hem in place. Edgestitch along the top fold of the hem through all layers.

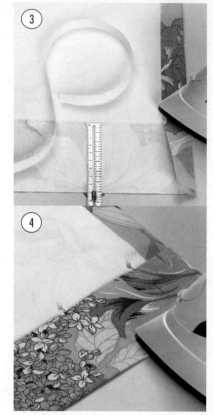

(5) **On the lining side**, draw a line across the top of the shade at the finished length. Draw a second line 1½" (3.8 cm) above it (equal to the board projection). Cut off excess fabric along the top line. Pin the layers together, and finish the upper edges together.

(6) **Diagram** the back of the shade on paper, indicating the finished length and width. Mark the hem 3" (7.6 cm) from the lower edge. Plan the locations of rings in columns spaced 8" to 12" (20 to 30.5 cm) apart, with the outer columns ¾" (1.9 cm) from the edges of the shade. Space them in even horizontal rows 5" to 8" (13 to 20 cm) apart with the bottom row at the top of the hem and the top row on the marked line.

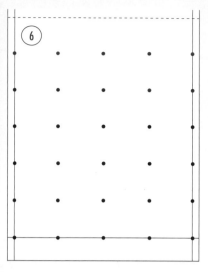

Here's how to do the math: Subtract 1½" (3.8 cm) from the finished width of the shade. Divide this adjusted width by 12" (30.5 cm) and round up to the nearest whole number to find the number of spaces between columns—there will be one more column than spaces. Divide the adjusted width by the number of spaces to find the distance between columns.

Measure the length of the shade from the top of the hem to the upper marked line. Divide this distance by 8" (20 cm) and round up to the nearest whole number to find the number of spaces between rows. Divide the distance by the number of spaces to find the distance between rows.

(7) **Mark** the placement for the rings on the lining side of the shade, following your diagram. The bottom row of rings is at the upper edge of the hem; the top row is the determined distance below the top marked line. (There are no rings on the top line.) Pin horizontally through both layers of fabric at each mark.

8 Stitch a ring at each mark through both layers of fabric, stitching either by machine or by hand. Reinforce the rings in the bottom row with extra stitches because they carry the weight of the shade.

9 Insert the flat weight bar into the hem pocket. Slipstitch the side openings closed.

10 Staple the shade to the top of the mounting board, aligning the marked line to the top front edge of the board.

11 Drill pilot holes and insert screw eyes, centered on the underside of the mounting board, aligning them to the columns of rings.

12 On the side where you want the cords to hang, run cord through the first column of rings, through the top screw eye, and at least halfway down the side. The extra length needed depends on the location of the window and whether or not you want it to be accessible to children. Cut the cord and tie a nonslip knot at the bottom ring. Repeat for each column in order, running the cords also through the previous screw eyes. Apply glue to the knots for security.

13 Reattach the mounting board to the angle irons for an outside mount or install the mounting board directly to the underside of the window frame, inserting screws through pilot holes, for an inside mount.

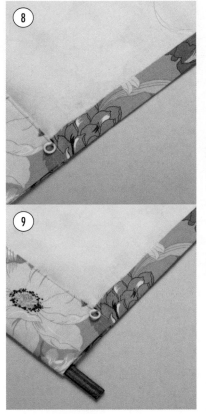

14 Adjust the cords with the shade down so the tension on all cords is equal. Tie the cords in a knot just below the first screw eye. Braid the cords, insert them through a drapery pull, if desired, and knot and trim the ends.

15 Secure an awning cleat to the edge of the window frame or on the wall. Pull gently on the cords to raise the shade, forming soft folds. Wind the cord around the cleat to hold the shade in its raised position. The first time you raise the shade, you may have to "train" it where to fold. As you raise the shade, pull the excess fabric between horizontal rows forward, forming gentle rolls. To help it "remember," leave the shade in the raised position for a day or two.

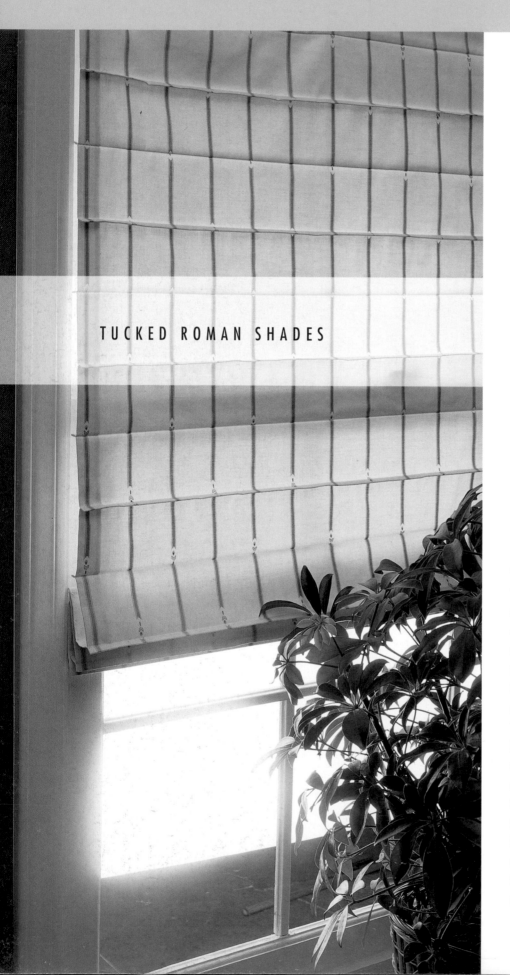

TUCKED ROMAN SHADES

Narrow, horizontal stitched tucks "remind" this shade where to fold when it is raised. With its clean-lined appearance, a tucked shade allows as much of the window to be exposed as desired and provides complete coverage when needed.

Design this shade with narrow tucks that alternate from front to back or with tucks in the back only. The rings are attached to the back tucks. When the shade is raised, the fabric folds along the tucks accordion-style, from the bottom. The folds take up minimal space when completely raised. To help the shade hang smoothly, a weight bar is inserted into the hem at the lower edge.

Use firmly woven decorator fabric for crisp, straight tucks. Because the tucks will break up the surface, this style is best for small all-over prints, solids, and stripes. If you want to use a large print, stitch only back tucks to avoid interupting the design. Lining provides added body and light control while helping support tucks. This shade is attached to a mounting board and may be installed as either an outside or inside mount. For an outside mount, the mounting board is installed above the window and extends to either the sill or ½" (1.3 cm) below the apron. The shade should extend at least 1" (2.5 cm) beyond the window frame on each side. Use a very narrow projection because the shade does not wrap over the ends of the board. For an inside mount, measure across the window inside the frame. To allow for variance in the width of the frame, measure it across the top, middle, and bottom. The finished width should be ⅛" (3 mm) less than the shortest of these three measurements.

For an outside-mounted shade, if the estimated finished length of the shade is not evenly divisible by the desired space between the tucks, the length can be increased until it is, if there is the necessary wall space above the window. For example, if you would like 4" (10 cm) spaces between the tucks and the estimated finished length is 45" (114 cm), you can make the shade 48" (122 cm) long, which is divisible by four. This allows for a 4" (10 cm) space between each of the tucks, a 4" (10 cm) space at the top, and a 4" (10 cm) hem depth at the bottom of the shade, for a total of twelve spaces.

Sometimes the length of the shade cannot be adjusted, as for an inside-mounted shade that must fit within the window frame. In this case, the spacing between the tucks can be adjusted. For example, if the estimated space between the tucks is 4" (10 cm) and the finished length of the shade is 45" (114 cm), you can have ten 4½" (11.4 cm) spaces; this includes the spaces between the tucks, the space at the top of the shade, and the space for the hem depth at the bottom. Or you can have nine 5"

(12.7 cm) spaces, including the top space and the hem depth.

Cutting Directions

• Cut a mounting board 2" (5 cm) longer than the outside measurement of the window frame for an outside mount or ½" (1.3 cm) shorter than the inside measurement for an inside mount. Cut a strip of fabric for covering the board ½" (1.3 cm) wider than the board circumference and 2" (5 cm) longer than the board length.

• Cut the decorator fabric to the desired finished length of the shade plus twice the hem depth plus the projection of the mounting board plus ¾" (1.9 cm) for each tuck. Also add 2" (5 cm) to allow for any reduction in the length that results from multiple rows of stitching. After the shade is sewn, excess length is trimmed off at the top.

• The cut width of the shade fabric is 3" (7.6 cm) wider than the finished width of the shade. If more than one fabric width is required for the shade, use one full width for a center panel and seam equal partial widths on each side, matching the pattern in the fabric.

• Cut the lining to the same length as the decorator fabric minus twice the depth of the hem at the bottom. The cut width of the lining is equal to the finished width of the shade; if necessary, seam equal partial widths on each side of a center panel, as for the decorator fabric.

YOU WILL NEED

• graph paper

• decorator fabric

• liquid fray preventer, optional

• paper-backed fusible adhesive strip, ¾" (1.9 cm) wide

• drapery lining

• plastic rings, ⅜" or ½" (1 or 1.3 cm)

• mounting board

• 1" (2.5 cm) angle irons with screws for outside mount

• tools for installation

• flat metal weight bar, ½" (1.3 cm) wide, cut ½" (1.3 cm) shorter than finished width of shade

• staple gun and staples

• screw eyes

• shade cord

• white glue

• drapery pull, optional

• awning cleat

How to make a Tucked Roman Shade

1 **Before** you cut the fabric, diagram the shade on paper, indicating the finished length and width, the number of tucks and spaces, and the columns of rings. Choose the distance between tucks according to the look you want; a spacing of about 4" (10 cm) between the tucks is attractive. The bottom tuck is a back tuck and is located just above the hem. Position the rings along the back tucks, starting 1" (2.5 cm) from the sides and spacing the remaining columns evenly 8" to 12" (20 to 30.5 cm) apart.

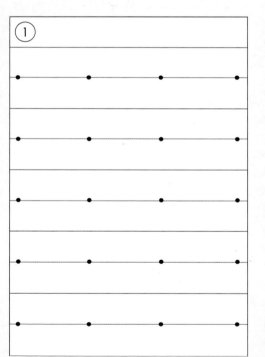

Here's how to do the math: Divide the desired space between the tucks into the finished length of the shade; if necessary, round the number up or down to the nearest whole number. This is the number of spaces, including the space at the top of the shade and the hem depth at the bottom. Then divide the number of spaces into the finished length of the shade to find the exact space between the tucks and the hem depth. There is one less tuck in the shade than there are spaces.

Subtract 2" (5 cm) from the finished width of the shade. Divide this adjusted width by 12" (30.5 cm) and round up to the nearest whole number to find the number of spaces between columns—there will be one more column than spaces. Divide the adjusted width by the number of spaces to find the distance between columns.

2 **Cut** the fabric. Seam fabric widths together, if necessary. Stabilize the side edges by applying liquid fray preventer, or finish the edges, using overlock or zigzag stitches.

3 **Press** under 1½" (3.8 cm) on each side for the hems. Cut strips of paper-backed fusible adhesive the length of each side. Turn back the hem and place the strips near the cut edge. Press over the strips to fuse them to the hem allowance, following the manufacturer's directions.

4 **Place** the lining over the shade fabric, wrong sides together, with the upper edges matching; tuck the

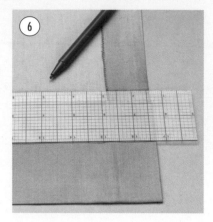

lining under the side hems. Remove the protective paper backing from the fusible web, and press to fuse the hems in place.

5 **Press** under an amount equal to the hem depth at the lower edge of the shade fabric; then press under again to make a double-fold hem. Pin in place. Stitch along the upper fold.

6 **Place** the shade facedown on a flat surface. On the lining, mark a line for the first back tuck ⅜" (1 cm) above the stitched upper fold of the hem.

7 **Mark** lines on the lining for the remaining back tucks. To determine the distance between the marked lines, multiply the space between tucks by two, and add 1½" (3.8 cm) if you will be making both front and back tucks; if you only want back tucks, add only ¾" (1.9 cm). For example, mark the lines 9½" (24 cm) apart for a shade with 4" (10 cm) spaces between the front and back tucks. Mark the lines 8¾" (22 cm) apart if you only want back tucks. Each tuck takes up ¾" (1.9 cm).

(8) **Pin** the lining to the shade fabric along the marked lines. Press the shade along the first marked line, right sides together. Stitch ⅜" (1 cm) from the fold. Repeat for the remaining back tucks. For the first tuck, it may be helpful to use a zipper foot, because the stitching line is even with the top fold of the hem.

(9) **Fold** the shade, wrong sides together, aligning the first two back tucks. From the right side, press the fold for the first front tuck. Pin along the fold.

(10) **Fold**, press, and pin the remaining front tucks. Stitch all the front tucks ⅜" (1 cm) from the folds.

(11) **Fold** the shade, stacking the front tucks and back tucks. Mark the placement for the rings on the back tucks, beginning 1" (2.5 cm) from the sides and spacing the remaining columns of rings, following your diagram.

(12) **Attach** a ring at each mark through both layers of fabric, stitching either by machine or by hand. By machine, place the fold under the presser foot with the ring next to the fold. Set the zigzag stitch at the widest setting; set the stitch length at 0. Stitch over the ring, securing it with about eight stitches. Then stitch in place for two or three stitches, with the stitch width and length set at 0 to secure threads. Reinforce the rings in the bottom row with extra stitches because they carry the weight of the shade.

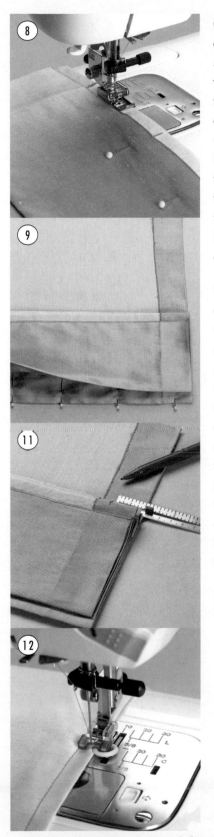

(13) **Cut** the mounting board and cover it with fabric (page 284). If the shade will be mounted outside the window frame, secure angle irons to the bottom of the board, near the ends and at 45" (114 cm) intervals, using pan-head screws. Mount the board (page 285), centered above the window frame. Measure for the finished size of the shade. Remove the screws that hold the mounting board to the angle irons, leaving the angle irons on the wall.

(14) **Place** the shade facedown on a flat surface. Pulling the fabric taut, measure from the lower edge of the shade to the desired finished length; mark a line on the lining fabric. This may change the upper space of the shade somewhat but ensures that the shade is the correct length. Mark a second line a distance away equal to the projection of the mounting board. Cut off excess fabric along the top line. Pin the layers together, and finish the upper edges together by serging or using wide zigzag stitches.

(15) **Complete** the shade as in steps 9 to 15 on page 299.

FLAT PANEL CURTAINS

One of the easiest curtains to make is also one of the most versatile. Flat panel curtains are just pieces of fabric that are hemmed on all four edges and hung from decorative rods with clip-on or sew-on rings. That's as basic as you can get, yet this style of curtain can easily be adapted to create a variety of looks: unlined sheers or semi-sheers that cover the window, lined or unlined side panels that reveal most or all of the glass, panels formally styled into uniform folds, panels allowed to casually drape and slouch.

Flat panel curtains can be designed as simple, casual, sill-length panels; semiformal floor-length styles, perfect for a contemporary interior; or spilling-onto-the-floor luxurious draperies. The look is strongly influenced by the fullness of the curtains, which can be sleek and spartan at one-and-one-half time fullness, full and opulent at three times fullness, or anywhere in between. See the examples for fullness and ring spacing on page 306.

Select firmly woven medium-weight fabric to create a simple tailored look, with an upper edge that can be styled into gentle rolling folds. Lightweight, slinky fabric will result in a relaxed, soft look, with an upper edge that dips gracefully between attachment points. Depending on the desired fullness, one full width of decorator fabric will cover an area 18" to 32" (46 to 81.5 cm) wide. If more width is desired, seam together full or half widths of fabric for each panel. You may prefer to line the curtain panels, to add body and prevent the decorator fabric from fading.

The panels can be hung from a decorative rod with clip-on or sew-on curtain rings, which are available in many styles. Choose the hardware and mount the rod before you begin so you can accurately measure for the finished length. The rod is usually mounted above the window frame far enough that the top of the curtain will cover the wood. Before you drill any holes, it is a good idea to mock up a small sample to determine the exact location of the curtain top in relation to the rod; the type of ring used also affects the measurement.

Cutting Directions

• The cut length of the fabric is equal to the finished length of the curtain plus the lower hem allowance (see chart on page 307) plus 3" (7.5 cm) for the upper hem.

• The cut width of the fabric is equal to the amount of space you want to cover multiplied by the desired fullness (see examples on page 314). Divide this amount by the width of the fabric and round up or down to the nearest whole or half width, to find the number of fabric widths you need. Use full or half widths of fabric for each curtain panel.

• Multiply the cut length by the total number of widths needed to determine the amount of fabric to buy. Buy an extra pattern repeat per fabric width for matching patterns (page 222).

• For lined curtains, cut the lining fabric 5" (13 cm) shorter than the decorator fabric for floor-length curtains; 3" (7.5 cm) shorter than the decorator fabric for sill- or apron-length curtains; the same length as the decorator fabric for curtains that puddle on the floor. The cut width of the lining is the same as the decorator fabric.

YOU WILL NEED

- decorative curtain rod
- tools and hardware for installation
- decorator fabric
- drapery lining for lined curtains
- drapery weights for floor-length curtains
- clip-on or sew-on rings

Fullness and Spacing Alternatives

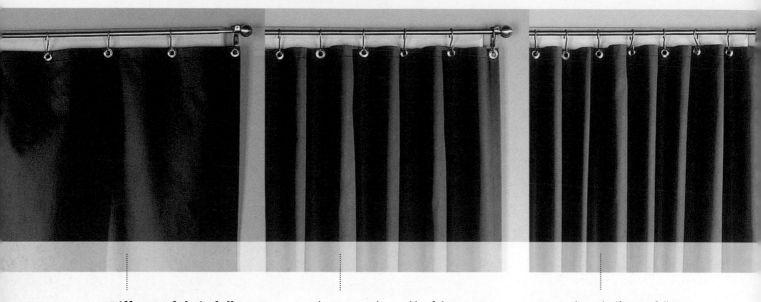

Different fabric fullnesses and same spacing between hooks.

For a flatter panel, one-and-one-half times fullness is used (left);

this means the width of the curtain measures one-and-one-half times the length of the rod. For a fuller panel, use two times fullness (center);

or two-and-one-half times fullness (right). In these photos, all rings are spaced 15½" (39 cm) apart.

Different spacing between rings and same fabric fullness.

For a controlled look along the top of the curtain, use more rings and space them close together (left).

For a softer look, use fewer rings with more space between them.

For dramatic swoops in the fabric, use a minimum of rings, spaced even farther apart. All of these curtain panels have two times fullness.

How to Make Unlined Flat Panel Curtains

(1) **Seam** the fabric widths together, if necessary, for each curtain panel. If half widths are needed, add them at the sides of the panels. Finish the seams together, and press them toward the side of the panel.

(2) **Press** under the lower edge the full amount of the hem allowance. Then unfold the pressed edge and turn the cut edge back, aligning it to the pressed foldline. Press the outer fold. If you are making floor-length curtains with more than one fabric width, tack a drapery weight to the upper layer of fabric at the base of each seam, with the bottom of the weight near the inner fold.

(3) **Refold** the lower edge, forming a double-fold hem. Pin. Stitch, using a blindstitch for an invisible hem or a straight stitch for a visible hem.

(4) **Press** under 3" (7.5 cm) on one side. Then unfold the pressed edge and turn the cut edge back, aligning it to the pressed foldline. Press the outer fold. If you are making floor-length curtains, insert a drapery weight between the layers of the lower hem, and tack it in place. Refold the edge, forming a 1½" (3.8 cm) double-fold side hem. Stitch, using a blindstitch. Repeat for each side of each panel.

(5) **Press** under a 1½" (3.8 cm) double-fold hem in the upper edge. Stitch the upper hem.

(6) **Mark** the placement for sew-on or clip-on rings along the top hem, placing the end marks ¾" (2 cm) from the sides. Space the remaining marks evenly 6" to 10" (15 to 25.5 cm) apart. Try different spacing patterns, using safety pins, to help you decide. See the examples opposite. Attach a ring at each mark.

(7) **Slide** the rings onto the drapery rod, and mount the rod on the brackets.

Hem Allowances

Curtain Length	Bottom Hem Allowance
To sill or apron	6" (15 cm)
½" (1.3 cm) above floor	8" (20.5 cm)
Brushing floor	8" (20.5 cm)
Puddling on floor	1" (2.5 cm)

Making lined flat panel curtains

(1) **Follow** steps 1 to 3 for unlined flat panel curtains at left. Repeat for the lining, but make a 2" (5 cm) double-fold hem in the lining.

(2) **Place** the curtain panel and lining panel wrong sides together, matching the raw edges at the sides and upper edge; pin. The lining panel will be 1" (2.5 cm) shorter than the curtain panel. Complete the curtain as in steps 4 to 7 (at left), handling the decorator fabric and lining as one fabric.

Making puddled curtains

(1) **Follow** step 1 at left for both decorator fabric and lining. Place the lining and decorator fabric wrong sides together, matching the raw edges. Complete steps 2 to 7, treating both fabrics as one.

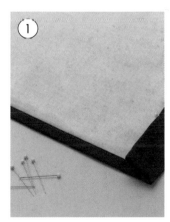

TAB CURTAINS

The eye is drawn upward when a window is dressed with tab curtains. Narrow straps that loop or tie over a decorative rod give this treatment the no-frill appeal of blending form with function. The tabs can loop, tie, or be buttoned.

Tab curtains are not intended to be opened and closed repeatedly, because the friction would put too much strain on the tabs. Therefore, this curtain style is often designed as two stationary panels at the sides of a window. For a narrow window, one panel can cover the entire width at the top and be drawn to one side to let light in. The tabs can be a continuous loop, two straps that are tied over the rod, or a single strap attached at one end and seemingly buttoned to the curtain at the front (to avoid strain on the buttons, the tabs are sewn in place and the buttons are just decorative). Each fabric width has five or six evenly spaced tabs.

Tab curtains can be lined or unlined, depending on the fabric selection and the degree of light control and privacy required. Medium-weight decorator fabrics offer the needed strength for the tabs and will keep the upper edge of the curtain in a controlled line. If a soft drape between tabs is desired, choose a lighter weight, drapable fabric for the curtain.

It is wise to mock up the treatment and hang the rod before cutting for accurate length measurements (see the steps opposite). Mount the rod high enough so the top of the window frame will not be visible above the curtain.

Measuring

① **Determine** the tab length by wrapping a cloth tape measure over the rod the desired distance to the top of the curtain. Add 1" (2.5 cm) for seam allowances and 2¾" (7 cm) more for button tabs. For tie tabs, mock up a tab with wide ribbon or strips of fabric in the style of knot you want to use. Then measure the length of each piece and add 1" (2.5 cm) for end seams.

② **Measure** the distance from the underside of the rod to the top of the curtain. Mount the rod a distance above the window equal to this distance plus 1" (2.5 cm). This ensures that the window frame will not show above the curtain.

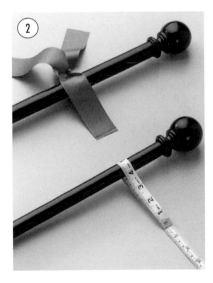

Cutting Directions

• The cut length of each curtain panel is equal to the finished length plus the bottom hem allowance (see chart on page 307) plus 3" (7.5 cm).

• The cut width of the fabric is equal to the amount of space you want to cover multiplied by two. Divide this amount by the width of the fabric and round up or down to the nearest whole or half width, to determine the number of fabric widths you need. Use full or half widths of fabric for each curtain panel.

• For lined tab curtains, the cut length of the lining is equal to the finished length of the curtain plus 3½" (9 cm). The cut width is the same as for the decorator fabric.

• You will need five tabs for the first full width plus four tabs for each additional full width and two tabs for each additional half width in each curtain panel. For loop or button tabs 1½" (3.8 cm) wide, cut a 4" (10 cm) strip of fabric for each tab, using the length measurement found at left. For tie tabs 1" (2.5 cm) wide, cut two 2½" (6.5 cm) strips for each tab, using the length measurement found at left.

• Multiply the cut length by the number of fabric widths needed to determine the total amount required for the curtains. For the tabs, add 12" (30.5 cm) for every two fabric widths needed to determine the total length to buy.

Making Unlined Loop Tab Curtains

1. **Seam** the fabric widths together as necessary for each curtain panel, adding any half widths at the return ends of the panels. Finish the seam allowances together, and press them toward the side of the panel.

2. **Press** under the lower edge 8" (20.5 cm) for the hem. Then unfold the pressed edge and turn the cut edge back, aligning it to the pressed foldline. Press the outer fold. If the panel has more than one fabric width, tack a drapery weight to the upper layer of fabric at the base of each seam, with the bottom of the weight near the inner fold.

3. **Refold** the lower edge, forming a 4" (10 cm) double-fold hem, encasing the weights at the seams. Pin. Stitch, using a blindstitch for an invisible hem or a straight stitch for a visible hem.

4. **Press** under ½" (1.3 cm) on the upper edge. Then fold 2" (5 cm) to the right side, forming a facing. At the outer corners, stitch the facing to the curtain 3" (7.5 cm) from the edges (arrow). Trim the facing to within ¼" (6 mm) of the stitching; trim off the top 1" (2.5 cm) of the side hem allowance.

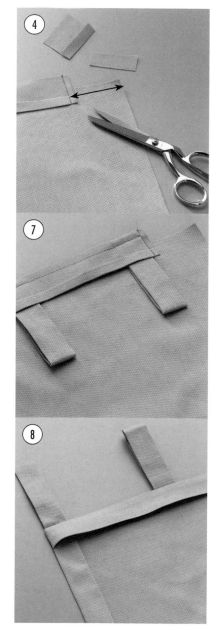

5. **Fold** each tab in half lengthwise, right sides together. Stitch a ½" (1.3 cm) seam along the cut edge.

6. **Turn** the tabs right side out. Center the seam in the back of each tab; press.

7. **Mark** the placement for the tabs, evenly spaced along the upper hem of the curtain, with the first and last tabs even with the outer edges. Fold the tabs in half and slide them under the facing with the raw edges in the fold; pin. Stitch across the curtain top, ½" (1.3 cm) from the fold.

8. **Press** under 1½" (3.8 cm) double-fold side hems. Turn the facing to the curtain back; press. Stitch the side hems, encasing a drapery weight in the hem layers at the lower corners of floor-length curtains. At the upper corners, the hem will disappear under the facing. Stitch along the lower fold of the facing.

9. **Hang** the curtain from the rod. Space the tabs evenly on the rod. Train the curtain to fall in soft folds, with the fabric at the tabs rolling forward and the fabric between the tabs rolling toward the window.

Making Button Tab Curtains

(1) **Follow** steps 1 to 5 opposite. Center the seam in the back of the tab; press, avoiding sharp creases on the outer edges. Mark a point ¼" (6 mm) from the lower edge on the seam; mark points 1¼" (3.2 cm) from the lower edge on the outer folds.

(2) **Sew** from the mark on the outer fold to the mark on the seam; pivot, and stitch to the mark on the opposite fold, forming the point of the tab. Trim the seam to ¼" (6 mm). Turn the tab right side out; press.

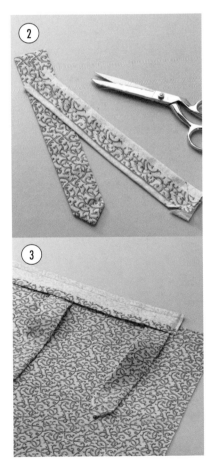

(3) **Follow** step 7, but secure only the open end of the tabs under the facing, with the seam against the right side of the curtain.

(4) **Finish** the curtains as in step 8. Turn the tabs down over the upper edge of the curtain, aligning the outer points of the tabs to the lower stitching line; pin. Tack the tabs securely with the sewing machine. Sew buttons over the stitches. Hang the curtains as in step 9.

Making Lined Tab Curtains

(1) **Follow** steps 1 to 3 for unlined tab curtains opposite. Repeat for the lining, but make a 2" (5 cm) double-fold hem in the lining and omit drapery weights in the lining.

(2) **Place** the curtain panel and lining panel wrong sides together, matching the raw edges at the sides. The upper edge of the lining will be 2½" (6.5 cm) below the upper edge of the curtain panel. At the bottom, the lining panel will be 1" (2.5 cm) shorter than the curtain panel. Pin.

(3) **Complete** the curtain as on page 318, steps 4 to 9, handling the decorator fabric and lining as one fabric.

Making Tie Tab Curtains

(1) **Follow** steps 1 to 4 for loop tab curtains. Fold each tab in half lengthwise, right sides together. Stitch a ¼" (6 mm) seam along the cut edge and one end. Turn the tabs right side out and press.

(2) **Follow** step 7, but stack two tabs with seams on opposite sides, securing only the open ends of the tabs under the facing.

(3) **Finish** the curtains as in step 8. Hang the curtains as in step 9, tying the tabs over the rod.

CLASSIC ROD-POCKET CURTAINS

Rod-pocket curtains are often chosen for a stationary window treatment that is stylish and easy to sew. With ample fullness and a deep, ruffly heading, classic rod-pocket curtains take on a feminine, romantic appearance. With less fullness and a shorter heading, the look becomes more tailored and modern. Either way, the fluid lines and gathered fabric soften the hard surfaces and edges of the window.

Rod-pocket curtains have a heading and rod pocket. The heading is the portion at the top of a rod-pocket curtain that forms a ruffle when the curtain is on the rod. The depth of the heading is the distance from the top of the curtain to the top stitching line of the rod pocket. The rod pocket is the "tunnel" where the rod or pole is inserted; stitching lines at the top and bottom of the rod pocket keep the rod in place. To determine the depth of the rod pocket, measure around the widest part of the rod or pole; add ½" (1.3 cm) ease to this measurement, and divide by two.

To design your rod-pocket curtains, first decide how you will hang them. Several types of rods can be used, including flat rods in widths of 1", 2½", and 4½" (2.5, 6.5, and 11.5 cm). Wood and metal pole sets with elbows or finials can also be used and are available in several diameters. When a curtain rod or pole set with elbows is used, sides of the curtain panels wrap to the wall. This portion is called the return. For curtains mounted on poles with finials, returns can be created by making an opening in the front of the rod pocket for inserting the pole.

Rod-pocket curtains work well with a variety of fabrics. Unlined rod-pocket curtains can be made from sheers or laces, creating a lightweight treatment that allows filtered light to enter the room. For curtains made from medium-weight decorator fabrics, lining can be used to make the curtains more durable and opaque, add extra body, and support the side hems and heading. For sheer fabrics, allow two-and-one-half to three times the length of the rod for fullness; for heavier fabrics, allow two to two-and-one-half times.

Before cutting the fabric, decide where the window treatment should be positioned and mount the curtain rod or pole. Brackets are usually mounted on the wall just outside the window frame so the bottom of the rod is even with the top of the frame. Measure from the lower edge of the rod to where you want the lower edge of the curtain. To determine the finished length of the curtain, add the desired depth of the heading and rod pocket to this measurement. This is the finished length of the curtain panel.

Cutting Directions

• The cut length of the fabric is equal to the finished length of the curtain plus the lower hem allowance (see chart on page 315) plus the depth of the heading and the rod pocket plus ½" (1.3 cm) for turn-under at the upper edge.

• The cut width of the fabric is equal to the amount of space you want to cover (including returns) multiplied by the desired fullness. Divide this amount by the width of the fabric and round up or down to the nearest whole or half width, to find the number of fabric widths you need. Use full or half widths of fabric for each curtain panel.

• Multiply the cut length by the total number of widths needed to determine the amount of fabric to buy. Buy an extra pattern repeat per fabric width for matching patterns (page 222).

• For lined curtains, cut the lining fabric 5" (12.7 cm) shorter than the decorator fabric. The cut width of the lining is the same as the decorator fabric.

Making Unlined Rod-Pocket Curtains

1. **Seam** the fabric widths together, if necessary, for each curtain panel. If half widths are needed, add them at the sides of the panels. Finish the seam allowances together, and press them toward the side of the panel.

2. **Press** under the lower edge the full amount of the hem allowance. Then unfold the pressed edge and turn the cut edge back, aligning it to the pressed foldline. Press the outer fold. If you are making floor-length curtains with more than one fabric width, tack a drapery weight to the upper layer of fabric at the base of each seam, with the bottom of the weight near the inner fold.

3. **Refold** the lower edge, forming a double-fold hem, encasing the weights at the seams. Pin. Stitch, using a blindstitch for an invisible hem or a straight stitch for a visible hem.

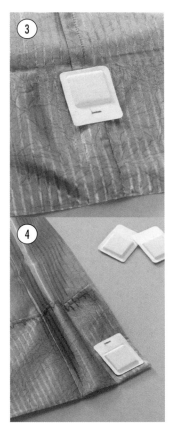

4. **Press** under 3" (7.5 cm) on one side. Then unfold the pressed edge and turn the cut edge back, aligning it to the pressed foldline. Press the outer fold. Insert a drapery weight between the layers of the lower hem, and tack it in place. Refold the edge, forming a 1½" (3.8 cm) double-fold side hem. Stitch, using a blindstitch. Repeat for each side of each curtain panel.

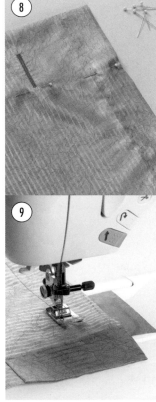

5. **Press** under ½" (1.3 cm) on the upper edge. Then press under an amount equal to the rod-pocket depth plus the heading depth. If the curtain will be mounted on a pole with elbow returns, omit steps 6 to 8.

6. **Mount** the rod on a wooden, keyhole, or elbow bracket. Measure the distance from the wall to the center of the pole.

7. **Unfold** the upper edge of the curtain on the return side of the panel. On the right side of the fabric, measure from the side of the curtain a distance equal to the measurement in step 6; mark at the center of the rod pocket. If the curtain will be mounted on a rod with keyhole brackets, omit step 8.

8. **Cut** a 1" (2.5 cm) strip of fusible interfacing, 1" (2.5 cm) longer than the depth of the rod pocket. Fuse the strip to the wrong side of the curtain panel, centering it directly under the mark made in step 7. On the right side of the panel, stitch a buttonhole at the mark, from the top to the bottom of the rod pocket. Refold the upper edge of the panel along the pressed lines and pin.

9. **Stitch** close to the first fold; stitch again at the depth of the heading, using tape on the bed of the sewing machine as a stitching guide.

Making Lined Rod-Pocket Curtains

1) **Follow** steps 1 to 3 for unlined rod-pocket curtains opposite. Repeat for the lining, but make a 2" (5 cm) double-fold hem in the lining and omit drapery weights in the lining.

2) **Place** the curtain panel and lining panel wrong sides together, matching the raw edges at the sides and upper edge; pin. At the bottom, the lining panel will be 1" (2.5 cm) shorter than the curtain panel. Complete the curtain as in steps 4 to 9, handling the decorator fabric and lining as one fabric.

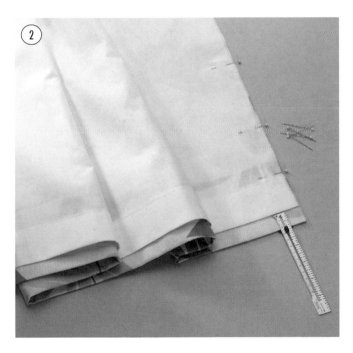

Installing Rod-pocket Curtains

a) Pole with wooden brackets and finials

Remove the finials; insert the pole into the rod pocket with ends of the pole extending through the buttonholes. Reattach the finials; mount the pole. Secure the return to the wooden bracket, using self-adhesive hook and loop tape.

b) Pole with keyhole bracket and finials

Slit center of the rod pocket at the point marked in step 7 opposite. Insert the pole into the rod pocket. Pull the return over the end of pole, aligning slit to finial screw hole; attach finials through slits, and mount the pole. Attach a pin-on ring to the inner edge of the return, and secure to a cup hook or tenter hook in wall.

c) Pole with elbows

Insert the pole through the rod pocket; pull the curtain back to expose small screws. Mount the pole on brackets. Slide the curtain over brackets.

PINCH-PLEATED DRAPERIES

Classic pleated draperies are the ultimate window treatment for versatility and style. Installed on traverse rods, they easily open to reveal the full window view. When closed, they offer privacy, light control, and even insulation. They can also be made as stationary draperies. Traditional threefold pinch pleats will create uniform, graceful folds.

The instructions that follow are for a pair of drapery panels mounted on a two-way-draw traverse rod. When designing the treatment, allow for the stacking space (page 273) at the sides of the window so the draperies will clear the window when they are open. The actual stacking space varies, depending on the weight of the fabric, the fullness of the draperies, and whether or not they are lined, but is estimated at one-third the width of the windows; allow for one-half of the stacking space on each side of the window.

A wide range of decorator fabrics can be used, including sheers, casements, semisheers, and medium-weight fabrics in both prints and solids. Two-and-one-half times fullness is used for most draperies, but for sheers, three times fullness can be used. For lace draperies, use two-and-one-half times fullness so the pattern of the lace is noticeable in the finished draperies.

After you measure the window and determine the stacking space, purchase the rod and mount it on the wall above and to the outside of the window frame. If the draperies will hang from a conventional traverse rod, measure for the finished length from the top of the rod to where you want the lower edge of the draperies; then add ½" (1.3 cm) so the draperies will extend above the rod. If the draperies will hang from a decorative rod, measure from the bottom of the rod to the desired finished length. If the draperies will hang from a pole set with rings, measure from the pin holes in the rings to the desired finished length.

Cutting Directions

• Use the fabric worksheet on page 319 to find the necessary measurements. Several widths of fabric are often required. Cut the number of fabric widths you need to the calculated cut length of the draperies.

Making Unlined Pinch-Pleated Draperies

(1) **Seam** the fabric widths together as necessary. If half widths are needed, add them at the sides of the panels. Finish the seams together, and press them toward the side of the panel.

(2) **Press** under the lower edge 8" (20.5 cm) for the hem. Then unfold the pressed edge and turn the cut edge back, aligning it to the pressed foldline. Press the outer fold. If the panel has more than one fabric width, tack a drapery weight to the upper layer of fabric at the base of each seam, with the bottom of the weight near the inner fold.

(3) **Refold** the lower edge, forming a 4" (10 cm) double-fold hem, encasing the weights at the seams. Pin. Stitch, using a blindstitch for an invisible hem or a straight stitch for a visible hem.

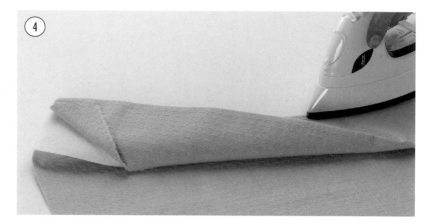

(4) **Press** under the upper edge 8" (20.5 cm). Then unfold the pressed edge and turn the cut edge back, aligning it to the pressed foldline. Press the outer fold. Cut buckram the width of each drapery panel. Slip the buckram under the first fold, and then refold the top, encasing the buckram. Pin in place.

(5) **Press** under 3" (7.5 cm) on one side. Then unfold the pressed edge and turn the cut edge back, aligning it to the pressed foldline. Press the outer fold. Insert a drapery weight between the layers of the lower hem, and tack it in place. Refold the edge, forming a 1½" (3.8 cm) double-fold side hem. Stitch. Repeat for each side of each curtain panel.

(6) **Determine** the number and size of pleats and spaces between them by working through the chart at right. The recommended amount of fabric for each pleat is 4" to 6" (10 to 15 cm). The recommended space between pleats is 3½" to 4" (9 to 10 cm). If the calculation from the worksheets results in pleats or spaces that are greater than the amount recommended, add one more pleat and space. If the calculation results in pleats or spaces smaller than the amount recommended, subtract one pleat and space.

Drapery Fabric Worksheet

Drapery Length

Desired finished length
+ 8" (20.5 cm) for heading
+ 8" (20.5 cm) for 4" (10 cm) double-fold lower hem
= cut length of drapery *

*If you buy fabric with a pattern repeat, your cut length must be rounded up to the next number evenly divisible by the pattern repeat.

Drapery Width

Rod width (from end bracket to end bracket on conventional rods; from end ring to end ring on decorative rods)
+ allowance for two returns (projection of rod plus ½" [1.3 cm] for each return)
+ 3½" (9 cm) for overlap
= finished width of drapery

Total Number of Drapery Fabric Widths

Finished drapery width
× multiplied by 2½ to 3 times fullness
÷ divided by width of fabric
= total number of fabric widths needed, rounded up or down to nearest full width "

Number of Fabric Widths per Panel

Total number of fabric widths
÷ divided by 2
= number of fabric widths per panel

Amount to Purchase

Total number of fabric widths
× multiplied by cut length
= amount to purchase

Lining Fabric Worksheet

Lining Length

Cut length of drapery
− 5" (13 cm)
= cut length of lining

Number of Lining Widths

Same as for total number of drapery fabric widths (above). Lining fabric width must be the same as the decorator fabric width.

Pleats Worksheet

Finished Panel Width

Finished drapery width (at left)
÷ divided by 2
= finished panel width

Number of Pleats per Panel

Number of drapery fabric widths per panel (see chart at left)
× multiplied by number of pleats per width*
= number of pleats per panel

Space between Pleats

Finished panel width (at left)
− overlap and return
= width to be pleated
÷ divided by number of spaces per panel (one less than number of pleats per panel)
= space between pleats

Pleat Size

Flat width of hemmed panel
− finished panel width (at left)
= total amount allowed for pleats
÷ divided by number of pleats per panel (figured above)
= pleat size

* Plan 5 pleats per width of 48" (122 cm) fabric, 6 pleats per width of 54" (137 cm) fabric. For example, for 54" (137 cm) fabric, 3 widths per panel = 18 pleats. If you have a half width of fabric, plan 2 or 3 pleats in that half width.

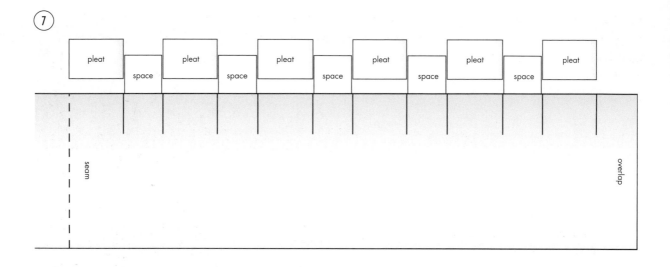

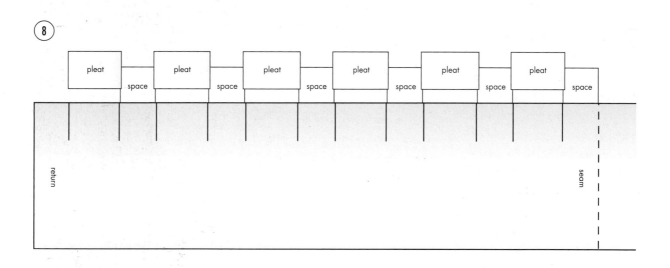

7 **Cut** buckram templates in sizes to match the determined pleats and spaces; cut five of each for 48" (122 cm) fabric or six of each for 54" (137 cm) fabric. Mark the overlap and return on the right side of one panel, using chalk. Arrange the templates on the first fabric width, with the first pleat starting at the overlap line and the last pleat ending at the seam line. There will be one less space. Adjust the pleat sizes to arrange the spaces evenly; spaces must remain uniform. Mark the heading even with the outer edges of the space templates.

8 **Arrange** the templates on the second fabric width from the overlap, with the first space starting at the first seam line from the overlap and the last pleat ending at the next seam line; use the same number of pleats as spaces. Repeat for each panel. (The last pleat ends at the return mark in the last fabric width.) Adjust the pleats as necessary; mark the spaces. If the return end of the panel has a half width of fabric, plan for two pleats if the fabric is 48" (122 cm) wide or for three pleats if the fabric is 54" (137 cm) wide. Transfer the markings to the opposite panel in mirror-image placement.

9 **Fold** each pleat by bringing the pleat lines together; pin. Crease the buckram on the fold.

10 **Stitch** on the pleat line from the top of the heading to the lower edge of the buckram; backstitch to secure. Repeat for each pleat in each panel.

11 **Check** the finished width of the panel along the heading. Adjust the size of a few pleats if necessary to adjust the width of the panel.

12 **To divide** each stitched pleat into three even pleats, grasp the center crease and push it down toward the stitching line, forcing the sides to spread out. Form the fabric into three even pleats and press creases in the buckram with your fingers.

13 **Bar-tack** pleats by machine just above the lower edge of the buckram; or tack pleats by hand, using a stabstitch and heavy-duty thimble.

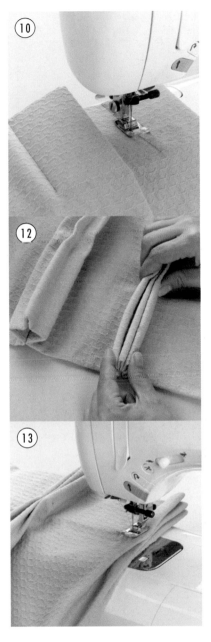

Hanging and Dressing the Draperies

1) Insert drapery hooks, with one hook at each pleat and one hook near each end of the panel. On a conventional traverse rod (a), the top of the hook is 1¾" (4.5 cm) from the upper edge of the overdrapery or 1¼" (3.2 cm) from the upper edge of the underdrapery. On a decorator traverse rod (b), the top of the hook is ¾" to 1" (2 to 2.5 cm) from the upper edge. On a pole set with rings (c), the top of the hook is ¼" (6 mm) from the upper edge. (Shown on traverse rods for clarity.)

2) Crease the buckram midway between each pleat; fold it forward if a conventional traverse rod is being used, or fold it to the back if a decorative traverse rod is being used. This is often referred to as "cracking" the buckram. After cracking the buckram, press the draperies, using a warm, dry iron.

3) Hang the end hook at the return in the hole on the side of the bracket (a). Hang the hook of the first pleat in the hole at the front corner of the bracket (b).

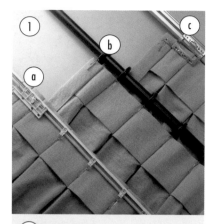

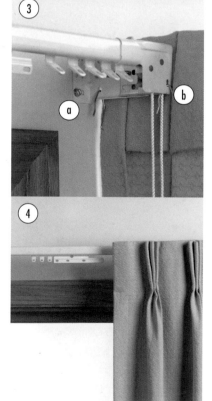

4) Hang the hooks for middle pleats on the slides; remove any slides that are not used. Hang the hook for the last pleat in the first hole of the master slide. Hang the end hook on the overlap of the drapery in the end hole of the master slide. Pinch the hooks on the master slides closed to keep them from catching when the draperies are drawn; also, pull the front master slide slightly forward, if necessary.

5) Open the draperies completely into the stacked position. Check the heading to be sure the buckram is folded as it was cracked in step 2. Starting at the heading, guide the pleats into evenly spaced soft folds of equal depth; follow the grain line of the fabric to keep the pleats perpendicular to the floor.

6) Staple a narrow strip of matching fabric or muslin around the drapery panel, midway between the heading and hem, to hold the pleats in place. Avoid pulling the fabric too tightly or you will create unwanted wrinkles.

7) Staple a second strip of fabric at the hemline. Check to see that the draperies hang straight down from the rod. Leave the draperies in this position for two weeks to set the pleats. In humid conditions, one week may be sufficient.

Making Lined Pleated Draperies

1 **Prepare** the drapery panels as in steps 1 to 3 on page 318. Repeat for the lining panels, making 2" (5 cm) double-fold lower hems and omitting weights.

2 **Place** the drapery panel on a large flat surface. Lay the lining panel on top of the drapery panel, wrong sides together, with the lower edge of the lining 1" (2.5 cm) above the lower edge of the drapery panel; raw edges should be even at the sides.

3 **Mark** the lining panel 8" (20.5 cm) from the upper edge of the drapery panel. Trim on the marked line. This will be even with the top fold of the heading.

4 **Finish** the draperies as in steps 4 to 13 on pages 318 to 321, treating the decorator fabric and lining as one. The lining will be caught in the stitches of the pleats and in the side hems.

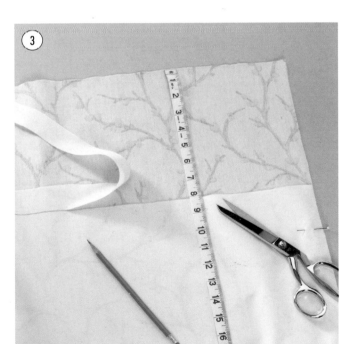

Pleat Alternatives

You can change the look of pleated draperies with any of these pleat variations. Follow the same directions up to the point of making the pleats. Then form the pleats in one of these styles.

a **Goblet Pleats**

Tack the pleats just above the lower edge of the buckram. Form each pleat into a rounded goblet shape. Insert wadded tissue paper into the pleats to help them retain their shape.

b **Fan Pleats**

Tack the pleats together at the upper edge of the drapery and let them fan out from the top.

c **Inverted Pinch Pleats**

Fold the pleats to the back instead of the front, and tack them together. The front of the heading will have a flat appearance.

d **Cartridge Pleats**

Plan for one more pleat per fabric width and half width. Do not crease the buckram when you stitch the pleats, but allow them to form a round tube shape. To hold the shape of the cartridges, insert a section of foam pipe insulation into each pleat.

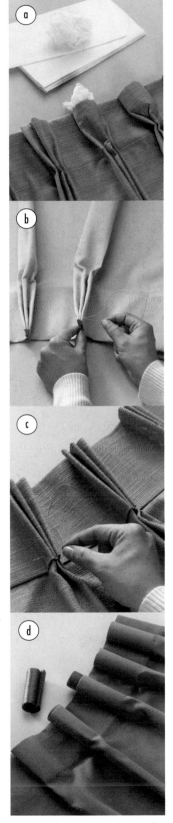

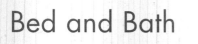

Bed and Bath

FLANGED PILLOW SHAMS

Flanged shams transform ordinary bed pillows into custom designer pillows. They can be made to fit standard-size, queen-size, or king-size pillows. An overlapping closure in the center of the back makes it easy to insert and remove the pillow. Select decorator fabric to coordinate with your duvet or bedspread.

Cutting Directions

• Cut a sham front and two sham back pieces according to the measurements given in the chart on page 326.

YOU WILL NEED

• 1⅝ yd. (1.5 m) decorator fabric for each pillow sham

• thread

• masking tape

How to Sew a Pillow Sham

① **Press** ½" (1.3 cm) double-fold hems on one long edge of each back piece (these will be the vertical, overlapping edges). Stitch the hems.

② **Place** the sham back pieces over the sham front, right sides together, aligning the cut edges and overlapping the back hemmed edges 3" (7.5 cm). Pin the layers together around the outer edge.

③ **Stitch** ½" (1.3 cm) from the edge, pivoting at the corners. Trim the seam allowances diagonally at the four corners to remove excess bulk.

Pillow Size	Cut size of front	Cut size of each back
Standard 20" x 26" (51 x 66 cm)	27" x 33" (68.5 x 84 cm)	27" x 19" (68.5 x 48.5 cm)
Queen 20" x 30" (51 x 76 cm)	27" x 37" (68.5 x 94 cm)	27" x 21" (68.5 x 53.5 cm)
King 20" x 36" (51 x 91.5 cm)	27" x 43" (68.5 x 109 cm)	27" x 24" (68.5 x 61 cm)

(4) **Insert** a heavy cardboard tube or a seam roll into the opening and place it under the seam. Press the seam allowances open, applying light pressure with the tip of the iron down the crease of the seam.

(5) **Turn** the pillow sham right side out, reaching in through the overlap to pull out each corner. Insert a point turner or similar tool into the sham, gently pushing the points out to form perfect corners.

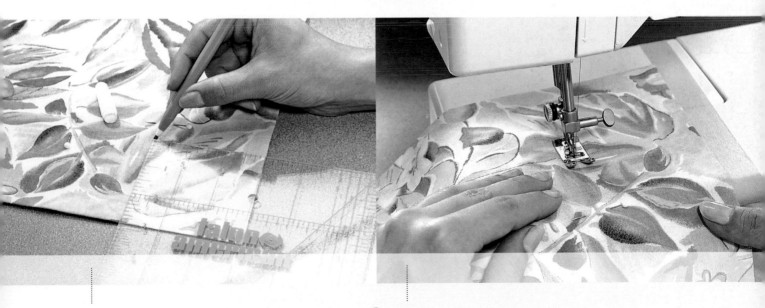

(6) **Press** the seamed edges. With the front facing up, pin the layers together about 3" (7.5 cm) from the four sides. Mark small dots 3" (7.5 cm) from the corners of the shams to help you know when to pivot.

(7) **Place** a piece of masking tape on the bed of your machine 3" (7.5 cm) to the right of the needle, parallel to the seam allowance guide. Stitch the pillow sham flange, guiding the seamed edge along the tape and pivoting at each corner.

DUVET COVER

A duvet cover keeps a duvet or comforter clean and is easily removed for laundering. The sewing steps are fairly simple; the difficulty comes in handling large expanses of fabric. Set up a card table next to your sewing machine station to help with the task. Duvet covers usually require two or more widths of fabric sewn together for the front and back: one full width down the center with equal partial widths along the sides. Choose a lightweight, firmly woven, washable fabric.

How to Sew a Duvet Cover

(1) **Measure** your duvet or comforter to determine the finished size of the cover. Use the formula on page 330 to determine the cut length and cut width of the pieces and the amount of fabric you will need. We are using numbers for a queen-size duvet cover; yours may be different.

(2) **Measure** and mark the location of each cut along the selvage. Cut the pieces, following the cutting guidelines (page 221). If you do not have to match a pattern (page 222), cut away the selvages. Cut one front and one back piece in half lengthwise.

(2)

FRONT			BACK		
half width	full width	half width	half width	full width	half width

Finished length of the duvet cover		86" (218.5 cm)
Add 1" (2.5 cm) for seam allowances	+	1" (2.5 cm)
to find the cut length of the front*	=	87" (221 cm)
Finished length of the duvet cover		86" (218.5 cm)
Add 8½" (22 cm)	+	8½" (21.8 cm)
to find the cut length of the back*	=	94½" (240 cm)
Finished width of the duvet cover		86" (218.5 cm)
Add 1" (2.5 cm) for seam allowances	+	1" (2.5 cm)
to find the cut width of the cover	=	87" (221 cm)
Divide the cut width	÷	87" (221 cm)
by the fabric width	×	54" (137 cm)
Round up to the next whole number		1.6
to find the number of widths needed		2
Multiply the number of widths		2
by the cut length of the front	×	87" (221 cm)
to find the amount needed for the front	=	174" (442 cm)
Multiply the number of widths		2
by the cut length of the back	×	94½" (240 cm)
to find the amount needed for the back	=	189" (480 cm)
Add the amount needed for the front		174" (442 cm)
to the amount needed for the back	+	189" (480 cm)
to find the total amount needed	=	363" (922 cm)
Convert to yards (meters); round up	=	10⅛ yd. (9.25 m)

*If you buy a fabric with a pattern repeat, the cut lengths must be rounded up to the next number evenly divisible by the pattern repeat length. In our example, if the repeat length is 7" (18 cm) the cut lengths are 91" and 98" (231 and 249 cm) instead of 87" and 94¹/2" (221 and 240 cm). Proceed with your figures using the revised cut lengths.

(3) **Pin** a half-width piece to the full-width front piece, right sides together, along the lengthwise edges. Match the pattern, if necessary, following the guidelines on page 222. Stitch ½" (1.3 cm) seam. Repeat for the other side. Finish the seam allowances and press them open.

(4) **Measure** and cut the duvet front to the exact cut width, as determined in the chart. Be sure to trim equal amounts from each side.

(5) **Repeat** steps 3 and 4 for the duvet cover back. Mark a line 12" (30.5 cm) from the lower edge of the back. Cut on the marked line.

(6) **Press** a 1½" (3.8 cm) double-fold hem in the upper edge of the small back piece. Stitch the hem.

(7) **Press** and stitch 1½" (3.8 cm) double-fold hem on the lower edge of the large back piece. Mark the placement and length for buttonholes on the hem of the large back piece, centered between the fold and stitching line. Place outer marks 6" (15 cm) from each side and the others spaced about 10" to 12" (25.5 to 30.5 cm) apart. Run the marks perpendicular to the hem edge.

(8) **Sew** buttonholes over the marked lines. Apply liquid fray preventer to the buttonholes; allow to dry and then cut the buttonholes open.

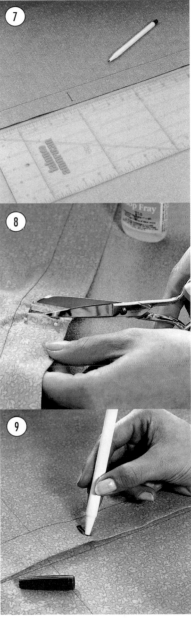

(9) **Overlap** the hemlines of the back pieces 1½" (3.8 cm), and pin them together at the outer edges. Mark the placement for the buttons on the hemline of the small back piece. Sew buttons over the marks.

10 Button the back pieces together. Place the duvet cover back over the front, right sides together, aligning the outer edges. Pin the layers together. Fold a 20" (51 cm) piece of twill tape in half. Align the folded edge to the outer edge of the duvet cover ½" (1.3 cm) from the corner, and pin in place. Repeat at each corner.

11 Stitch a ½" (1.3 cm) seam around the edge of the duvet cover, pivoting at each corner and catching the folded end of the twill tape in the stitching. Trim the seam allowances diagonally at the four corners to remove excess bulk. Avoid cutting through the twill tape.

12 Unbutton the opening. Insert a heavy cardboard tube or a seam roll into the opening and place it under the seam. Press the seam allowances open, applying light pressure with the tip of the iron down the crease of the seam.

13 Stitch a plastic ring at each corner of your duvet or comforter. Spread the duvet or comforter out over your new duvet cover and tie the twill tape to the rings at each corner. Now turn the duvet cover right side out, encasing the duvet or comforter inside.

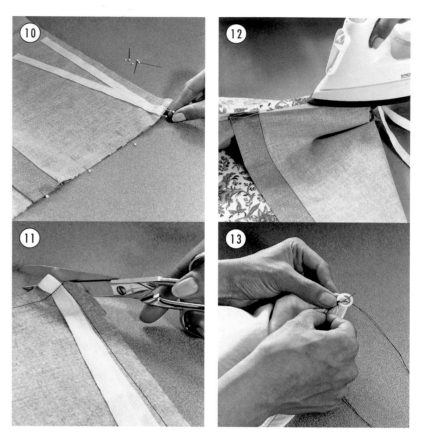

BED SKIRTS

Bed skirts hide the box springs and legs of a bed when a comforter or duvet is used for the top cover. Gathered skirts give a soft effect; pleated skirts are more tailored. Both styles cover the sides and foot of the bed, and can be made with split corners (to accommodate bed posts and foot boards) or continuous corners (for beds without footboards).

Gathered skirts can be made with one layer or two. When making a two-layered skirt, prepare the panels separately and then gather them together as one piece. The weight of the fabric and the desired look will determine the fullness of the skirt. Allow up to three times fullness for very lightweight, semi-sheer fabric, if you want a full look. Double fullness works better for medium-weight fabric.

Pleated skirts have box pleats at the foot corners and centers of each side. For king-size beds, you may also want to add a pleat in the center of the foot. The directions that follow allow for 6" (15 cm) pleats. There is a 1" (2.5 cm) double-fold hem at the lower edge and front edges.

Bed skirts you buy in a store are attached to a plain fabric deck that slides between the mattress and box spring. The directions for the pleated skirt incorporate a deck, which can be made from muslin, broadcloth, or a flat sheet. When you make your own bed skirt, you can sew it to a fitted sheet, which keeps the skirt from shifting out of position. The directions for the gathered skirt show how to attach it to a fitted sheet. Both styles can be made either way.

Cutting Directions

- For gathered dust ruffle length, cut two pieces each the length of the box spring times the desired fullness, plus 4" (10 cm) for 1" (2.5 cm) double fold side hems. Cut one piece the width of the box spring times the desired fullness, plus 4" (10 cm) for 1" (2.5 cm) double-fold hems. The skirt depth is equal to the distance from the top of the box spring to the floor plus 4" (10 cm).

- For pleated skirt, cut the deck 1" (2.5 cm) wider and 1" (2.5 cm) longer than the box spring. Cut bed skirt on lengthwise grain of fabric. Cut two pieces the length of the box spring plus 18" (46 cm). Cut one piece the width of the box spring plus 18" (46 cm). Bed skirt depth equals distance from top of box spring to floor minus ¼" (6 mm), plus 2½" (6.5 cm) for the seam and hem.

How to Sew a Gathered Skirt with Open Corners

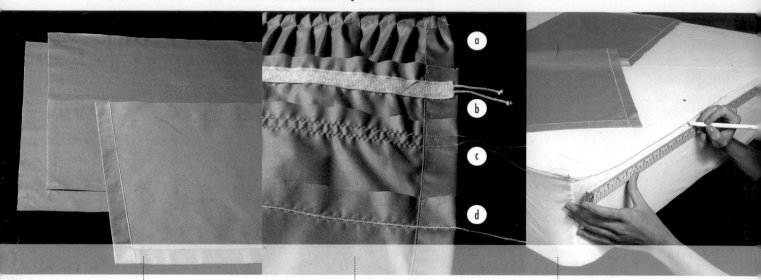

1. **Stitch** 1" (2.5 cm) double-fold hem along lower edges of the three pieces, then turn under and stitch 1" (2.5 cm) double-fold hem on both ends of each piece.

2. **Gather** 1" (2.5 cm) from upper edge with ruffler attachment (a), two-string shirring tape (b), two rows of basting (c), or zigzag stitching over a cord (d).

3. **Place** fitted sheet on box spring. On sheet, mark upper edge of box spring. Mark every 12" (30.5 cm) along this line for matching to skirt. Mark upper edge of skirt every 24" (61 cm) if using double fullness; every 36" (91.5 cm) for triple fullness.

4. **Pin** right sides of skirt pieces along three sides of sheet, raw edges on marked line and hems overlapping at corners. Match markings on skirt pieces to markings on sheet. Pull up gathers to fit.

5. **Remove** sheet from box spring, keeping skirt pinned in place. Stitch 1" (2.5 cm) from raw edge of skirt.

6. **Turn** skirt down over lower edge of sheet. Topstitch ½" (1.3 cm) from seam, stitching through skirt and sheet.

How to Sew a Pleated Bed Skirt

① **Fold** deck in half lengthwise, then crosswise so corners are together. Using saucer as a guide, cut corners in gentle curve.

② **Fold** curved corners in half to determine centers; mark fold with ¼" (6 mm) clips. Also, mark center of each side with clip.

③ **Stitch** skirt pieces, right sides together, on narrow ends, with shorter piece in center. Stitch 1" (2.5 cm) double-fold hem on lower edge of skirt and on unstitched narrow ends of skirt pieces.

3" (7.5 cm)

3" (7.5 cm)

④ **Pin** skirt to deck, right sides together, with stitching of side hem at clip on one end of deck (arrow). Form 6" (15 cm) pleats at clips on sides and corners of deck. Seam will fall inside pleats.

⑤ **Remove** skirt and machine-baste pleats. Reposition skirt on deck. Pin, right sides together. Clip center of corner pleats. Stitch ½" (1.3 cm) seam.

⑥ **Press** seam allowance toward deck. Press ¼" (6 mm) double-fold hem at open end of deck; stitch hem. Topstitch the skirt seam allowance to deck. Press pleats.

SHOWER CURTAIN

A bathroom shower curtain is easy to sew. You can choose fabric to coordinate with your fixtures, tile color, and window treatment fabric. This shower curtain has grommets along the upper hem, spaced to align with the grommets in a standard shower curtain liner. Join the fabric panels with a French seam to give the curtain a neat appearance from both sides. To make the shower curtain washable, select a washable fabric and preshrink it before you cut it.

Cutting Directions

• Cut two full-width pieces 82" (208.5 cm) long. Curtain will be trimmed to necessary cut width in step 2.

How to Sew a Shower Curtain

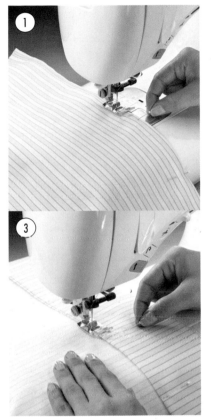

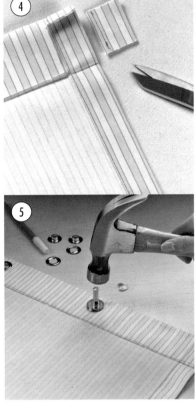

(1) **Cut** away the selvages evenly.
Join the two lengths together using
a French seam (page 106). The
total seam allowance width is ½"
(1.3 cm), so use ¼" (6 mm) seams
for each pass.

(2) **Cut** one vertical edge of the
shower curtain so the total width is
76" (193 cm). The finished width
of a standard shower curtain is 72"
(183 cm). This allows 2" (5 cm) on
each side for hemming.

(3) **Press** a 3" (7.6 cm) double-
fold hem into the lower edge; stitch
the hem.

(4) **Press** a 2" (7.6 cm) double-fold
hem into each side. Unfold the fabric
at the upper corners. Trim out the
excess fabric from the inner layer, as
shown, trimming to within ⅜" (1 cm)
of the fold. Refold the upper edge,
and pin; stitch the upper hem.

(5) **Mark** the placement for twelve
evenly spaced grommets along the
upper hem, using a fabric marker.
Position them ¾" (2 cm) from the
upper edge with the outer marks
centered in the side hems. Read the
manufacturer's directions for attaching the grommets, and test the technique on a sample of fabric folded
several times. Attach the grommets.

Table Fashions

Customized tabletop fashions are a simple, cost-effective way to change the look of a dining room or kitchen. Home-sewn tablecloths and napkins, unlike purchased ones, are not limited to a small selection of standard sizes. You can scale tablecloths to fit the exact size and shape of your table. With an abundant supply of fabric colors, patterns, and textures, you can make choices that complement your room décor.

Selecting Fabrics

You may find a small selection of 72" (183 cm)-wide tablecloth fabrics in basic colors at the fabric store. In most cases, you simply buy the length you need and hem the edges for an instant tablecloth. Many decorator fabrics are good choices for tablecloths but they are not wide enough to provide the needed coverage in one fabric width, so you must piece widths together. Avoid a center seam by using a full fabric width in the center and stitching narrow, equal side panels to it.

Measuring the Table

The length of the tablecloth from the edge of the table to the bottom of the cloth is called the drop. The usual drop length for tablecloths is 10" to 12" (25.5 to 30.5 cm), which is at or near chair seat height. Be sure to include the drop length in your measurements.

Three common drop lengths are: short, 10" to 12" (25.5 to 30.5 cm); mid-length, 16" to 24" (40.5 to 61 cm); and floor-length, 28" to 29" (71 to 73.5 cm). Short cloths end at about seat height and are good for everyday use. Mid-length cloths are more formal. Elegant floor-length coverings are used for buffet and decorator tables.

Round tablecloth. Measure the diameter of the table, then determine the drop length of the cloth. The size of the tablecloth is the diameter of the table plus twice the drop length plus 1" (2.5 cm) for a narrow hem allowance. A narrow hem is the easiest way to finish the curved edge of a round tablecloth.

Square or rectangular tablecloth. Measure the length and width of the tabletop; then determine the drop length of the cloth. Add the drop length twice to both length and width measurements to find the finished tablecloth size. To find the cut size, add 1" (2.5 cm) to each measurement for a narrow hem or 4" (10.2 cm) for a wider hem.

Oval tablecloth. Measure the length and width of the tabletop, then determine the drop length of the cloth. Add the drop length twice to both length and width measurements to find the finished tablecloth size. To find the cut size, add 1" (2.5 cm) to each measurement for a narrow hem. Because oval tables vary in shape, mark the finished size with the fabric on the table. Center the fabric on the table and keep it in place with weights. Then use a hem marker or cardboard gauge to mark the drop length evenly around the curves.

ROUND TABLECLOTHS

● Option ⓑ. Use two seams when the diameter of the tablecloth is more than one-and one-half times the fabric width. Cut one fabric piece in half lengthwise.

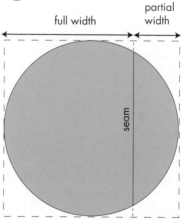

ⓐ

full width | partial width

seam

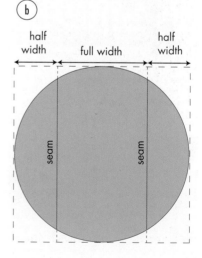

ⓑ

half width | full width | half width

seam | seam

There are two ways to finish the edge of a round tablecloth: a ¼" (6 mm) double-fold hem or by adding fabric-covered welting. To determine the yardage for a round tablecloth, divide the tablecloth diameter by the fabric width less 1" (2.5 cm). Count fractions as one width. This is the number of widths you need. Then multiply the number of widths by the diameter and divide by 36" (100 cm) to find the total yards (meters).

Cutting Directions

● The cut size of the tablecloth is the diameter of the table plus twice the drop length. Add 1" (2.5 cm) for a narrow hem allowance. If you want to finish the edge with welting, the cut size is the same as the finished size. Determine where you want the seams in your tablecloth, using one of these options:

● Option ⓐ. Use one seam when the diameter of the tablecloth is less than one-and-one-half times the fabric width. Subtract the fabric width from the tablecloth diameter. Cut a strip on the lengthwise grain of one fabric piece that is 2" (5.1 cm) wider than this measurement.

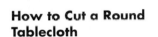

How to Cut a Round Tablecloth

(1) **Join** fabric panels, right sides together, with ½" (1.3 cm) seams to form a square. Fold square into fourths. Pin layers together to prevent slipping.

(2) **Tie** a string to a marking pencil. Pin the other end of the string to the center folded corner of the fabric a distance from the pencil equal to the cut radius of the tablecloth. Mark the arc. Cut on the marked lines; remove the pins.

How to Sew a Narrow Hem

Stitch around tablecloth ¼" (6 mm) from edge. Press under on stitching line. Press under ¼" (6 mm) again, easing fullness around curves. Edge-stitch close to folded edge.

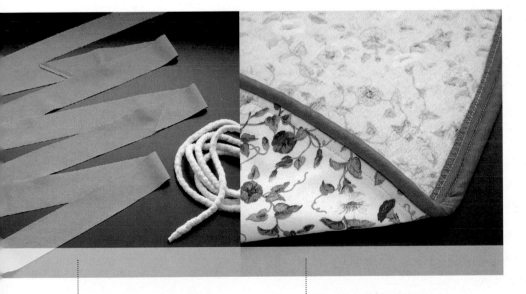

How to Sew a Welted Hem

(1) **Multiply** diameter of tablecloth by 3½ to determine length of welting needed. Cut and join bias strips, right sides together, to cover welting (page 248).

(2) **Cover** cording and attach to right side of cloth. Zigzag seam and press to back of tablecloth. Topstitch ¼" (6 mm) from welted seam.

SQUARE AND RECTANGULAR TABLECLOTHS

Make tablecloths the desired width by joining fabric widths as necessary, using full widths in the center and partial widths on the lengthwise edges. Straighten the crosswise ends of fabric (page 221) to square the corners. Use plain, French, or overedge seams.

Hem the edges with double-fold hems of ¼" (6 mm) width or use 1" (2.5 cm) width to give them more weight. Mitering is the neatest way to square the corners because it covers raw edges and eliminates bulk.

To determine the amount of fabric you need, divide the total width of the tablecloth by the width of your fabric, less 1" (2.5 cm) for seam allowances. Count fractions as one width. Multiply this figure, which is the number of panels needed by the total length of the tablecloth. Divide this number by 36" (100 cm) to get the total yards (meters) required.

Cutting Directions

• The cut length of the tablecloth is the length of the tabletop plus twice the drop length plus 4" (10 cm) for hems. The cut width is the width of the tabletop plus twice the drop length plus 4" (10 cm) for hems. For tablecloths wider than one fabric width, cut two pieces to the necessary length and sew them together, following the guidelines at left. Then cut to the necessary width.

How to Sew a Wide Mitered Hem

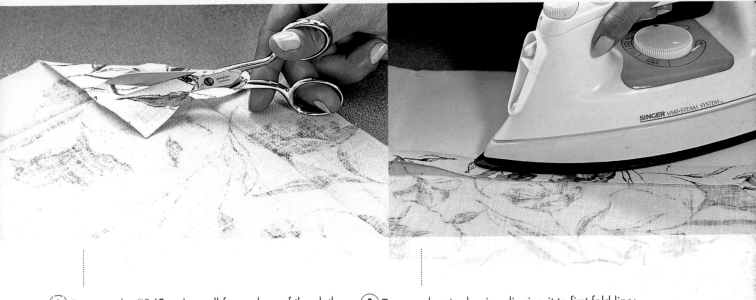

1) **Press** under 2" (5 cm) on all four edges of the cloth. Unfold. Press each corner diagonally at point where creases intersect. Trim off corner diagonally from one foldline to the other. Use dot of fabric glue stick to hold corner in place.

2) **Turn** each cut edge in, aligning it to first fold line; press outer fold.

3) **Refold** hem, encasing raw edge. Pin. At corners, creases will meet, forming miter. Use more glue stick to hold folds in place.

4) **Edgestitch** along inner fold. Pivot at corners. Press.

REVERSIBLE PLACEMATS

Spark up your dining room table or breakfast nook with reversible octagonal placemats. These placemats are lined to the edge and can be made reversible by selecting two decorator fabrics. Welting (page 248), sewn into the outer edge of the placemat, is available in different sizes and colors, or you can make your own. For ease of application, choose welting no larger than ³⁄₁₆" (4.5 mm).

How to Sew a Reversible Placemat

① **Draw** a 13" × 19" (33 × 48.5 cm) rectangle xon paper. Mark point 3½" (9 cm) from each corner. Draw diagonal lines across each corner connecting marks; cut off corners.

② **Preshrink** fabrics (page 220). To preshrink welting, wrap it into large loops and tie it in the middle with large loose knot. Soak welting in warm water; squeeze out excess moisture. Place in net laundry bag or nylon stocking before tossing in dryer. This will keep it from getting too tangled. Press the flat edge of the welting when dry.

③ **Cut** out front and back for each placemat, using pattern. Make sure edges are parallel to grainlines.

YOU WILL NEED

for four placemats:

- paper for drawing a pattern
- ¾ yd. (0.7 m) fabric for placemat fronts
- ¾ yd. (0.7 m) fabric for placemat backs
- 7 yd. (6.4 m) welting
- thread to match fabrics

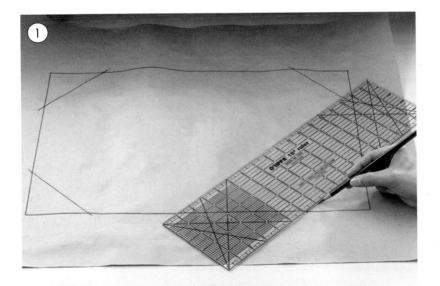

4 **Pin** welting to right side of placemat front. Keep welting relaxed. Clip into seam allowance of welting at each corner of placemat at exact point where welting must bend. Clip to, but not through stitching line, so that welting seam allowances spread open and lie flat.

5 **Sew** welting to placemat front as for welted pillow, page 248.

6 **Pin** placemat front over back, right sides together, encasing welting between layers and aligning outer edges. Stitch just inside first stitching line, leaving an opening for turning along one side.

7 **Trim** seam allowances diagonally at each corner. Turn back and press back seam allowance ½" (1.3 cm) from the edge at opening.

8 **Turn** placemat right side out through opening. Use point turner to push out corners. Press placemat up to welting as you smooth and tug welting out to the edge with your fingers. Slipstitch opening closed.

NAPKINS

Coordinating napkins are the finishing touch to your tabletop fashions. Standard finished napkins are 14" or 17" (35.5 or 43 cm) square. Before cutting the fabric, square the ends, using a carpenter's square. For fringed napkins, square the ends by pulling a thread.

Napkin hems can be decorative. Experiment with some of the decorative stitches on your sewing machine. The hemming techniques shown here can also be used for tablecloths and single-layer placemats.

Cutting Directions

• Cut napkins 1" (2.5 cm) larger than finished size. One yard (meter) of 36" (100 cm)-wide fabric yields four 17" (43 cm) napkins. A piece of fabric 45" (115 cm) square yields nine 14" (35.5 cm) napkins.

Six Ways to Hem Napkins

Satin Stitch. Turn under ½" (1.3 cm) on all sides. Miter corners (page 343). Edgestitch along raw edge to use as guide. Use wide, closely spaced zigzag to stitch from right side over edgestitching.

Zigzag overedge. Trim loose threads from napkin edges. Stitch over raw edge, using wide, closely spaced zigzag. Use overedge foot or special-purpose foot to maintain zigzag width.

Decorative stitch. Press under ¼" (6 mm) and stitch. From right side, stitch with a decorative stitch, using straight stitching as the guideline. Blanket stitch (shown above) gives a hemstitched look.

Double-fold hem. Turn under ¼" (6 mm) on all edges and press. Turn under another ¼" (6 mm). Miter corners as on page 343. Edgestitch close to fold.

Fringe. Cut napkins on a pulled thread to straighten edges. Stitch ½" (1.3 cm) from raw edges with short straight stitches or narrow closely spaced zigzag. Pull out threads up to the stitching line.

Serged edge. Overlock edges with your serger. Thread loopers with wooly nylon thread for better coverage. Stitch two opposite sides, then remaining sides, leaving long tails. Weave tails back under overlock stitches for 1" (2.5 cm) (a); cut off remaining tail. Or apply liquid fray preventer at corners (b); allow to dry, and cut off tails.

Index